Microsoft®
Office 97

SIMPLIFIED

IN FULL COLOR

VISUAL 3D SERIES

by: maranGraphics' Development Group

Corporate Sales

Contact maranGraphics
Phone: (905) 890-3300
     (800) 469-6616
Fax: (905) 890-9434

Canadian Trade Sales

Contact Prentice Hall Canada
Phone: (416) 293-3621
     (800) 567-3800
Fax: (416) 299-2529

Visit our Web site at:
http://www.maran.com

Microsoft® Office 97 Simplified

Copyright© 1996 by maranGraphics Inc.
5755 Coopers Avenue
Mississauga, Ontario, Canada
L4Z 1R9

Screen shots reprinted by permission from Microsoft Corporation.

Canadian Cataloguing in Publication Data

Maran, Ruth, 1970-
    Office 97 simplified

(Visual 3-D series)
Written by Ruth Maran.
Includes index.
ISBN 1-896283-26-8

1. Microsoft Office for Windows   (Computer file) .
2. Microsoft Word for Windows   (Computer file) .
3. Microsoft Excel for Windows   (Computer file) .
4. Microsoft PowerPoint for Windows   (Computer file) .
5. Microsoft Outlook   (Computer file) .   I. maranGraphics'
Development Group. II. MaranGraphics Inc.   III. Title.
IV. Series.

HF5548.4.M525M372   650'.0285'5369   C96-932432-4

Printed in the United States of America

10   9   8   7   6   5   4   3   2

Trademark Acknowledgments

maranGraphics Inc. has attempted to include trademark information
for products, services and companies referred to in this guide.
Although maranGraphics Inc. has made reasonable efforts in
gathering this information, it cannot guarantee its accuracy.

All other brand names and product names used in this book
are trademarks, registered trademarks, or trade names of their
respective holders. maranGraphics Inc. is not associated with any
product or vendor mentioned in this book.

**FOR PURPOSES OF ILLUSTRATING THE CONCEPTS AND
TECHNIQUES DESCRIBED IN THIS BOOK, THE AUTHOR HAS
CREATED VARIOUS NAMES, COMPANY NAMES, MAILING
ADDRESSES, E-MAIL ADDRESSES AND PHONE NUMBERS,
ALL OF WHICH ARE FICTITIOUS. ANY RESEMBLANCE OF
THESE FICTITIOUS NAMES, COMPANY NAMES, MAILING
ADDRESSES, E-MAIL ADDRESSES AND PHONE NUMBERS TO
ANY ACTUAL PERSON, COMPANY AND/OR ORGANIZATION IS
UNINTENTIONAL AND PURELY COINCIDENTAL.**

©1996
maranGraphics, Inc.

The animated characters are the
copyright of maranGraphics, Inc.

Microsoft® Office 97

SIMPLIFIED

IN FULL COLOR

VISUAL 3D SERIES

maranGraphics™

*Every maranGraphics book represents
the extraordinary vision and commitment of a unique family:
the Maran family of Toronto, Canada.*

Back Row (from left to right): Sherry Maran, Rob Maran, Richard Maran, Maxine Maran, Jill Maran.
Front Row (from left to right): Judy Maran, Ruth Maran.

Richard Maran is the company founder and its inspirational leader. He developed maranGraphics' proprietary communication technology called "visual grammar." This book is built on that technology—empowering readers with the easiest and quickest way to learn about computers.

Ruth Maran is the Author and Architect—a role Richard established that now bears Ruth's distinctive touch. She creates the words and visual structure that are the basis for the books.

Judy Maran is the Project Manager. She works with Ruth, Richard, and the highly talented maranGraphics illustrators, designers, and editors to transform Ruth's material into its final form.

Rob Maran is the Technical and Production Specialist. He makes sure the state-of-the-art technology used to create these books always performs as it should.

Sherry Maran manages the Reception, Order Desk, and any number of areas that require immediate attention and a helping hand.

Jill Maran is a jack-of-all-trades and dynamo who fills in anywhere she's needed anytime she's back from university.

Maxine Maran is the Business Manager and family sage. She maintains order in the business and family—and keeps everything running smoothly.

Oh, and three other family members are seated on the sofa. These graphic disk characters help make it fun and easy to learn about computers. They're part of the extended maranGraphics family.

Credits

Author & Architect:
Ruth Maran

**Copy Development
& Screen Captures:**
Alison MacAlpine

Project Manager:
Judy Maran

**Editors for Excel, Outlook
and Internet Chapters:**
Brad Hilderley
Susan Beytas
Richard Warren

**Editors for Introduction, Word
and PowerPoint Chapters:**
Karen Derrah
Wanda Lawrie

**Layout, Illustrations
& Cover Design:**
Tamara Poliquin

Illustrations & Screens:
Chris K.C. Leung
Russell Marini
Ben Lee

**Screens & Layout
Corrections:**
Christie Van Duin

Indexer:
Kelleigh Wing

Post Production:
Robert Maran

Acknowledgments

Thanks to the dedicated staff of maranGraphics, including Susan Beytas, Karen Derrah, Francisco Ferreira, Brad Hilderley, Jeff Jones, Wanda Lawrie, Ben Lee, Chris K.C. Leung, Alison MacAlpine, Michael W. M^{ac}Donald, Jill Maran, Judy Maran, Maxine Maran, Robert Maran, Sherry Maran, Russ Marini, Tamara Poliquin, Christie Van Duin, Richard Warren, Paul Whitehead and Kelleigh Wing.

Finally, to Richard Maran who originated the easy-to-use graphic format of this guide. Thank you for your inspiration and guidance.

TABLE OF CONTENTS

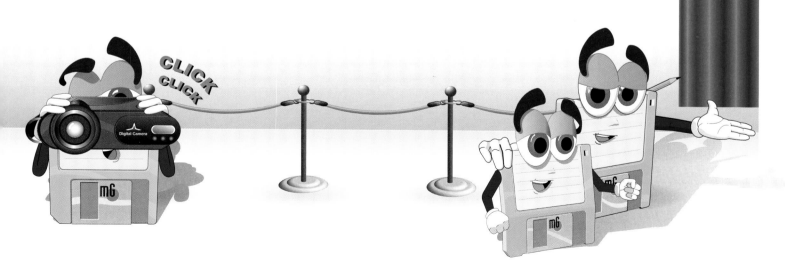

TABLE OF CONTENTS

Microsoft Office

WORD

1 GETTING STARTED

Introduction to Word 16
Start Word 17
Enter Text 18
The Word Screen 19
Select Text 20
Move Through a Document 22

2 SAVE, PRINT AND OPEN A DOCUMENT

Save a Document 24
Preview a Document 26
Print a Document 28
Create a New Document 30
Switch Between Documents 31
Close a Document 32
Exit Word 33
Open a Document 34

3 CHANGE DOCUMENT DISPLAY

Change the View 36
Zoom In or Out 38
Display the Ruler 39
Display Toolbars 40

INTRODUCTION

INTRODUCTION

Introduction to Microsoft Office 4
Using the Mouse 6
Start a Program 8
Switch Between Programs 10
Exit a Program 11
Getting Help 12

4 EDIT A DOCUMENT

Insert Text 42

Delete Text 44

Undo Last Change 47

Move Text 48

Copy Text 50

Find Text 52

Replace Text 54

Check Spelling and Grammar 56

Using the Thesaurus 58

5 FORMAT TEXT

Bold, Italic and Underline...............................60

Change Alignment of Text 61

Change Font of Text 62

Change Size of Text......................................63

Change Appearance of Text 64

Change Text Color 66

Highlight Text 67

Copy Formatting 68

Add a Border...69

Insert a Symbol 70

Add Bullets or Numbers 72

Change Line Spacing......................................74

Indent Paragraphs 76

Change Tab Settings 78

6 FORMAT PAGES

Add Page Numbers 82

Add Footnotes 84

Add a Header and Footer 86

Insert a Page Break 88

Insert a Section Break....................................90

Center Text on a Page 92

Change Margins 94

Create Newspaper Columns 96

7 WORKING WITH TABLES

Create a Table 98

Change Row Height or Column Width 100

Erase Lines 102

Enter Text 103

Add a Row or Column...................................104

Delete a Row or Column 106

Delete a Table 107

Format a Table 108

TABLE OF CONTENTS

EXCEL

1 GETTING STARTED

Introduction to Excel 112

Start Excel 113

Worksheet Basics 114

The Excel Screen 115

Enter Data 116

Complete a Series 118

Select Cells 120

Scroll Through a Worksheet 122

Zoom In or Out 124

Display Toolbars 125

2 SAVE AND OPEN A WORKBOOK

Save a Workbook 126

Create a New Workbook 128

Switch Between Workbooks 129

Close a Workbook 130

Exit Excel 131

Open a Workbook 132

3 EDIT A WORKSHEET

Edit Data 134

Delete Data 136

Undo Last Change 137

Move Data 138

Copy Data 140

Insert a Row or Column 142

Delete a Row or Column 144

4 USING FORMULAS AND FUNCTIONS

Enter a Formula 146

Enter a Function..150

Using AutoCalculate 156

Add Numbers..158

Errors in Formulas 160

Copy a Formula 162

5 FORMAT A WORKSHEET

Change Column Width 166
Change Row Height 167
Change Appearance of Numbers.............................168
Bold, Italic and Underline......................................169
Change Font of Data...170
Change Size of Data...171
Change Alignment of Data.....................................172
Indent Data...173
Add Borders 174
Change Color...176
Copy Formatting..178
Center Data Across Columns..................................179
Quickly Apply a Design 180

6 PRINT A WORKSHEET

Preview a Worksheet...182
Change Margins 184
Print a Worksheet...186
Center Data on a Page 188
Change Page Orientation.......................................189
Change Print Options..190
Insert a Page Break 192

7 USING MULTIPLE WORKSHEETS

Switch Between Worksheets 194
Insert a Worksheet 196
Delete a Worksheet 197
Rename a Worksheet 198
Move a Worksheet..199

8 WORKING WITH CHARTS

Create a Chart 200
Change Chart Type..204
Move or Resize a Chart 206
Print a Chart 208

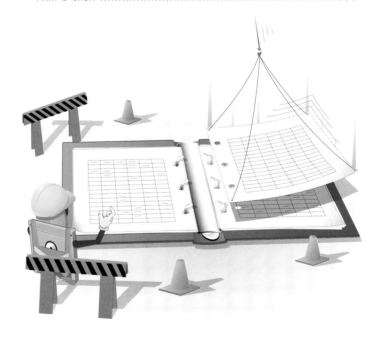

TABLE OF CONTENTS

POWERPOINT

1 GETTING STARTED

Introduction to PowerPoint 212
Start PowerPoint 213
Create a Presentation.......................................214
Change the View..220
Browse Through a Presentation 222
Save and Exit..224
Open a Presentation...226

2 EDIT SLIDES

Select Text...228
Replace Text...230
Undo Last Change 231
Insert Text 232
Delete Text 234
Move Text...236
Change Importance of Text...............................237
Check Spelling 238

3 ADD OBJECTS TO SLIDES

Change the Slide Layout 240
Add a New Slide 242
Add Clip Art or Pictures....................................244
Add a Chart...246
Add an AutoShape 250
Move or Resize an Object 252

4 ENHANCE A PRESENTATION

Change Slide Design 254
Change Color Scheme..256
Emphasize Text..258
Change Alignment of Text 259
Change Font of Text..260
Change Size of Text..261
Change Text Color 262
Change Object Color...263
Add Header and Footer 264
Animate Slides...266

5 FINE-TUNE A PRESENTATION

Reorder Slides 268
Delete a Slide..269
Create Speaker Notes..270
View a Slide Show 272
Add Slide Transitions 274
Print a Presentation 276

OUTLOOK

1 START OUTLOOK
Start Outlook...280

2 USING INBOX
View Inbox 282
Display the Mail Folders 283
Open a Message 284
Delete a Message..285
Send a Message..286
Reply to a Message 288
Forward a Message..290

3 USING NOTES
Create a Note..292
Open a Note..294
Resize a Note..295

4 USING TASKS
Create a Task 296
Mark a Task as Complete 298
Sort Tasks...299

5 USING CALENDAR
View Calendar 300
Add an Appointment.......................................302
Day, Week and Month Views 304

6 USING CONTACTS
Add a Contact..306
Update a Contact 308
Browse Through Contacts 310
Change Views..311

7 USING JOURNAL
View Journal Entries 312
Open a Journal Entry.......................................314
Select Activities to Record 316

8 PRINT
Print 318

9 USING DELETED ITEMS
Recover a Deleted Item 320
Empty Deleted Items Folder.............................322

TABLE OF CONTENTS

OFFICE AND THE INTERNET

OFFICE AND THE INTERNET

Create a Hyperlink 326

Display the Web Toolbar 330

Move Between Documents 331

Open a Document 332

Stop the Connection 334

Refresh a Document 335

Display the Start Page 336

Display the Search Page 337

Add Document to Favorites 338

Save Document as a Web Page 340

In this section you will learn the basic skills you need to use Microsoft Office programs.

Word

Excel

PowerPoint

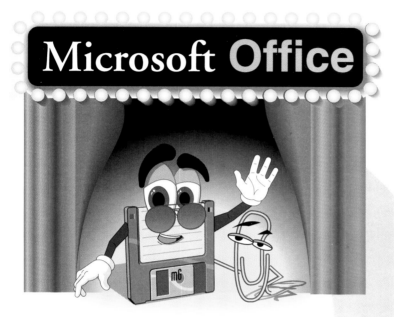

Outlook

Microsoft Office includes several programs to help you accomplish many tasks.

Each Office program has features that make it easy for you to take advantage of the World Wide Web.

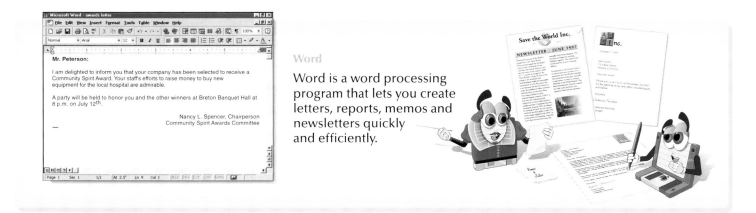

Word

Word is a word processing program that lets you create letters, reports, memos and newsletters quickly and efficiently.

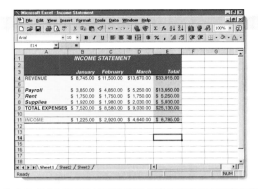

Excel

Excel is a spreadsheet program that helps you organize, analyze and present data.

PowerPoint

PowerPoint is a program that helps you plan, organize and design professional presentations.

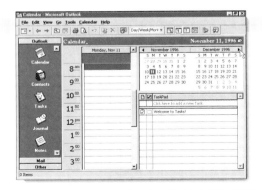

Outlook

Outlook is an information management program that helps you organize messages, appointments, contacts, tasks and activities.

USING THE MOUSE

A mouse is a hand-held device that lets you select and move items on the screen.

Holding the Mouse

Resting your hand on the mouse, use your thumb and two rightmost fingers to move the mouse on your desk. Use your two remaining fingers to press the mouse buttons.

Moving the Mouse

When you move the mouse on your desk, the mouse pointer on the screen moves in the same direction.

The mouse pointer assumes different shapes (examples: ▷, I or ✛), depending on its location on the screen and the task you are performing.

Cleaning the Mouse

A ball under the mouse senses movement. You should occasionally remove and clean this ball to ensure smooth motion of the mouse.

MOUSE ACTIONS

Click

Press and release the left mouse button.

Double-Click

Quickly press and release the left mouse button twice.

Drag and Drop

Move the mouse pointer (⬚) over an object on your screen and then press and hold down the left mouse button. Still holding down the mouse button, move the mouse to where you want to place the object and then release the mouse button.

MICROSOFT INTELLIMOUSE

The new Microsoft IntelliMouse has a wheel between the left and right mouse buttons. Moving this wheel lets you quickly scroll through information on the screen.

You can also zoom in or out with the Microsoft IntelliMouse by holding down **Ctrl** on your keyboard as you move the wheel.

START A PROGRAM

You can easily start a Microsoft Office program to create a letter, analyze finances, design a presentation or manage information.

START A PROGRAM

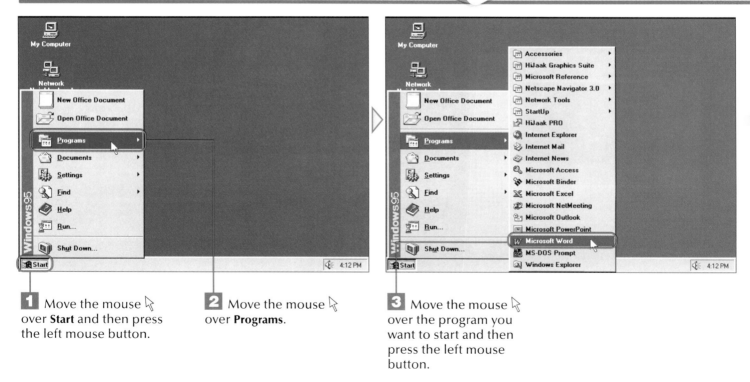

1 Move the mouse over **Start** and then press the left mouse button.

2 Move the mouse over **Programs**.

3 Move the mouse over the program you want to start and then press the left mouse button.

8

What is the difference between a toolbar and a menu bar?

Each button on a toolbar provides a fast method of selecting a command on a menu. For example, you can use the **Save** button to quickly select the **Save** command.

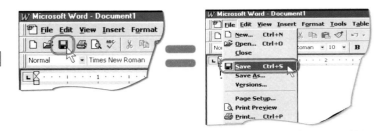

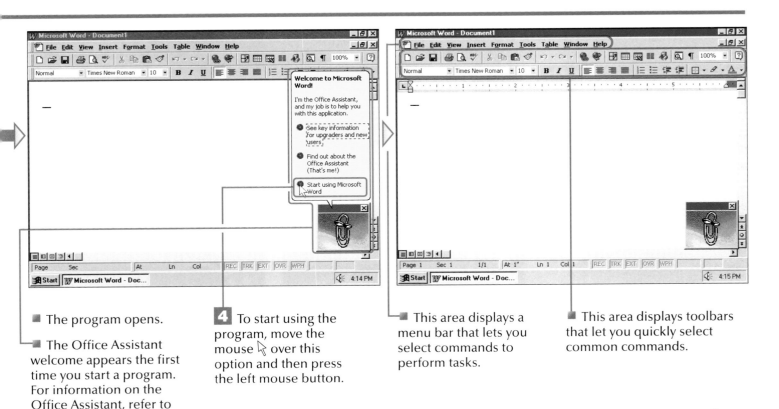

■ The program opens.

■ The Office Assistant welcome appears the first time you start a program. For information on the Office Assistant, refer to page 12.

4 To start using the program, move the mouse over this option and then press the left mouse button.

■ This area displays a menu bar that lets you select commands to perform tasks.

■ This area displays toolbars that let you quickly select common commands.

SWITCH BETWEEN PROGRAMS

You can have more than one program open at a time. You can easily switch between the open programs.

Think of each program as a separate piece of paper. Switching between programs lets you place a different piece of paper at the top of the pile.

SWITCH BETWEEN PROGRAMS

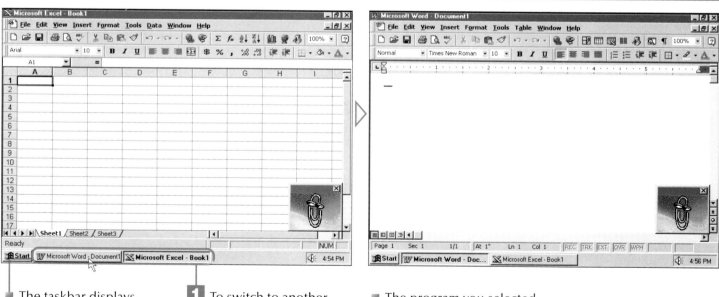

■ The taskbar displays the name of each program you have opened.

Note: To start a program, refer to page 8.

1 To switch to another program, move the mouse over the name of the program and then press the left mouse button.

■ The program you selected appears on top of all other open programs.

10

EXIT A PROGRAM

When you finish using a program, exit the program.

You should always exit all programs before turning off your computer.

EXIT A PROGRAM

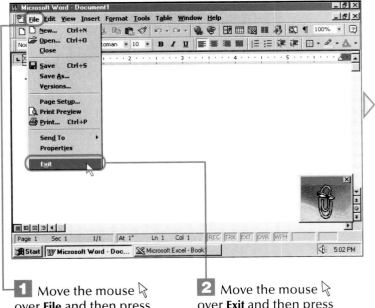

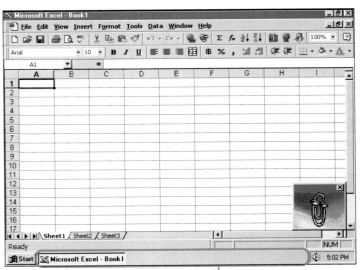

1 Move the mouse over **File** and then press the left mouse button.

2 Move the mouse over **Exit** and then press the left mouse button.

■ The program disappears from the screen.

■ The name of the program disappears from the taskbar.

If you do not know how to perform a task you can ask the Office Assistant for help.

GETTING HELP

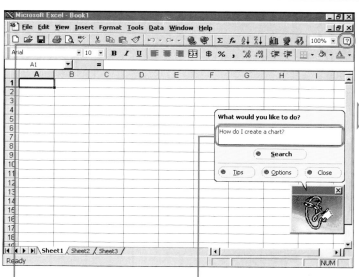

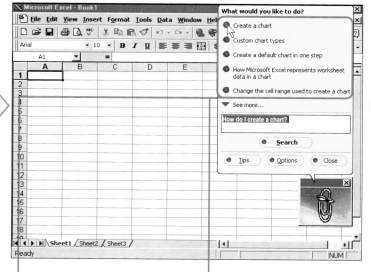

1 To display the Office Assistant, move the mouse ⍜ over 🔲 and then press the left mouse button.

2 Type the question you want to ask and then press **Enter** on your keyboard.

■ The Office Assistant displays a list of help topics that relate to the question you asked.

Note: If you do not see a help topic of interest, try rephrasing your question. Type the new question and then press **Enter** *on your keyboard.*

3 Move the mouse ⍜ over the help topic you want information on and then press the left mouse button.

How do I display the name of each toolbar button?

To display the name of a toolbar button, move the mouse ⌖ over the button. After a few seconds, the name of the button appears.

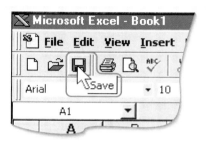

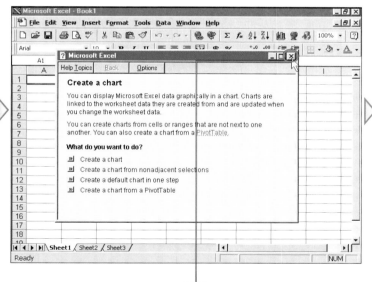

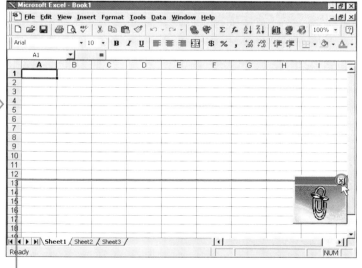

■ The Help window appears, displaying information about the topic you selected.

4 When you finish reading the information, move the mouse ⌖ over ⊠ and then press the left mouse button to close the Help window.

5 To hide the Office Assistant, move the mouse ⌖ over ⊠ and then press the left mouse button.

Microsoft Word allows you to create letters, reports, memos and newsletters.

Insert a Section Break
Page 90

I like to type.

Enter Text
Page18

Add Bullets or Numbers
Page 72

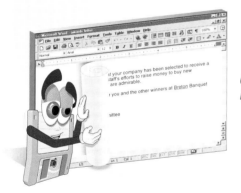

Close a Document
Page 32

Start Word
Page 17

WORD

Save a Document
Page 24

Delete Text
Page 44

Dear Susan,

I'm delighted you'll be coming to Chicago
this summer. I've requested the same vacation
time, so we'll be able to spend lots of time
together.

I've enclosed a newspaper article about
upcoming musical and ... Be sure to
write to me se... let me know what you
would lik... ee so I can order a couple of

... have to spend lots of time in Rose Park,
which is one of the city's most beautiful
spots. We can rent bicycles and enjoy the
park's scenic trails. I also know where all the
best restaurants are.

Nancy

1 Getting Started
Pages 16-23

2 Save, Print and Open a Document
Pages 24-35

3 Change Document Display
Pages 36-41

4 Edit a Document
Pages 42-59

5 Format Text
Pages 60-81

6 Format Pages
Pages 82-97

7 Working With Tables
Pages 98-109

> Word lets you produce professional documents quickly and efficiently.

You can use Word to create letters, reports, manuals, newsletters and brochures.

Editing

Word offers many features that help you work with text in a document. You can easily edit text, rearrange paragraphs and check for spelling mistakes.

Formatting

Word offers many features that help you change the appearance of a document. You can add page numbers, center text and use various fonts in a document.

Printing

You can produce a paper copy of a Word document. Word lets you see on the screen exactly what the printed document will look like.

When you start Word, a blank document appears. You can type text into this document.

START WORD

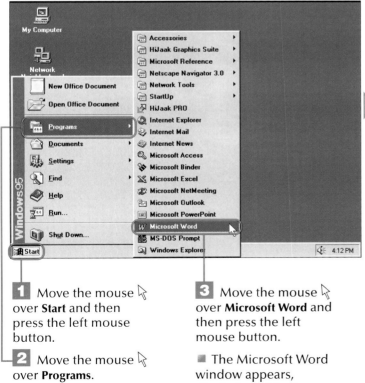

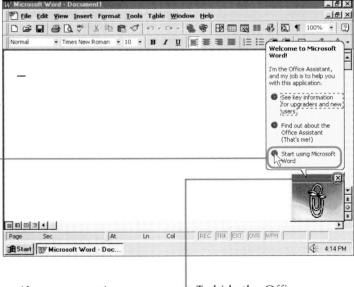

1 Move the mouse ⌖ over **Start** and then press the left mouse button.

2 Move the mouse ⌖ over **Programs**.

3 Move the mouse ⌖ over **Microsoft Word** and then press the left mouse button.

■ The Microsoft Word window appears, displaying a blank document.

■ If you are starting Word for the first time, the Office Assistant welcome appears.

4 To start using Word, move the mouse ⌖ over this option and then press the left mouse button.

■ To hide the Office Assistant, move the mouse ⌖ over ⊠ and then press the left mouse button.

Note: For more information on the Office Assistant, refer to page 12.

Word lets you type text into your document quickly and easily.

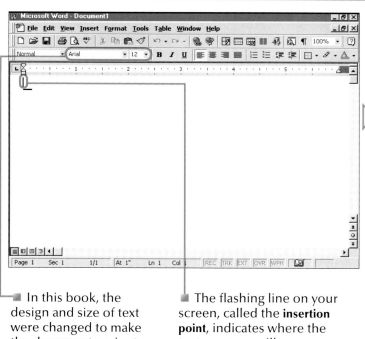

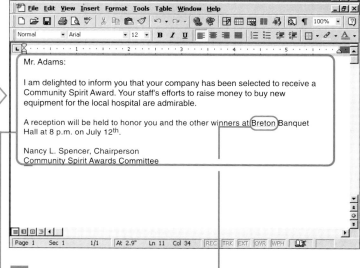

■ In this book, the design and size of text were changed to make the document easier to read. To change the design and size of text, refer to pages 62 and 63.

■ The flashing line on your screen, called the **insertion point**, indicates where the text you type will appear.

1 Type the text.

■ When you reach the end of a line, Word automatically wraps the text to the next line. You only need to press **Enter** when you want to start a new line or paragraph.

■ Word underlines misspelled words in red and grammar mistakes in green.

Note: For information on how to check spelling and grammar, refer to page 56.

THE WORD SCREEN

The Word screen displays several bars to help you perform tasks efficiently.

Standard Toolbar

Contains buttons to help you quickly select commonly used commands, such as opening a document.

Formatting Toolbar

Contains buttons to help you quickly select formatting and layout features, such as **bold** and <u>underline</u>.

Ruler

Allows you to change margin and tab settings for your document.

Status Bar

Displays information about the area of the document displayed on your screen and the position of the insertion point.

Page 1

The page displayed on your screen.

Sec 1

The section of the document displayed on your screen.

1/1

The page displayed on the screen and the total number of pages in the document.

At 1"

The distance from the top of the page to the insertion point.

Ln 1

The number of lines from the top of the page to the insertion point.

Col 1

The number of characters from the left margin to the insertion point, including spaces.

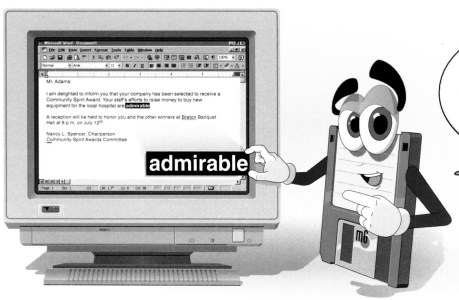

Before performing many tasks in Word, you must select the text you want to work with. Selected text appears highlighted on your screen.

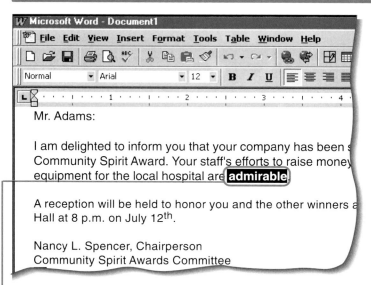

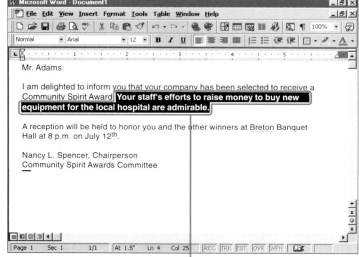

SELECT A WORD

1 Move the mouse I anywhere over the word you want to select and then quickly press the left mouse button twice.

■ To deselect text, move the mouse I outside the selected area and then press the left mouse button.

SELECT A SENTENCE

1 Press and hold down **Ctrl** on your keyboard.

2 Still holding down **Ctrl**, move the mouse I anywhere over the sentence you want to select and then press the left mouse button. Then release **Ctrl**.

How do I select all the text in a document?

To quickly select all the text in your document, press and hold down **Ctrl** and then press **A** on your keyboard. Then release both keys.

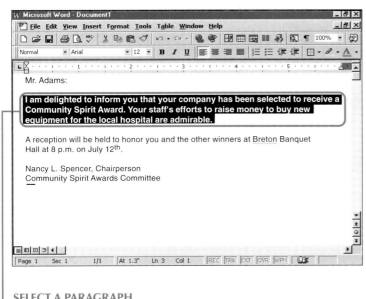

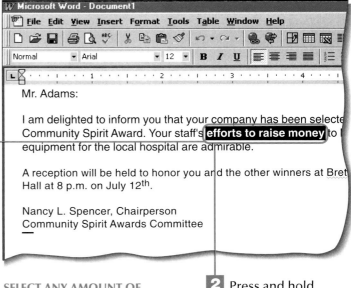

SELECT A PARAGRAPH

1 Move the mouse I anywhere over the paragraph you want to select and then quickly press the left mouse button **three** times.

SELECT ANY AMOUNT OF TEXT

1 Move the mouse I over the first word you want to select.

2 Press and hold down the left mouse button as you move the mouse I over the text you want to select. Then release the mouse button.

You can easily move to another location in your document.

If you create a long document, your computer screen cannot display all the text at the same time. You must scroll up or down to view and edit other parts of the document.

MOVE THE INSERTION POINT

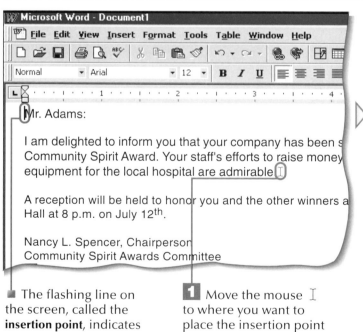

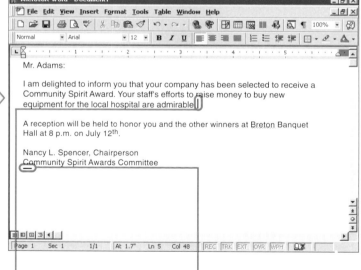

■ The flashing line on the screen, called the **insertion point**, indicates where the text you type will appear.

1 Move the mouse I to where you want to place the insertion point and then press the left mouse button.

■ The insertion point appears in the new position.

Note: You can also press ↑, ↓, ← *or* → *on your keyboard to move the insertion point one line or character in any direction.*

■ You cannot move the insertion point below the horizontal line displayed on the screen. To move this line, position the insertion point after the last character in the document and then press Enter several times.

How do I use the new Microsoft IntelliMouse to scroll?

The Microsoft IntelliMouse has a wheel between the left and right mouse buttons. Moving this wheel lets you quickly scroll through a document.

SCROLL UP OR DOWN

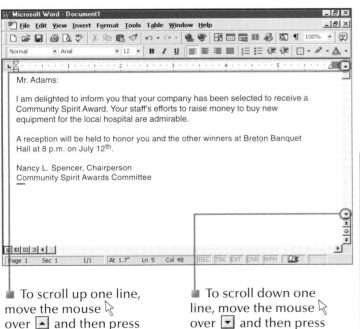

■ To scroll up one line, move the mouse ⌖ over ▲ and then press the left mouse button.

■ To scroll down one line, move the mouse ⌖ over ▼ and then press the left mouse button.

SCROLL TO ANY POSITION

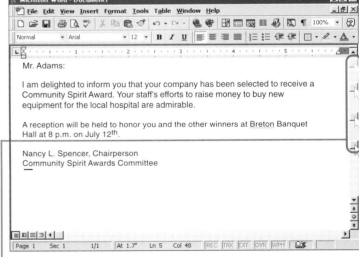

1 To quickly scroll through your document, move the mouse ⌖ over the scroll box □.

2 Press and hold down the left mouse button and then move the mouse ⌖ up or down the scroll bar. Then release the mouse button.

■ The location of the scroll box indicates which part of the document you are viewing. To view the middle of the document, move the scroll box halfway down the scroll bar.

SAVE A DOCUMENT

You should save your document to store it for future use. This lets you later retrieve the document for reviewing or editing.

SAVE A DOCUMENT

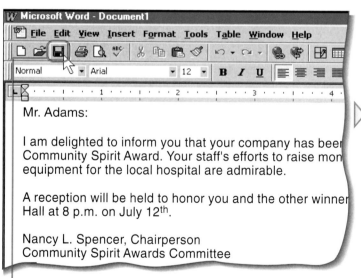

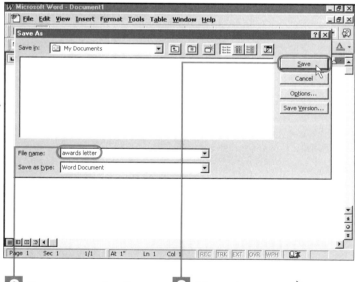

1 Move the mouse ⬚ over 🔲 and then press the left mouse button.

■ The **Save As** dialog box appears.

*Note: If you previously saved the document, the **Save As** dialog box will not appear since you have already named the document.*

2 Type a name for the document.

Note: You can use up to 255 characters to name a document.

3 Move the mouse ⬚ over **Save** and then press the left mouse button.

When you want to make major changes to a document, save the document with a different name before you begin. This gives you two copies of the document—the original document and a document with all the changes.

SAVE A DOCUMENT WITH A NEW NAME

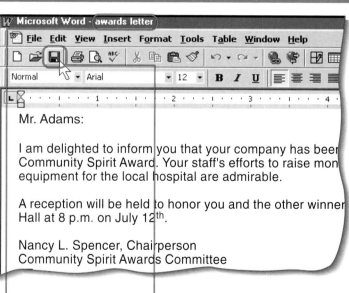

■ Word saves the document and displays the name at the top of the screen.

SAVE CHANGES

To avoid losing your work, you should regularly save changes you make to the document.

1 Move the mouse ⌖ over 🖬 and then press the left mouse button.

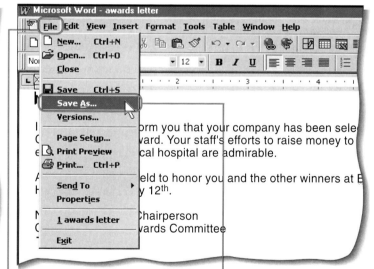

1 Move the mouse ⌖ over **File** and then press the left mouse button.

2 Move the mouse ⌖ over **Save As** and then press the left mouse button.

3 Perform steps 2 and 3 on page 24.

You can use the Print Preview feature to see how your document will look when printed.

PREVIEW A DOCUMENT

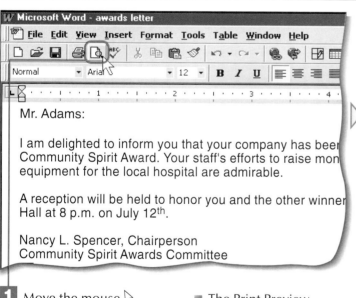

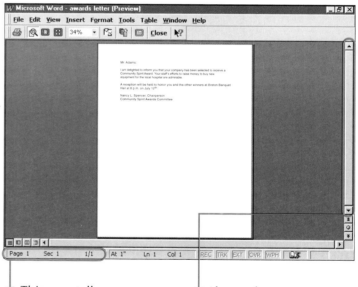

1 Move the mouse over 🔍 and then press the left mouse button.

■ The Print Preview window appears.

■ This area tells you which page is displayed and the number of pages in the document. In this example, the document contains one page.

■ If your document contains more than one page, use the scroll bar to view the other pages.

When can I edit my document in the Print Preview window?

Note: To change the shape of the mouse, perform step **3** below.

If the mouse looks like ⊥ when over your document, you can edit the document.

If the mouse looks like ⊕ or ⊖ when over your document, you can magnify or shrink the page displayed on your screen.

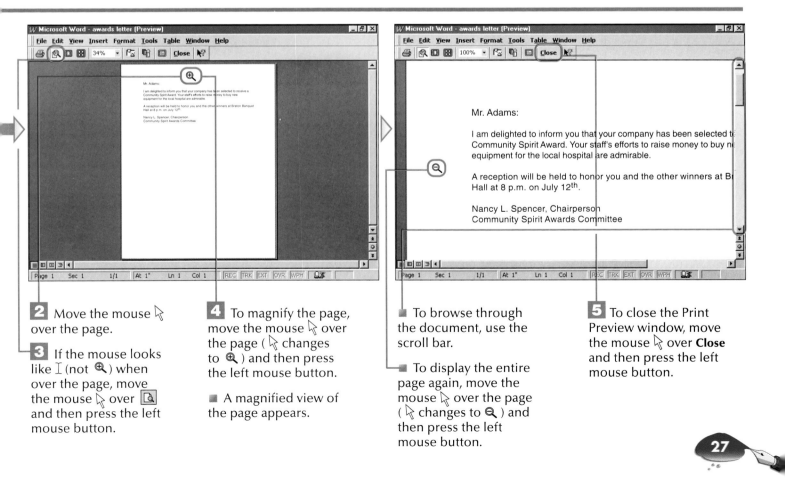

2 Move the mouse ▷ over the page.

3 If the mouse looks like ⊥ (not ⊕) when over the page, move the mouse ▷ over 🔍 and then press the left mouse button.

4 To magnify the page, move the mouse ▷ over the page (▷ changes to ⊕) and then press the left mouse button.

■ A magnified view of the page appears.

■ To browse through the document, use the scroll bar.

■ To display the entire page again, move the mouse ▷ over the page (▷ changes to ⊖) and then press the left mouse button.

5 To close the Print Preview window, move the mouse ▷ over **Close** and then press the left mouse button.

PRINT A DOCUMENT

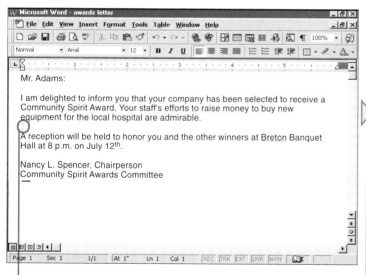

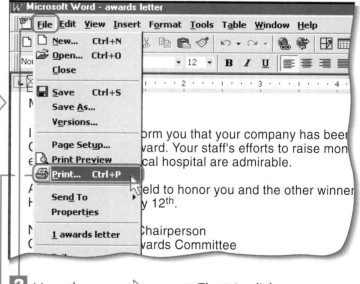

1 Move the mouse I anywhere over the document or page you want to print and then press the left mouse button.

■ To print part of the document, select the text you want to print. To select text, refer to page 20.

2 Move the mouse ⬡ over **File** and then press the left mouse button.

3 Move the mouse ⬡ over **Print** and then press the left mouse button.

■ The **Print** dialog box appears.

How do I prepare my printer to print documents?

Before printing, always make sure your printer is turned on and contains paper.

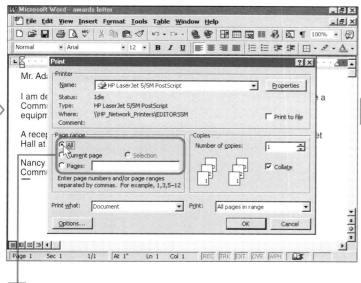

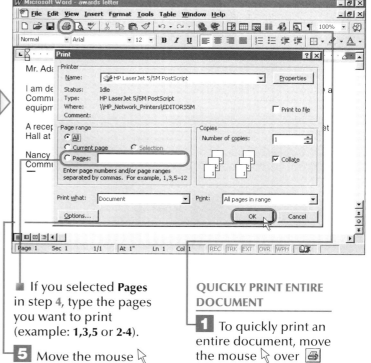

4 Move the mouse ⌖ over the print option you want to use and then press the left mouse button (○ changes to ●).

All - Prints every page in the document.

Current page - Prints the page containing the insertion point.

Pages - Prints the pages you specify.

Selection - Prints the text you selected.

■ If you selected **Pages** in step **4**, type the pages you want to print (example: **1,3,5** or **2-4**).

5 Move the mouse ⌖ over **OK** and then press the left mouse button.

QUICKLY PRINT ENTIRE DOCUMENT

1 To quickly print an entire document, move the mouse ⌖ over 🖨 and then press the left mouse button.

CREATE A NEW DOCUMENT

You can create a new document to start writing a letter, report or memo.

CREATE A NEW DOCUMENT

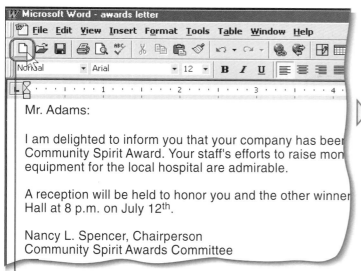

1 Move the mouse ↖ over 🗋 and then press the left mouse button.

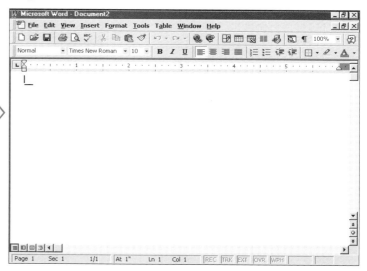

■ A new document appears. The previous document is now hidden behind the new document.

■ Think of each document as a separate piece of paper. When you create a document, you are placing a new piece of paper on the screen.

Word lets you have many documents open at once. You can easily switch from one open document to another.

SWITCH BETWEEN DOCUMENTS

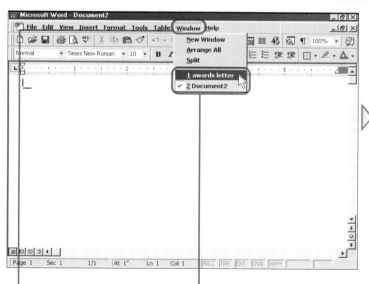

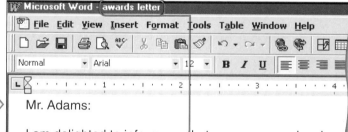

Mr. Adams:

I am delighted to inform you that your company has been Community Spirit Award. Your staff's efforts to raise mon equipment for the local hospital are admirable.

A reception will be held to honor you and the other winner Hall at 8 p.m. on July 12th.

Nancy L. Spencer, Chairperson
Community Spirit Awards Committee

1 To display a list of all open documents, move the mouse over **Window** and then press the left mouse button.

2 Move the mouse over the document you want to display and then press the left mouse button.

■ The document appears.

■ Word displays the name of the document at the top of your screen.

When you finish working with a document, you can close the document to remove it from your screen.

When you close a document, you do not exit the Word program. You can continue to work on other Word documents.

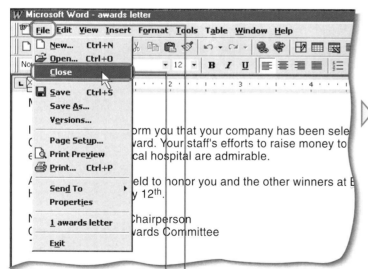

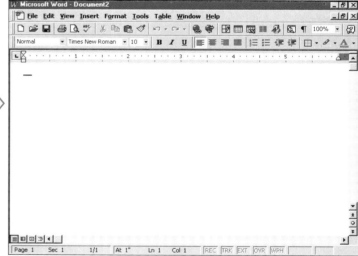

◼ To save the document displayed on the screen before closing, refer to page 24.

1 To close the document, move the mouse ⟍ over **File** and then press the left mouse button.

2 Move the mouse ⟍ over **Close** and then press the left mouse button.

◼ Word removes the document from the screen.

◼ If you had more than one document open, the second last document you worked on appears on the screen.

EXIT WORD

When you finish using Word, you can exit the program.

You should always exit all programs before turning off your computer.

EXIT WORD

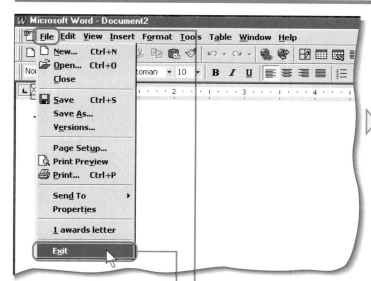

■ Save all open documents before exiting Word. To save a document, refer to page 24.

1 Move the mouse over **File** and then press the left mouse button.

2 Move the mouse over **Exit** and then press the left mouse button.

■ The Word window disappears from the screen.

Note: To restart Word, refer to page 17.

OPEN A DOCUMENT

You can open a saved document and display it on your screen. This allows you to review and make changes to your document.

OPEN A DOCUMENT

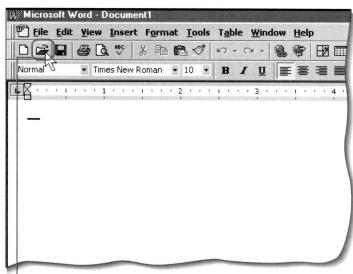

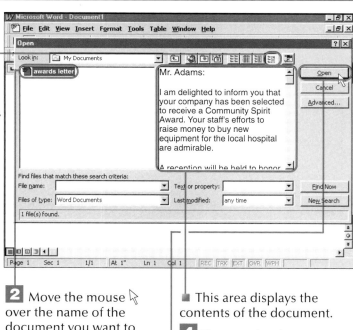

1 Move the mouse ⊳ over 📂 and then press the left mouse button.

■ The **Open** dialog box appears.

2 Move the mouse ⊳ over the name of the document you want to open and then press the left mouse button.

3 To see the contents of the document, move the mouse ⊳ over 🖽 and then press the left mouse button.

■ This area displays the contents of the document.

4 To open the document, move the mouse ⊳ over **Open** and then press the left mouse button.

Word remembers the names of the last four documents you worked with. You can quickly open any of these documents.

QUICKLY OPEN A DOCUMENT

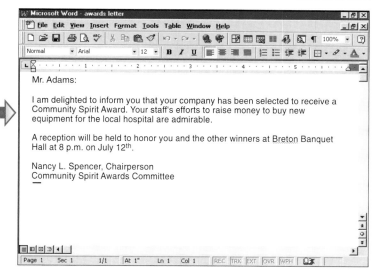

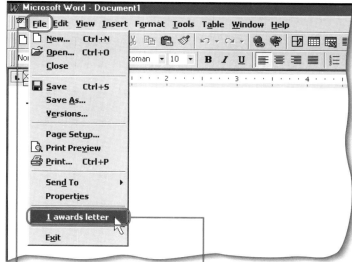

■ Word opens the document and displays it on the screen. You can now review and make changes to the document.

1 Move the mouse over **File** and then press the left mouse button.

2 Move the mouse over the name of the document you want to open and then press the left mouse button.

CHANGE THE VIEW

> Word offers four different ways to display your document. You can choose the view that best suits your needs.

CHANGE THE VIEW

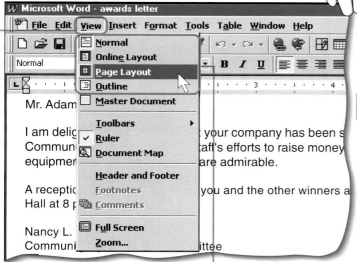

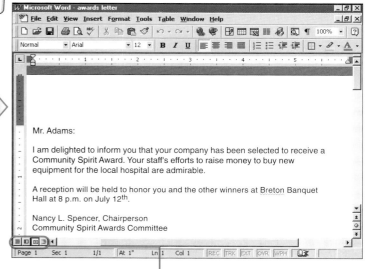

When you first start Word, the document appears in the Normal view.

1 To change the view, move the mouse over **View** and then press the left mouse button.

2 Move the mouse over the view you want to use and then press the left mouse button.

■ The document appears in the new view.

QUICKLY CHANGE THE VIEW

1 To quickly change the view, move the mouse over one of the following options and then press the left mouse button.

- ▤ Normal
- ▤ Online Layout
- ▤ Page Layout
- ▤ Outline

THE FOUR VIEWS

Normal View

This view simplifies the document so you can quickly enter, edit and format text. The Normal view does not display top or bottom margins, headers, footers or page numbers.

Outline View

This view helps you review and work with the structure of a document. You can focus on the main headings by hiding the remaining text.

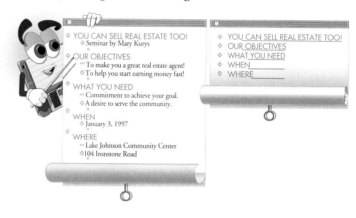

Page Layout View

This view displays the document exactly as it will appear on a printed page. The Page Layout view displays top and bottom margins, headers, footers and page numbers.

Online Layout View

This view displays documents so they are easy to read on the screen. The Online Layout view displays a document map, which lets you move quickly to specific locations in your document.

Word lets you enlarge or reduce the display of text on your screen.

Changing the zoom setting will not affect the way the document appears on a printed page.

ZOOM IN OR OUT

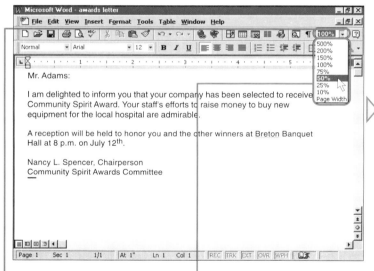

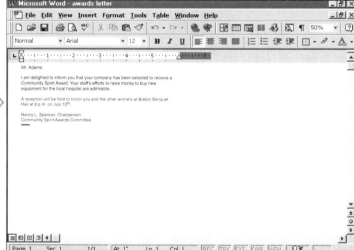

■ When you first start Word, the document appears in the 100% zoom setting.

1 To display a list of zoom settings, move the mouse ⬐ over 🔽 in this area and then press the left mouse button.

2 Move the mouse ⬐ over the setting you want to use and then press the left mouse button.

■ The document appears in the new zoom setting. You can edit your document as usual.

■ To return to the normal zoom setting, repeat steps **1** and **2**, selecting **100%** in step **2**.

You can use the ruler to position text on a page. You can display or hide the ruler at any time.

When you first start Word, the ruler is displayed on your screen. Hiding the ruler provides a larger and less cluttered working area.

DISPLAY THE RULER

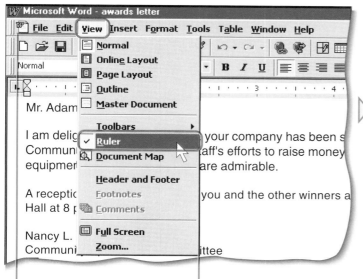

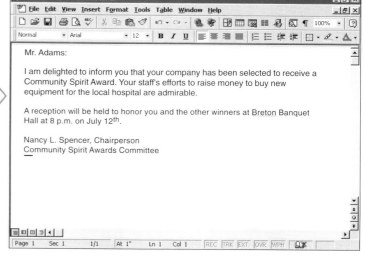

1 To display or hide the ruler, move the mouse ⬧ over **View** and then press the left mouse button.

2 Move the mouse ⬧ over **Ruler** and then press the left mouse button. A check mark (✓) beside **Ruler** tells you the ruler is currently displayed.

■ Word displays or hides the ruler.

Word offers several toolbars that you can hide or display at any time. Each toolbar contains buttons that help you quickly perform common tasks.

DISPLAY TOOLBARS

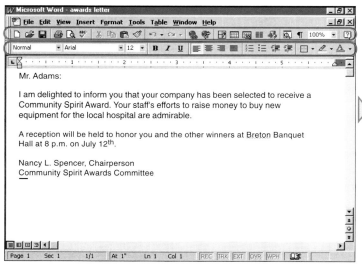

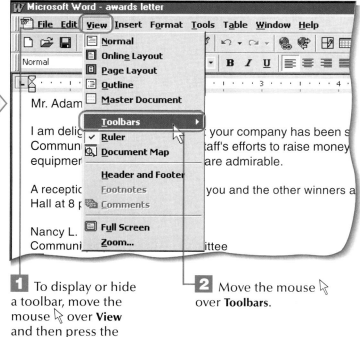

When you first start Word, the Standard and Formatting toolbars appear on the screen.

Standard toolbar

Formatting toolbar

1 To display or hide a toolbar, move the mouse over **View** and then press the left mouse button.

2 Move the mouse over **Toolbars**.

Why would I want to hide a toolbar?

A screen displaying fewer toolbars provides a larger and less cluttered working area.

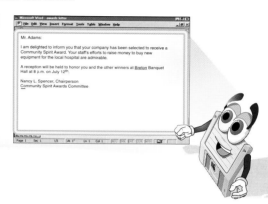

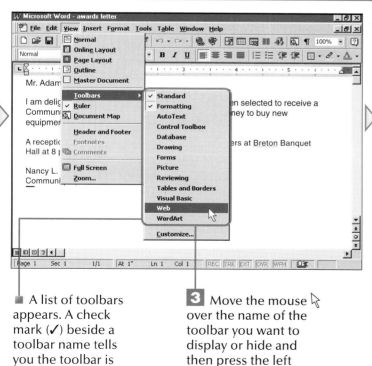

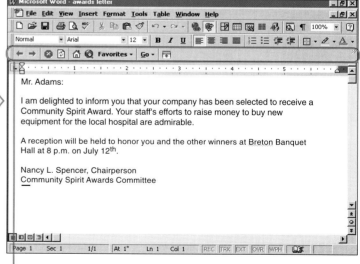

■ A list of toolbars appears. A check mark (✓) beside a toolbar name tells you the toolbar is currently displayed.

3 Move the mouse over the name of the toolbar you want to display or hide and then press the left mouse button.

■ Word displays or hides the toolbar you selected.

INSERT TEXT

You can easily add new text to your document. The existing text will move to make room for the text you add.

INSERT CHARACTERS

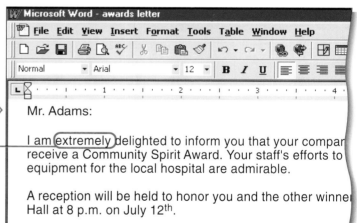

1 Move the mouse I to where you want to insert the new text and then press the left mouse button.

2 Type the text you want to insert. To insert a blank space, press the **Spacebar.**

■ The words to the right of the new text move forward.

How do I insert symbols into my document?

Word will automatically replace specific characters you type with symbols. This lets you quickly enter symbols that are not available on your keyboard.

Note: For more information on inserting symbols, refer to page 70.

INSERT A BLANK LINE

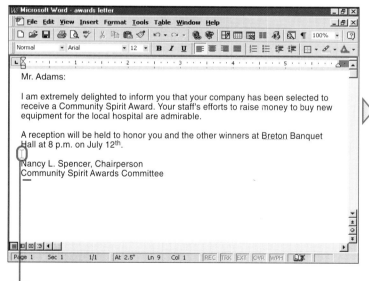

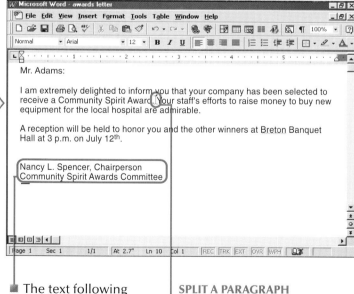

1 Move the mouse I to where you want to insert a blank line and then press the left mouse button.

2 Press **Enter** on your keyboard to insert the blank line.

■ The text following the blank line moves down one line.

SPLIT A PARAGRAPH

1 Move the mouse I to where you want to split a paragraph in two and then press the left mouse button.

2 Press **Enter** on your keyboard twice.

DELETE TEXT

You can easily remove text you no longer need. The remaining text moves to fill any empty spaces.

DELETE CHARACTERS

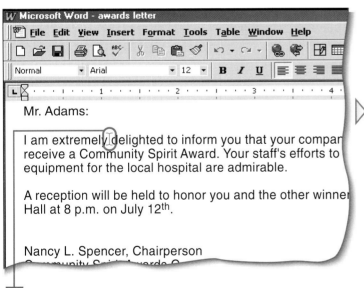

1 Move the mouse I to the **right** of the first character you want to delete and then press the left mouse button.

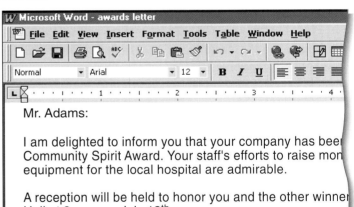

2 Press **←Backspace** on your keyboard once for each character or space you want to delete.

■ You can also use **Delete** on your keyboard to remove characters. Move the mouse I to the **left** of the first character you want to remove and then press the left mouse button. Press **Delete** once for each character or space you want to remove.

Can I recover text I accidentally delete?

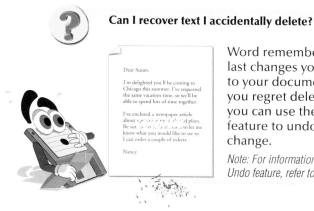

Word remembers the last changes you made to your document. If you regret deleting text, you can use the Undo feature to undo the change.

Note: For information on the Undo feature, refer to page 47.

DELETE A BLANK LINE

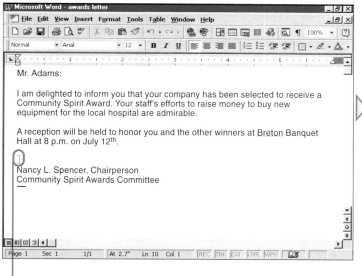

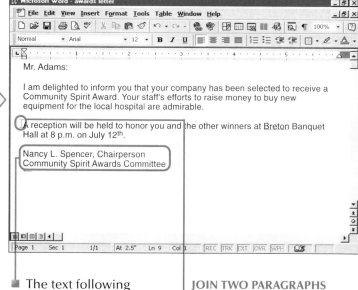

1 Move the mouse I to the beginning of the blank line you want to delete and then press the left mouse button.

2 Press **◆Backspace** on your keyboard to remove the blank line.

■ The text following the blank line moves up one line.

JOIN TWO PARAGRAPHS

1 Move the mouse I to the left of the first character in the second paragraph and then press the left mouse button.

2 Press **◆Backspace** on your keyboard until the paragraphs are joined.

DELETE TEXT

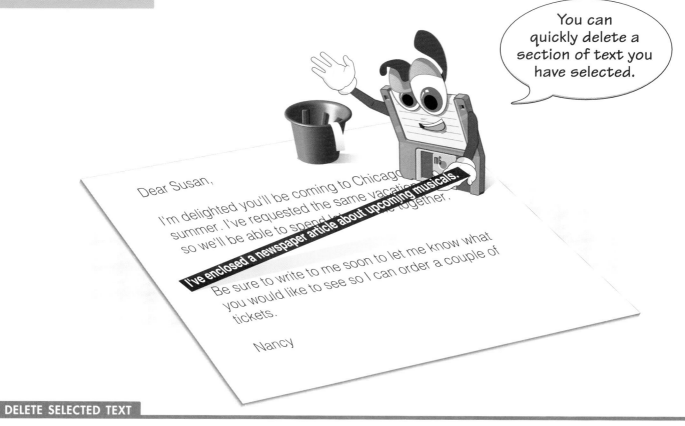

You can quickly delete a section of text you have selected.

Dear Susan,

I'm delighted you'll be coming to Chicago summer. I've requested the same vacation so we'll be able to spend time together.

~~I've enclosed a newspaper article about upcoming musicals.~~

Be sure to write to me soon to let me know what you would like to see so I can order a couple of tickets.

Nancy

DELETE SELECTED TEXT

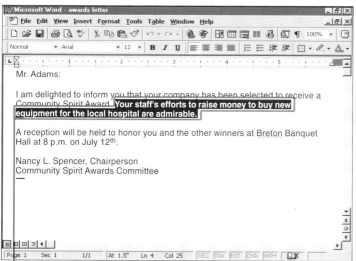

1 Select the text you want to delete. To select text, refer to page 20.

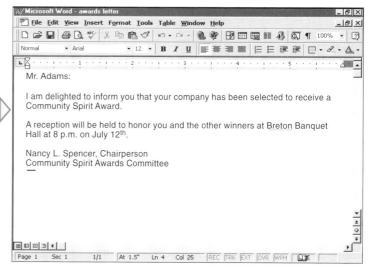

2 Press **Delete** on your keyboard to remove the text.

Word remembers the last changes you made to your document. If you regret these changes, you can cancel them by using the Undo feature.

UNDO LAST CHANGE

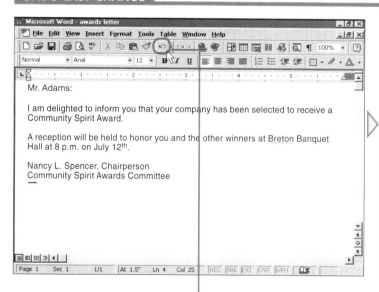

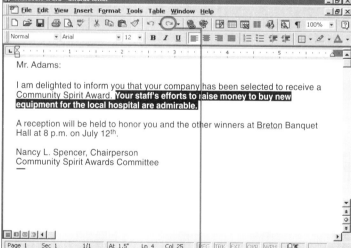

The Undo feature can cancel your last editing and formatting changes.

1 To undo your last change, move the mouse over and then press the left mouse button.

■ Word cancels the last change you made to your document.

■ You can repeat step 1 to cancel previous changes you made.

■ To reverse the results of using the Undo feature, move the mouse over and then press the left mouse button.

MOVE TEXT

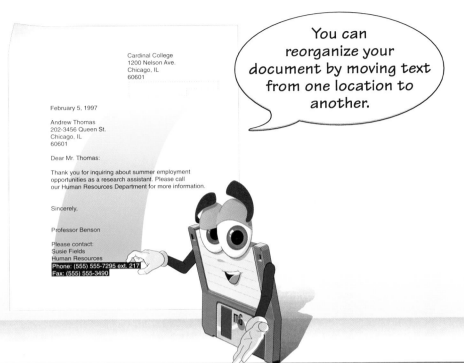

You can reorganize your document by moving text from one location to another.

MOVE TEXT

1 Select the text you want to move. To select text, refer to page 20.

2 Move the mouse I anywhere over the selected text (I changes to ⬚).

3 Press and hold down the left mouse button as you move the mouse ⬚ to where you want to place the text.

■ The text will appear where you position the dotted insertion point on your screen.

Can moving text help me edit my document?

Moving text lets you easily try out different ways of organizing the text in a document. You can find the most effective structure for your document by experimenting with different placements of sentences and paragraphs.

MOVE TEXT USING TOOLBAR

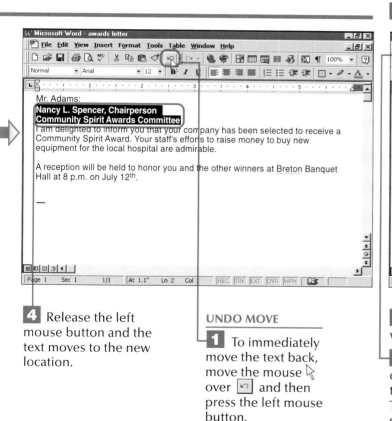

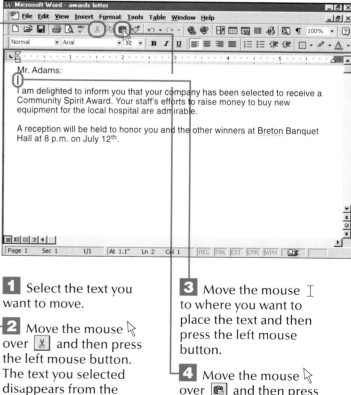

4 Release the left mouse button and the text moves to the new location.

UNDO MOVE

1 To immediately move the text back, move the mouse ⌖ over 🔄 and then press the left mouse button.

1 Select the text you want to move.

2 Move the mouse ⌖ over ✂ and then press the left mouse button. The text you selected disappears from the screen.

3 Move the mouse I to where you want to place the text and then press the left mouse button.

4 Move the mouse ⌖ over 📋 and then press the left mouse button. The text appears in the new location.

49

You can place a copy of text in a different location in your document. This will save you time since you do not have to retype the text.

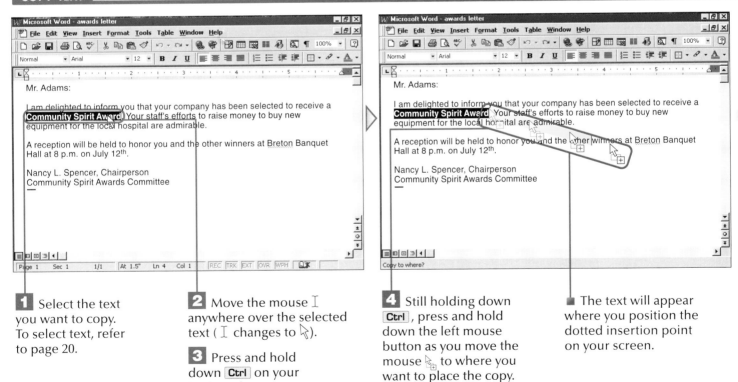

1 Select the text you want to copy. To select text, refer to page 20.

2 Move the mouse I anywhere over the selected text (I changes to ⤢).

3 Press and hold down **Ctrl** on your keyboard.

4 Still holding down **Ctrl**, press and hold down the left mouse button as you move the mouse ⤢ to where you want to place the copy.

■ The text will appear where you position the dotted insertion point on your screen.

How can copying text help me edit my document?

If you plan to make major changes to a paragraph, you may want to copy the paragraph before you begin. This gives you two copies of the paragraph—the original paragraph and a paragraph with all the changes.

There is a **10th** anniversary High School Reunion on August 8, 9 and 10 at **Woodblock** High School. We all hope to see you there. **Contact Susan Hughes** for more information.

There is an **11th** anniversary High School Reunion on August 8, 9 and 10 at **Brown** High School. We all hope to see you there. **Call Bob Maki** for more information.

COPY TEXT USING TOOLBAR

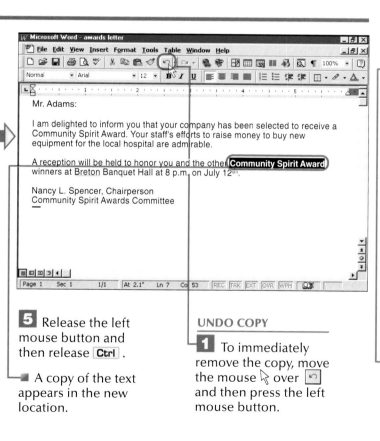

5 Release the left mouse button and then release **Ctrl**.

■ A copy of the text appears in the new location.

UNDO COPY

1 To immediately remove the copy, move the mouse ♐ over 🔙 and then press the left mouse button.

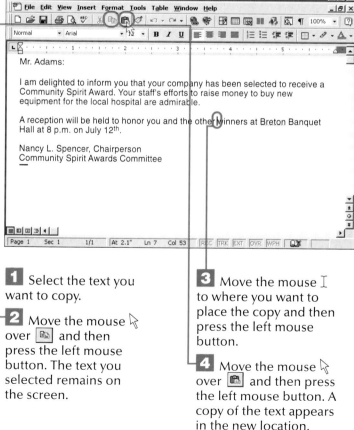

1 Select the text you want to copy.

2 Move the mouse ♐ over 🔳 and then press the left mouse button. The text you selected remains on the screen.

3 Move the mouse I to where you want to place the copy and then press the left mouse button.

4 Move the mouse ♐ over 🔳 and then press the left mouse button. A copy of the text appears in the new location.

You can use the Find feature to locate a word or phrase in your document.

sniff
sniff sniff

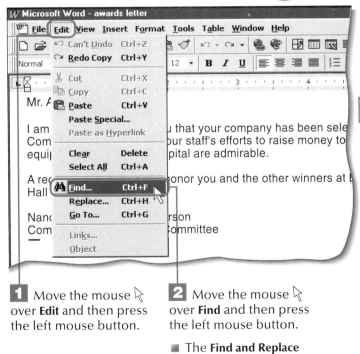

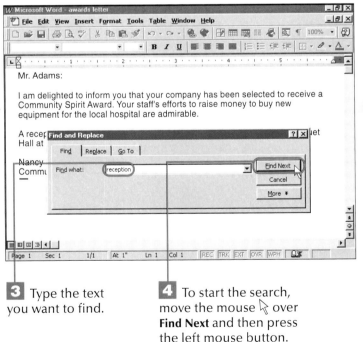

1 Move the mouse over **Edit** and then press the left mouse button.

2 Move the mouse over **Find** and then press the left mouse button.

■ The **Find and Replace** dialog box appears.

3 Type the text you want to find.

4 To start the search, move the mouse over **Find Next** and then press the left mouse button.

Can I search for part of a word?

When you search for text in your document, Word will find the text even if it is part of a larger word. For example, if you search for **place**, Word will also find **place**s, **place**ment and common**place**.

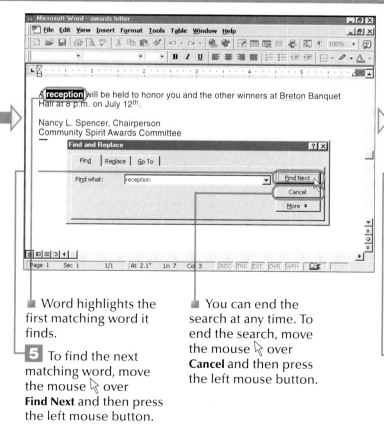

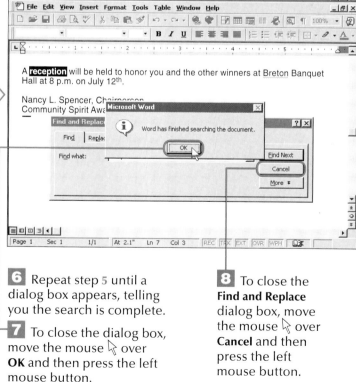

■ Word highlights the first matching word it finds.

5 To find the next matching word, move the mouse ➤ over **Find Next** and then press the left mouse button.

■ You can end the search at any time. To end the search, move the mouse ➤ over **Cancel** and then press the left mouse button.

6 Repeat step 5 until a dialog box appears, telling you the search is complete.

7 To close the dialog box, move the mouse ➤ over **OK** and then press the left mouse button.

8 To close the **Find and Replace** dialog box, move the mouse ➤ over **Cancel** and then press the left mouse button.

The Replace feature can locate and replace every occurrence of a word or phrase in your document. This is ideal if you have frequently misspelled a name.

REPLACE TEXT

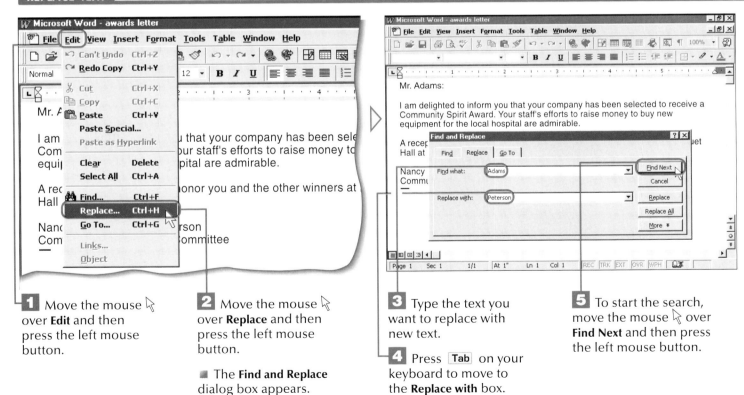

1 Move the mouse ᐃ over **Edit** and then press the left mouse button.

2 Move the mouse ᐃ over **Replace** and then press the left mouse button.

■ The **Find and Replace** dialog box appears.

3 Type the text you want to replace with new text.

4 Press **Tab** on your keyboard to move to the **Replace with** box. Then type the new text.

5 To start the search, move the mouse ᐃ over **Find Next** and then press the left mouse button.

Can I use the Replace feature to enter text more quickly?

The Replace feature is useful if you have to type a long word or phrase (example: University of Massachusetts) many times in a document. You can type a short form of the word or phrase (example: UM) throughout your document and then have Word replace the short form with the full word or phrase.

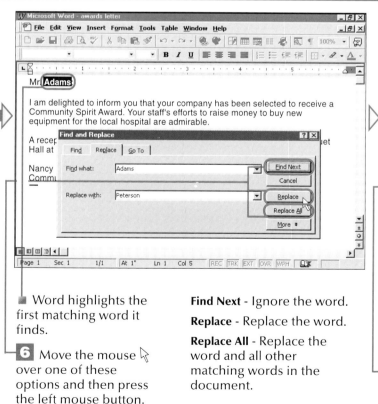

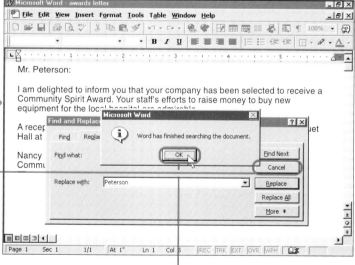

■ Word highlights the first matching word it finds.

6 Move the mouse ⌖ over one of these options and then press the left mouse button.

Find Next - Ignore the word.

Replace - Replace the word.

Replace All - Replace the word and all other matching words in the document.

■ In this example, Word replaces the text and searches for the next matching word.

■ You can end the search at any time. To end the search, move the mouse ⌖ over **Cancel** or **Close** and then press the left mouse button.

7 Repeat step 6 until a dialog box appears, telling you the search is complete.

8 To close the dialog box, move the mouse ⌖ over **OK** and then press the left mouse button.

CHECK SPELLING AND GRAMMAR

Word offers a Spelling and Grammar feature to help you find and correct errors in your document.

spelling error
wether

Suggestions
weather
wetter
whether
wither

grammar error
I did not buy no books.

I did not buy any books.

Word automatically underlines misspelled words in red and grammar mistakes in green. The red and green underlines will not appear when you print your document.

CHECK SPELLING AND GRAMMAR

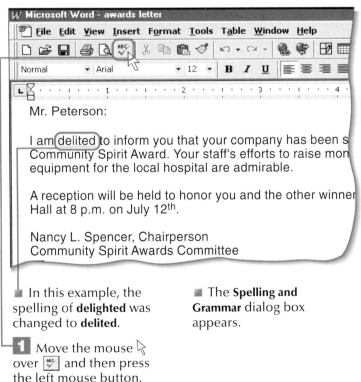

Mr. Peterson:

I am (delited) to inform you that your company has been s
Community Spirit Award. Your staff's efforts to raise mon
equipment for the local hospital are admirable.

A reception will be held to honor you and the other winner
Hall at 8 p.m. on July 12th.

Nancy L. Spencer, Chairperson
Community Spirit Awards Committee

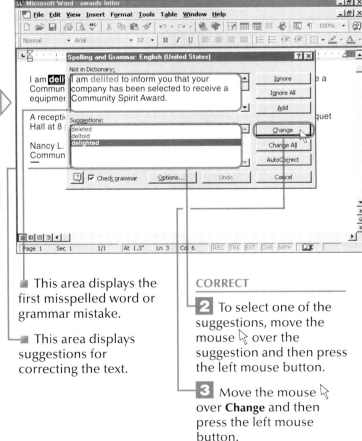

■ In this example, the spelling of **delighted** was changed to **delited**.

1 Move the mouse ⌖ over 🔤 and then press the left mouse button.

■ The **Spelling and Grammar** dialog box appears.

■ This area displays the first misspelled word or grammar mistake.

■ This area displays suggestions for correcting the text.

CORRECT

2 To select one of the suggestions, move the mouse ⌖ over the suggestion and then press the left mouse button.

3 Move the mouse ⌖ over **Change** and then press the left mouse button.

Can Word automatically correct my typing mistakes?

Word automatically corrects common spelling errors as you type.

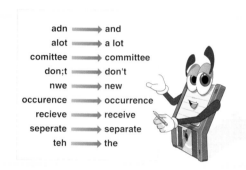

adn ⟹ and
alot ⟹ a lot
comittee ⟹ committee
don;t ⟹ don't
nwe ⟹ new
occurence ⟹ occurrence
recieve ⟹ receive
seperate ⟹ separate
teh ⟹ the

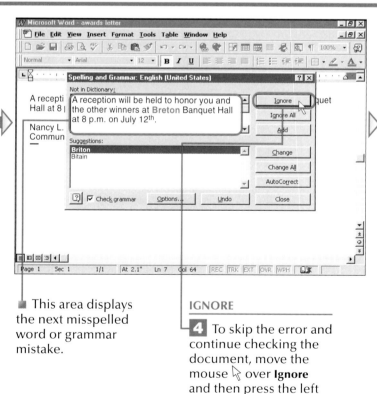

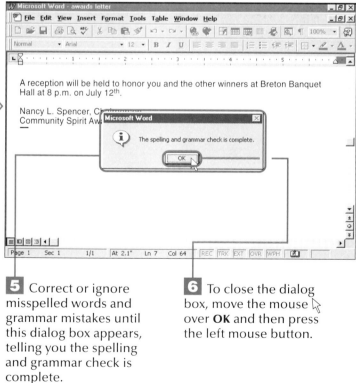

■ This area displays the next misspelled word or grammar mistake.

IGNORE

4 To skip the error and continue checking the document, move the mouse ⥄ over **Ignore** and then press the left mouse button.

*Note: To skip the error and all occurrences of the error, move the mouse ⥄ over **Ignore All** and then press the left mouse button.*

5 Correct or ignore misspelled words and grammar mistakes until this dialog box appears, telling you the spelling and grammar check is complete.

6 To close the dialog box, move the mouse ⥄ over **OK** and then press the left mouse button.

USING THE THESAURUS

You can use the Thesaurus to replace a word in your document with one that is more suitable.

Word big

Suggestions large immense huge gigantic

USING THE THESAURUS

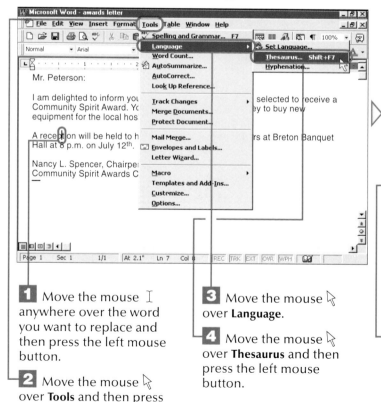

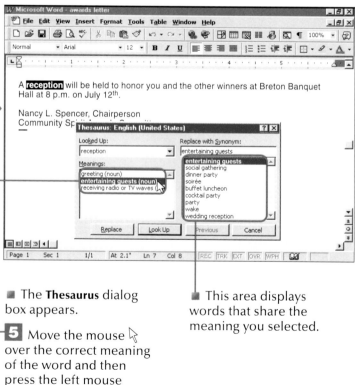

1 Move the mouse I anywhere over the word you want to replace and then press the left mouse button.

2 Move the mouse Ⓚ over **Tools** and then press the left mouse button.

3 Move the mouse Ⓚ over **Language**.

4 Move the mouse Ⓚ over **Thesaurus** and then press the left mouse button.

■ The **Thesaurus** dialog box appears.

5 Move the mouse Ⓚ over the correct meaning of the word and then press the left mouse button.

■ This area displays words that share the meaning you selected.

How can the Thesaurus feature help me?

Using the Thesaurus included with Word is faster and more convenient than searching through a printed thesaurus.

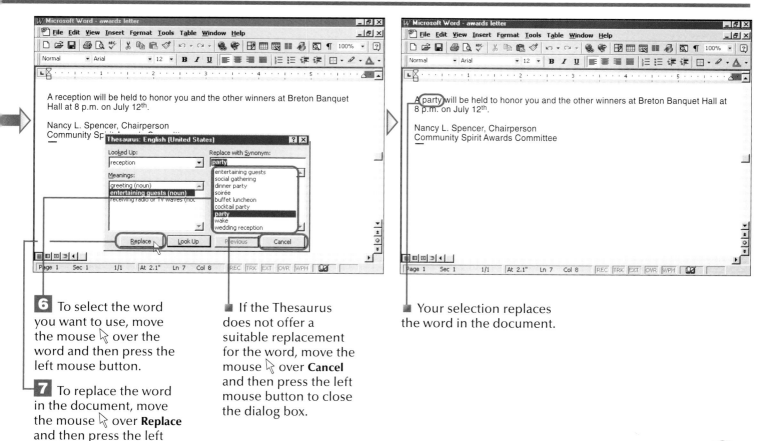

6 To select the word you want to use, move the mouse ⬚ over the word and then press the left mouse button.

7 To replace the word in the document, move the mouse ⬚ over **Replace** and then press the left mouse button.

■ If the Thesaurus does not offer a suitable replacement for the word, move the mouse ⬚ over **Cancel** and then press the left mouse button to close the dialog box.

■ Your selection replaces the word in the document.

BOLD, ITALIC AND UNDERLINE

You can use the Bold, Italic and Underline features to emphasize information in your document.

Bold   *Italic*   <u>Underline</u>

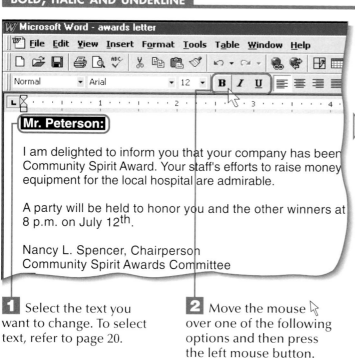

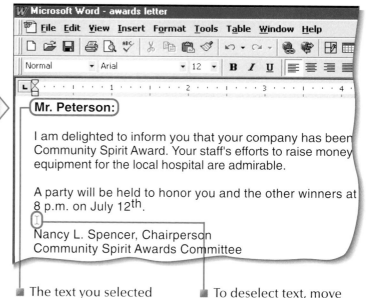

1 Select the text you want to change. To select text, refer to page 20.

2 Move the mouse ⬚ over one of the following options and then press the left mouse button.

   B Bold
   I Italic
   <u>U</u> Underline

■ The text you selected appears in the new style.

■ To deselect text, move the mouse Ⅰ outside the selected area and then press the left mouse button.

■ To remove a bold, italic or underline style, repeat steps **1** and **2**.

You can enhance the appearance of your document by aligning text in different ways.

CHANGE ALIGNMENT OF TEXT

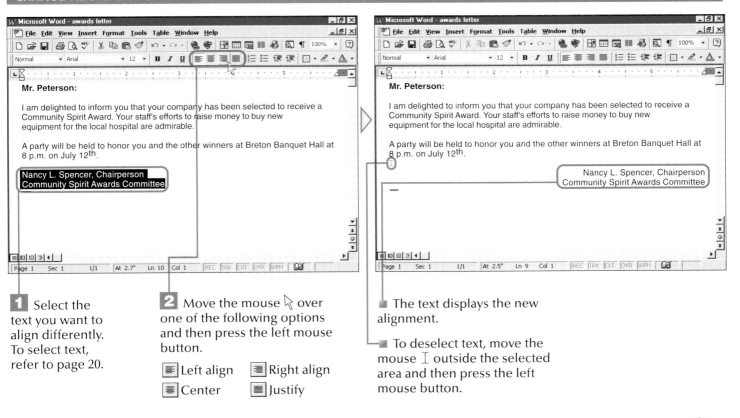

1 Select the text you want to align differently. To select text, refer to page 20.

2 Move the mouse ⬚ over one of the following options and then press the left mouse button.

▤ Left align ▤ Right align
▤ Center ▤ Justify

■ The text displays the new alignment.

■ To deselect text, move the mouse I outside the selected area and then press the left mouse button.

You can enhance the appearance of your document by changing the design of the text.

CHANGE FONT OF TEXT

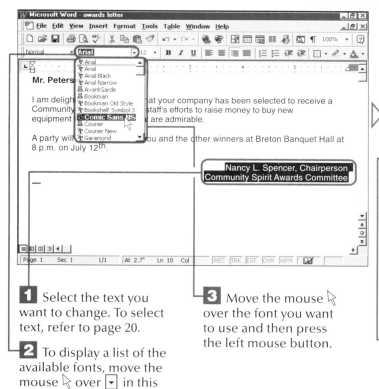

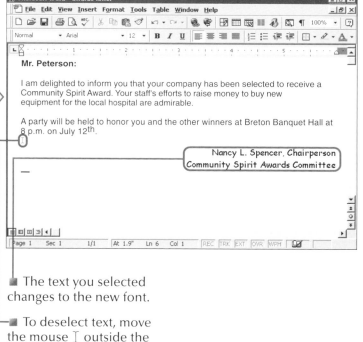

1 Select the text you want to change. To select text, refer to page 20.

2 To display a list of the available fonts, move the mouse ⌖ over ▾ in this area and then press the left mouse button.

3 Move the mouse ⌖ over the font you want to use and then press the left mouse button.

■ The text you selected changes to the new font.

■ To deselect text, move the mouse Ⅰ outside the selected area and then press the left mouse button.

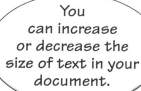

You can increase or decrease the size of text in your document.

8 point
12 point
14 point
18 point
24 point

Word measures the size of text in points. There are approximately 72 points in one inch.

Smaller text lets you fit more information on a page, but larger text is easier to read.

CHANGE SIZE OF TEXT

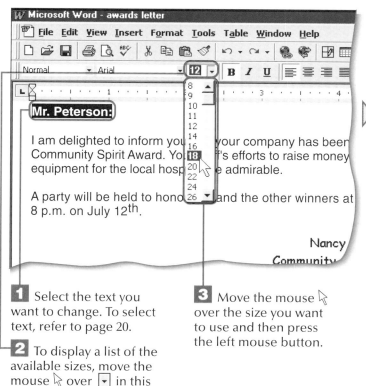

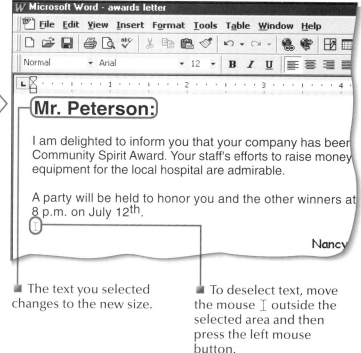

1 Select the text you want to change. To select text, refer to page 20.

2 To display a list of the available sizes, move the mouse ⬚ over 🔽 in this area and then press the left mouse button.

3 Move the mouse ⬚ over the size you want to use and then press the left mouse button.

■ The text you selected changes to the new size.

■ To deselect text, move the mouse ⌶ outside the selected area and then press the left mouse button.

You can make text in your document look attractive by using various fonts, sizes, styles, underlines and special effects.

CHANGE APPEARANCE OF TEXT

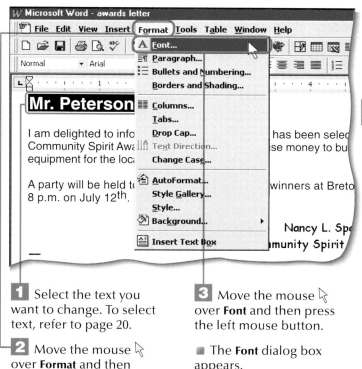

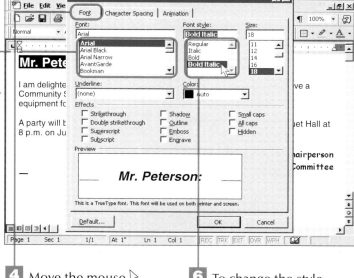

1 Select the text you want to change. To select text, refer to page 20.

2 Move the mouse ⌖ over **Format** and then press the left mouse button.

3 Move the mouse ⌖ over **Font** and then press the left mouse button.

■ The **Font** dialog box appears.

4 Move the mouse ⌖ over the **Font** tab and then press the left mouse button.

5 To change the design of the text, move the mouse ⌖ over the font you want to use and then press the left mouse button.

6 To change the style of the text, move the mouse ⌖ over the style you want to use and then press the left mouse button.

What underline styles and special effects can I add to my document?

Word offers many underline styles and special effects.

Underline Styles	Effects
Single	Strikethrough
Double	Shadow
Dash	Emboss
Wave	Engrave

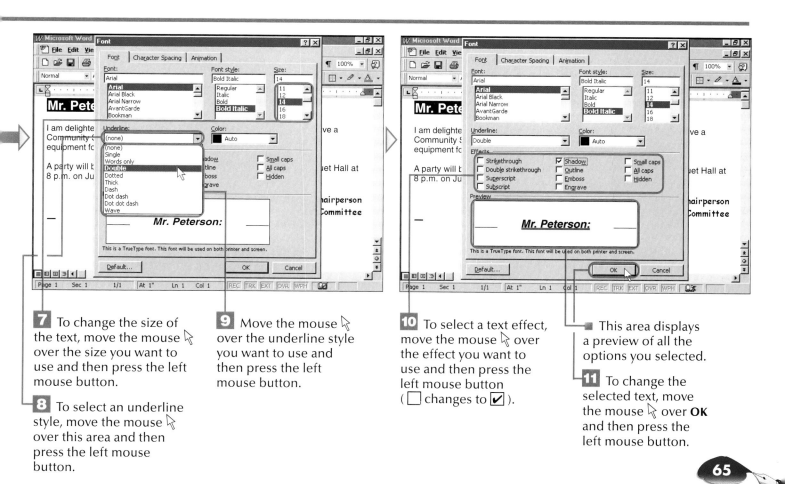

7 To change the size of the text, move the mouse over the size you want to use and then press the left mouse button.

8 To select an underline style, move the mouse over this area and then press the left mouse button.

9 Move the mouse over the underline style you want to use and then press the left mouse button.

10 To select a text effect, move the mouse over the effect you want to use and then press the left mouse button (☐ changes to ☑).

■ This area displays a preview of all the options you selected.

11 To change the selected text, move the mouse over **OK** and then press the left mouse button.

You can change the color of text to draw attention to headings or important information in your document.

CHANGE TEXT COLOR

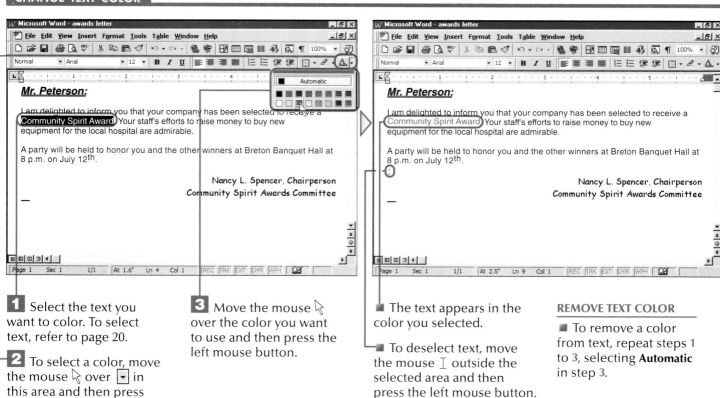

1 Select the text you want to color. To select text, refer to page 20.

2 To select a color, move the mouse ⟨ over ⏷ in this area and then press the left mouse button.

3 Move the mouse ⟨ over the color you want to use and then press the left mouse button.

◼ The text appears in the color you selected.

◼ To deselect text, move the mouse I outside the selected area and then press the left mouse button.

REMOVE TEXT COLOR

◼ To remove a color from text, repeat steps **1** to **3**, selecting **Automatic** in step **3**.

You can highlight important text in your document. Highlighting text is useful for marking text you want to verify later.

HIGHLIGHT TEXT

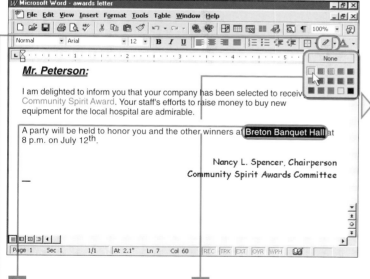

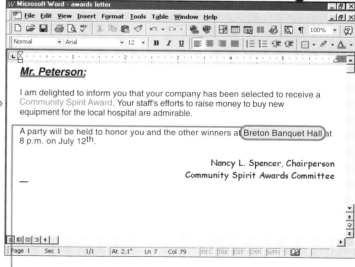

1 Select the text you want to highlight. To select text, refer to page 20.

2 To select a color, move the mouse ⌖ over ▾ in this area and then press the left mouse button.

3 Move the mouse ⌖ over the color you want to use and then press the left mouse button.

■ The text appears highlighted in the color you selected.

REMOVE HIGHLIGHT

■ To remove a highlight, repeat steps **1** to **3**, selecting **None** in step **3**.

COPY FORMATTING

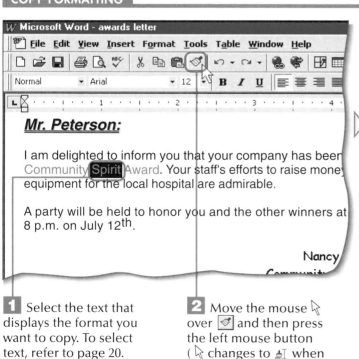

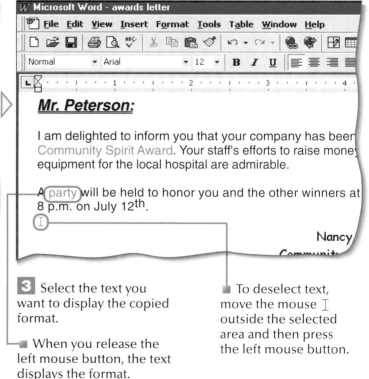

1 Select the text that displays the format you want to copy. To select text, refer to page 20.

2 Move the mouse ⌖ over 🖌 and then press the left mouse button (⌖ changes to 🖌I when over the document).

3 Select the text you want to display the copied format.

■ When you release the left mouse button, the text displays the format.

■ To deselect text, move the mouse I outside the selected area and then press the left mouse button.

ADD A BORDER

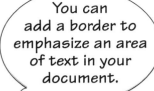

You can add a border to emphasize an area of text in your document.

ADD A BORDER

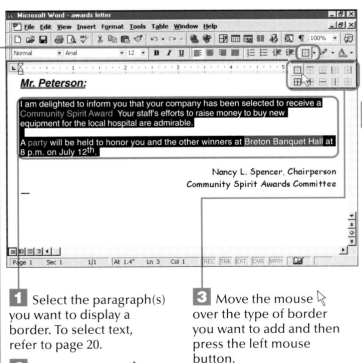

1 Select the paragraph(s) you want to display a border. To select text, refer to page 20.

2 Move the mouse over ▾ in this area and then press the left mouse button.

3 Move the mouse over the type of border you want to add and then press the left mouse button.

■ The border you selected appears.

■ To deselect text, move the mouse ⊥ outside the selected area and then press the left mouse button.

REMOVE A BORDER

■ Select the paragraph(s) you no longer want to display a border. Then perform steps **2** and **3**, selecting ⊞ in step **3**.

INSERT A SYMBOL

You can insert symbols that do not appear on your keyboard into your document.

INSERT A SYMBOL

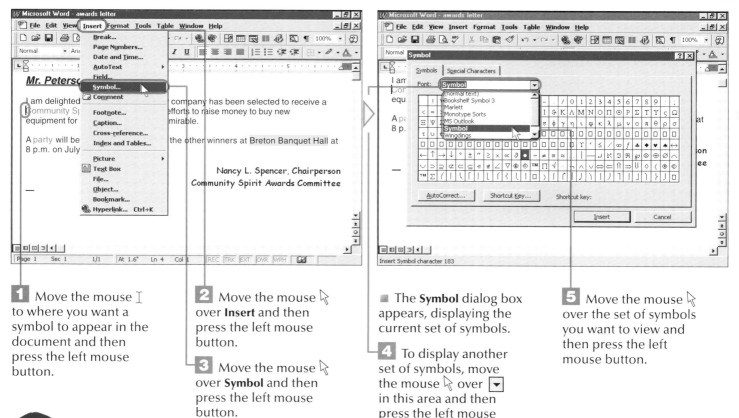

1 Move the mouse I to where you want a symbol to appear in the document and then press the left mouse button.

2 Move the mouse over **Insert** and then press the left mouse button.

3 Move the mouse over **Symbol** and then press the left mouse button.

■ The **Symbol** dialog box appears, displaying the current set of symbols.

4 To display another set of symbols, move the mouse over ▼ in this area and then press the left mouse button.

5 Move the mouse over the set of symbols you want to view and then press the left mouse button.

70

How can I quickly enter symbols into my document?

If you type one of the following sets of characters, Word will instantly replace the characters with a symbol. This lets you quickly enter symbols that are not available on your keyboard.

(c)	→	©
(r)	→	®
(tm)	→	TM
:(	→	☹
:)	→	☺
:l	→	☺
<--	→	←
-->	→	→
<==	→	⬅
==>	→	➡
<=>	→	⇔

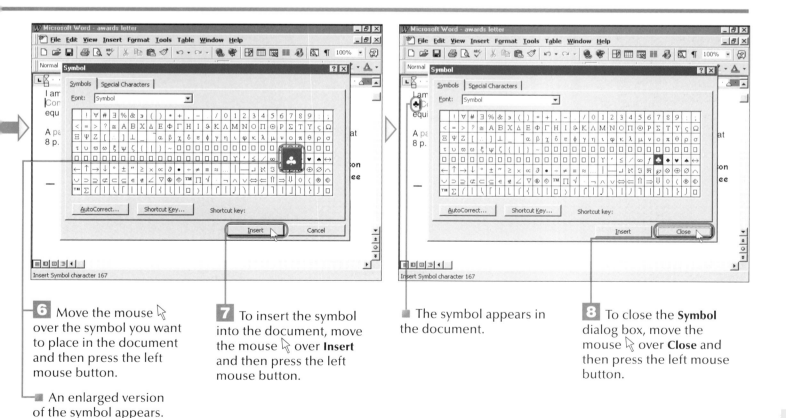

6 Move the mouse ⌖ over the symbol you want to place in the document and then press the left mouse button.

■ An enlarged version of the symbol appears.

7 To insert the symbol into the document, move the mouse ⌖ over **Insert** and then press the left mouse button.

■ The symbol appears in the document.

8 To close the **Symbol** dialog box, move the mouse ⌖ over **Close** and then press the left mouse button.

You can separate items in a list by beginning each item with a bullet or number.

ADD BULLETS OR NUMBERS

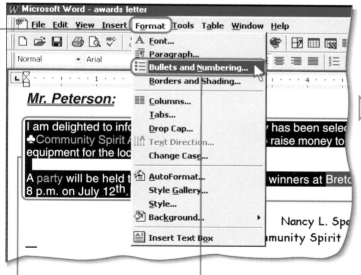

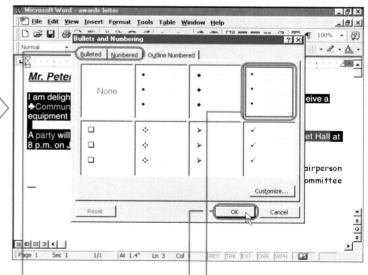

1 Select the text you want to display bullets or numbers. To select text, refer to page 20.

2 Move the mouse ⌖ over **Format** and then press the left mouse button.

3 Move the mouse ⌖ over **Bullets and Numbering** and then press the left mouse button.

■ The **Bullets and Numbering** dialog box appears.

4 Move the mouse ⌖ over the tab for the type of list you want to create and then press the left mouse button.

5 Move the mouse ⌖ over the style you want to use and then press the left mouse button.

6 Move the mouse ⌖ over **OK** and then press the left mouse button.

Should I use bullets or numbers in my list?

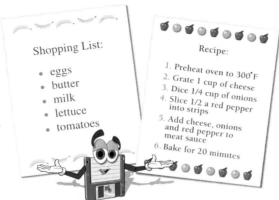

Bullets are useful for items in no particular order, such as a shopping list.

Numbers are useful for items in a specific order, such as a recipe.

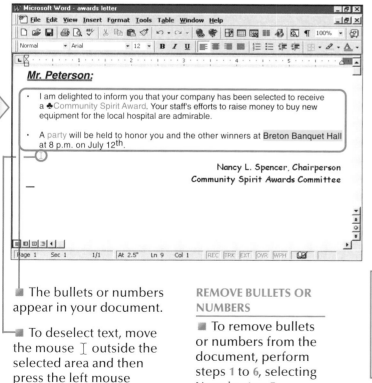

🔲 The bullets or numbers appear in your document.

🔲 To deselect text, move the mouse I outside the selected area and then press the left mouse button.

REMOVE BULLETS OR NUMBERS

🔲 To remove bullets or numbers from the document, perform steps **1** to **6**, selecting **None** in step **5**.

ADD BULLETS OR NUMBERS AS YOU TYPE

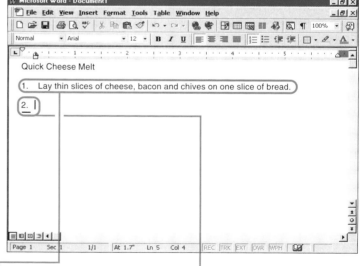

1 Move the mouse I to where you want the first number or bullet to appear and then press the left mouse button.

2 Type **1.** or ***** followed by a space. Then type the first item in the list.

3 Press **Enter** on your keyboard and Word automatically starts the next item with a number or bullet.

🔲 To end the numbered or bulleted list, press **Enter** on your keyboard twice.

CHANGE LINE SPACING

You can change the amount of space between the lines of text in your document to make your document easier to review and edit.

Single

There is a 10th anniversary High School Reunion on August 8, 9 and 10 at Woodblock High School. We all hope to see you there. Contact Susan Hughes for more information.

1.5 Lines

There is a 10th anniversary High School Reunion on August 8, 9 and 10 at Woodblock High School. We all hope to see you there. Contact Susan Hughes for more information.

Double

There is a 10th anniversary High School Reunion on August 8, 9 and 10 at Woodblock High School. We all hope to see you there. Contact Susan Hughes for more information.

CHANGE LINE SPACING

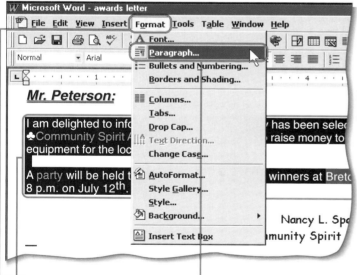

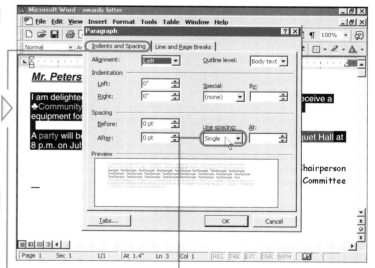

1 Select the paragraph(s) you want to change to a new line spacing. To select text, refer to page 20.

2 Move the mouse over **Format** and then press the left mouse button.

3 Move the mouse over **Paragraph** and then press the left mouse button.

■ The **Paragraph** dialog box appears.

4 Move the mouse over the **Indents and Spacing** tab and then press the left mouse button.

■ This area displays the line spacing for the paragraph(s) you selected.

5 To display a list of the available line spacing options, move the mouse over this area and then press the left mouse button.

Does Word ever automatically adjust the line spacing?

Word automatically increases the spacing of lines that contain large characters.

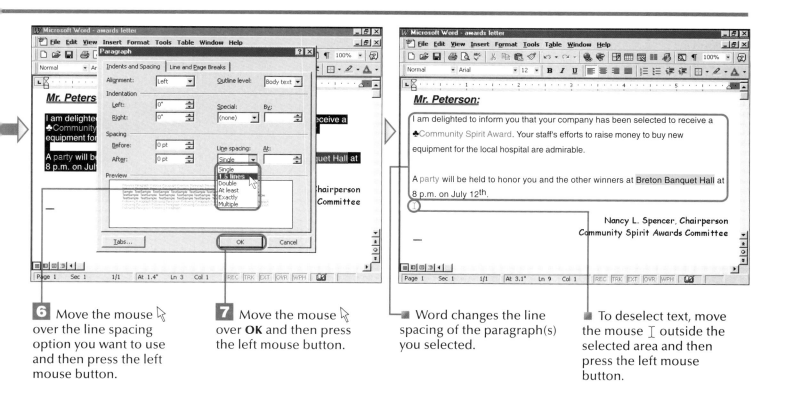

6 Move the mouse ⤵ over the line spacing option you want to use and then press the left mouse button.

7 Move the mouse ⤵ over **OK** and then press the left mouse button.

■ Word changes the line spacing of the paragraph(s) you selected.

■ To deselect text, move the mouse I outside the selected area and then press the left mouse button.

INDENT PARAGRAPHS

You can use the Indent feature to set off paragraphs in your document.

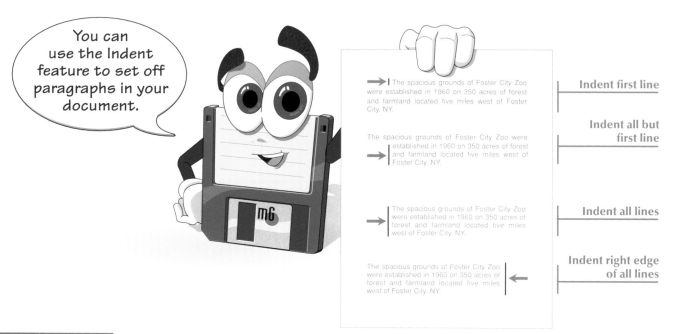

Indent first line

Indent all but first line

Indent all lines

Indent right edge of all lines

INDENT PARAGRAPHS

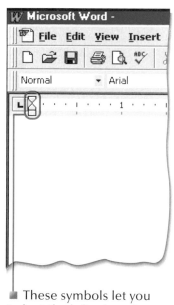

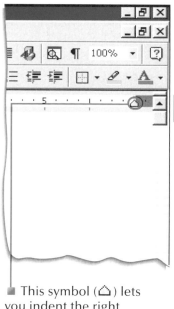

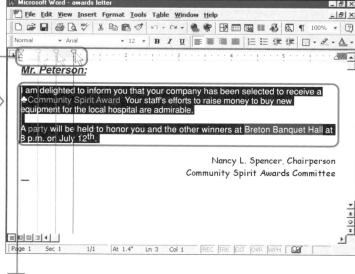

■ These symbols let you indent the left edge of a paragraph.

▽ Indent first line

△ Indent all but first line

▢ Indent all lines

■ This symbol (△) lets you indent the right edge of all lines.

Note: If the ruler is not displayed on the screen, refer to page 39 to display the ruler.

1 Select the paragraph(s) you want to indent. To select text, refer to page 20.

2 Move the mouse ⩘ over an indent symbol and then press and hold down the left mouse button as you move the symbol to a new position.

■ A line shows the new indent position.

What is a hanging indent?

A hanging indent moves all but the first line of a paragraph to the right. Hanging indents are useful when you are creating a résumé, glossary or bibliography.

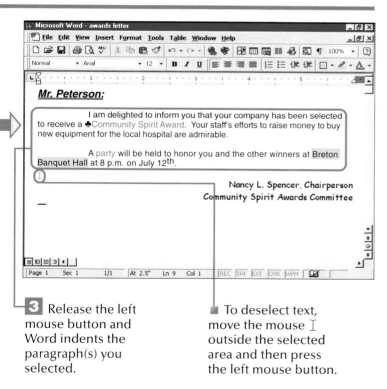

QUICKLY INDENT ALL LINES IN A PARAGRAPH

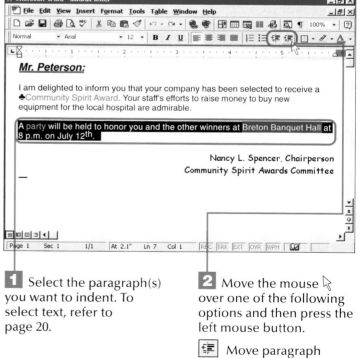

3 Release the left mouse button and Word indents the paragraph(s) you selected.

■ To deselect text, move the mouse I outside the selected area and then press the left mouse button.

1 Select the paragraph(s) you want to indent. To select text, refer to page 20.

2 Move the mouse ⌖ over one of the following options and then press the left mouse button.

🔳 Move paragraph to the left

🔳 Move paragraph to the right

CHANGE TAB SETTINGS

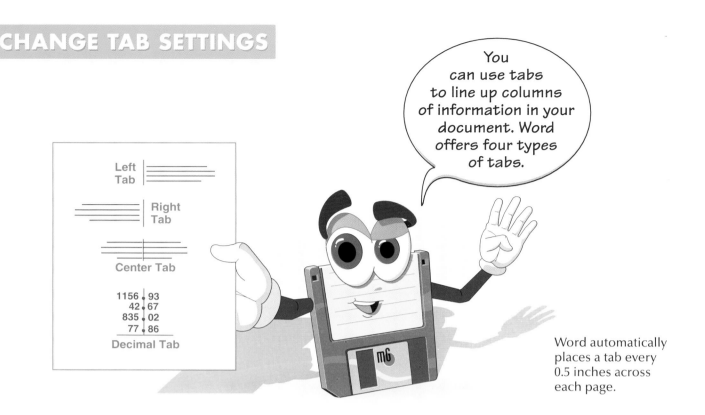

You can use tabs to line up columns of information in your document. Word offers four types of tabs.

Left Tab

Right Tab

Center Tab

1156 . 93
42 . 67
835 . 02
77 . 86

Decimal Tab

Word automatically places a tab every 0.5 inches across each page.

ADD A TAB

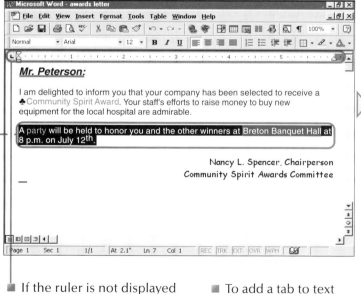

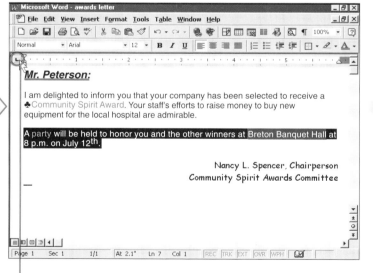

■ If the ruler is not displayed on the screen, refer to page 39 to display the ruler.

1 To add a tab, select the text you want to contain the new tab. To select text, refer to page 20.

■ To add a tab to text you are about to type, move the mouse I to where you want to type the text and then press the left mouse button.

2 Move the mouse ⊳ over this area and then press the left mouse button until the type of tab you want to add appears.

L Left tab
⊥ Center tab
⅃ Right tab
⅃. Decimal tab

What happens if I use spaces instead of tabs to line up columns of text?

Your document may not print correctly if you use spaces instead of tabs to line up columns of text.

◄■ Spaces were used to line up these columns.

◄■ Tabs were used to line up these columns.

USING TABS

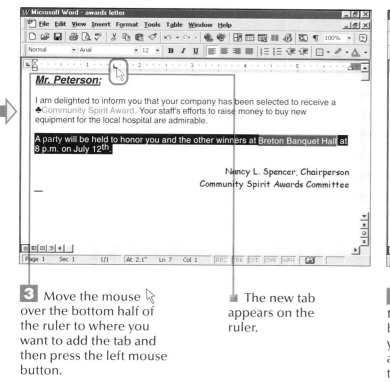

3 Move the mouse ⌖ over the bottom half of the ruler to where you want to add the tab and then press the left mouse button.

■ The new tab appears on the ruler.

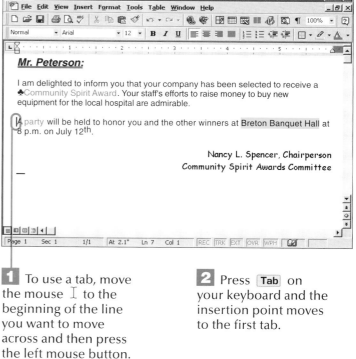

1 To use a tab, move the mouse I to the beginning of the line you want to move across and then press the left mouse button.

2 Press **Tab** on your keyboard and the insertion point moves to the first tab.

CHANGE TAB SETTINGS

You can easily move a tab to a different position on the ruler.

MOVE A TAB

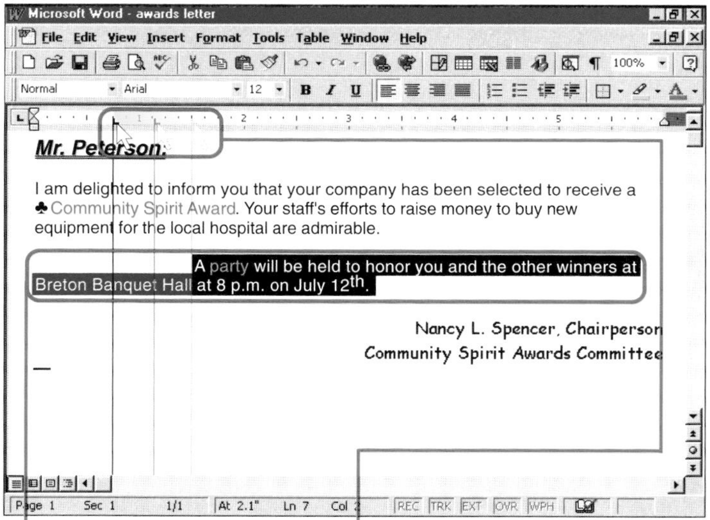

Microsoft Word - awards letter
File Edit View Insert Format Tools Table Window Help
Mr. Peterson:
I am delighted to inform you that your company has been selected to receive a Community Spirit Award. Your staff's efforts to raise money to buy new equipment for the local hospital are admirable.
A party will be held to honor you and the other winners at Breton Banquet Hall at 8 p.m. on July 12th.
Nancy L. Spencer, Chairperson
Community Spirit Awards Committee
Page 1 Sec 1 1/1 At 2.1" Ln 7 Col 2

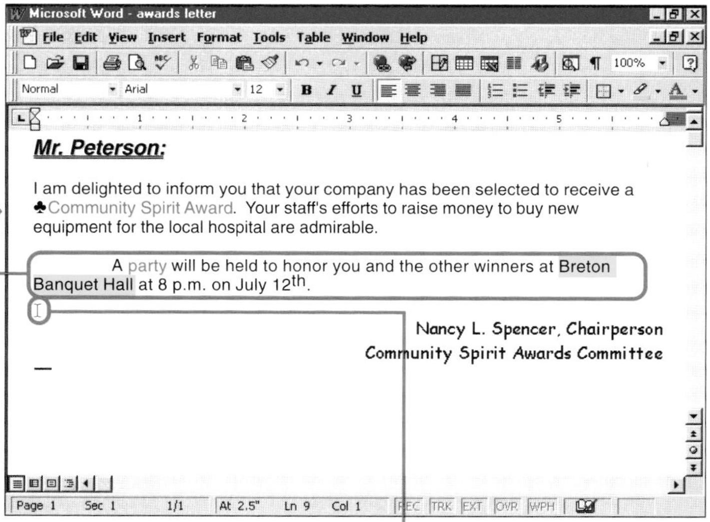

Microsoft Word - awards letter
File Edit View Insert Format Tools Table Window Help
Mr. Peterson:
I am delighted to inform you that your company has been selected to receive a Community Spirit Award. Your staff's efforts to raise money to buy new equipment for the local hospital are admirable.
A party will be held to honor you and the other winners at Breton Banquet Hall at 8 p.m. on July 12th.
Nancy L. Spencer, Chairperson
Community Spirit Awards Committee
Page 1 Sec 1 1/1 At 2.5" Ln 9 Col 1

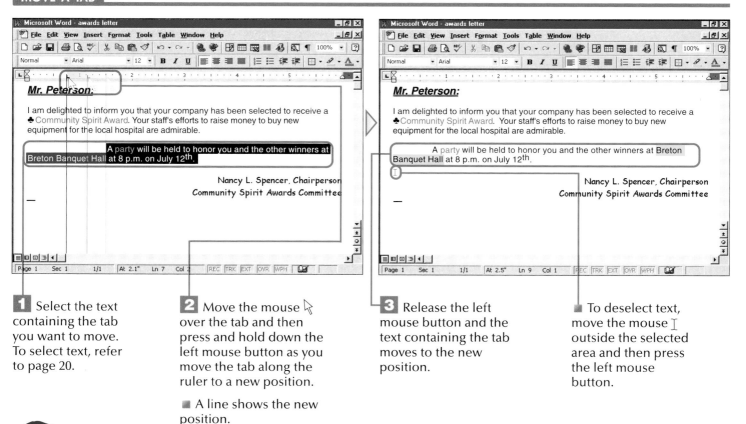

1 Select the text containing the tab you want to move. To select text, refer to page 20.

2 Move the mouse over the tab and then press and hold down the left mouse button as you move the tab along the ruler to a new position.

- A line shows the new position.

3 Release the left mouse button and the text containing the tab moves to the new position.

- To deselect text, move the mouse outside the selected area and then press the left mouse button.

When you no longer need a tab, you can remove it from the ruler.

REMOVE A TAB

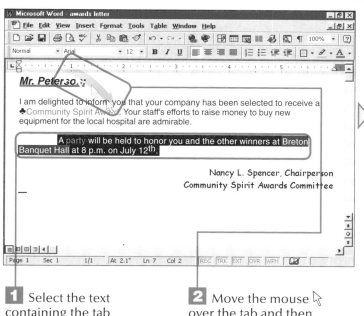

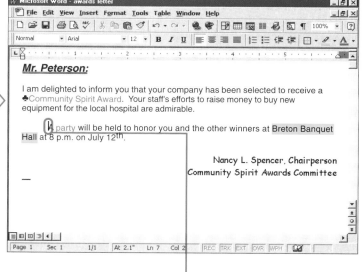

1 Select the text containing the tab you want to remove. To select text, refer to page 20.

2 Move the mouse over the tab and then press and hold down the left mouse button as you move the tab downward off the ruler.

3 Release the left mouse button and the tab disappears from the ruler.

■ To move text back to the left margin, move the mouse I to the left of the first character in the paragraph(s) and then press the left mouse button. Then press **+Backspace** on your keyboard.

You can have Word number the pages in your document.

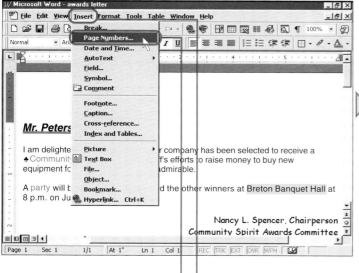

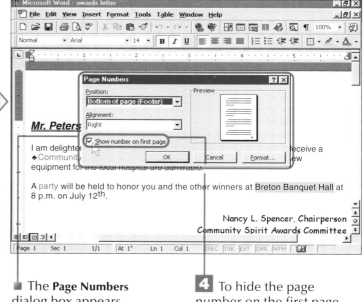

1 Display the document in the Page Layout view. To change the view, refer to page 36.

Note: Word does not display page numbers in the Normal view.

2 Move the mouse over **Insert** and then press the left mouse button.

3 Move the mouse over **Page Numbers** and then press the left mouse button.

■ The **Page Numbers** dialog box appears.

4 To hide the page number on the first page of the document, move the mouse over this option and then press the left mouse button (☑ changes to ☐).

Note: This option is useful if the first page of the document is a title page.

Will Word adjust the page numbers if I change my document?

If you add, remove or rearrange text in your document, Word will automatically adjust the page numbers for you.

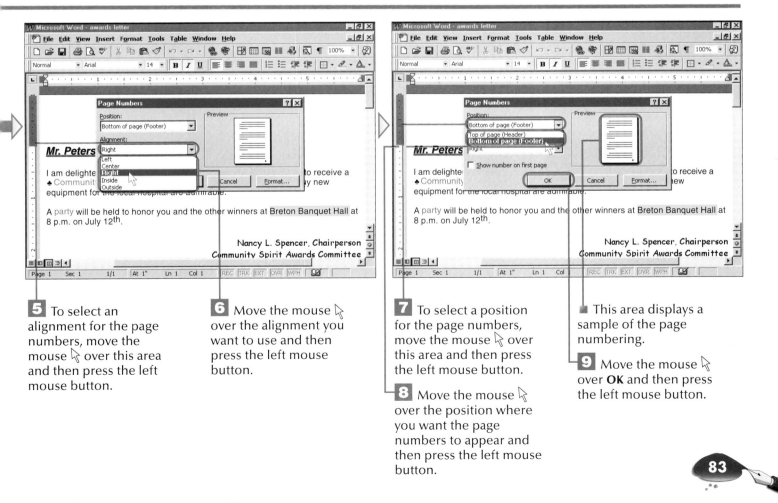

5 To select an alignment for the page numbers, move the mouse ⍟ over this area and then press the left mouse button.

6 Move the mouse ⍟ over the alignment you want to use and then press the left mouse button.

7 To select a position for the page numbers, move the mouse ⍟ over this area and then press the left mouse button.

8 Move the mouse ⍟ over the position where you want the page numbers to appear and then press the left mouse button.

■ This area displays a sample of the page numbering.

9 Move the mouse ⍟ over **OK** and then press the left mouse button.

A footnote appears at the bottom of a page to provide additional information about text in your document.

Word ensures that the footnote text always appears on the same page as the footnote number.

ADD FOOTNOTES

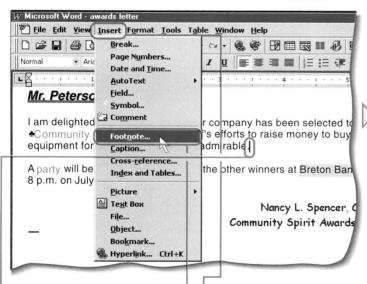

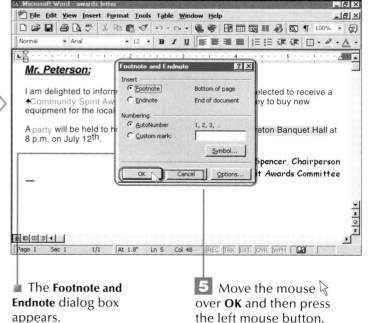

1 Display the document in the Normal view. To change the view, refer to page 36.

2 Move the mouse I to where you want the number of the footnote to appear and then press the left mouse button.

3 Move the mouse ⌖ over **Insert** and then press the left mouse button.

4 Move the mouse ⌖ over **Footnote** and then press the left mouse button.

■ The **Footnote and Endnote** dialog box appears.

5 Move the mouse ⌖ over **OK** and then press the left mouse button.

Will Word adjust the footnote numbers if I add or remove footnotes?

If you add or remove footnotes in your document, Word will automatically renumber the footnotes for you.

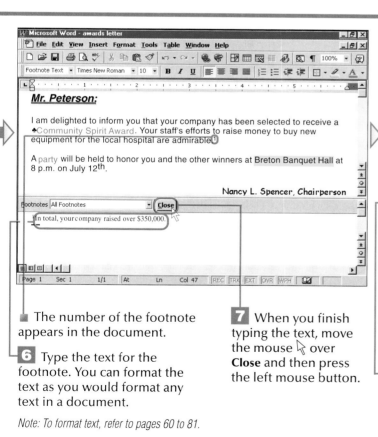

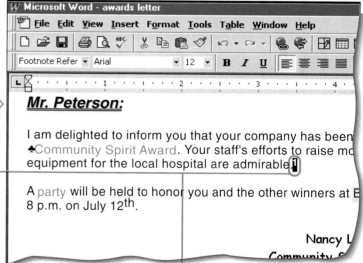

■ The number of the footnote appears in the document.

6 Type the text for the footnote. You can format the text as you would format any text in a document.

Note: To format text, refer to pages 60 to 81.

7 When you finish typing the text, move the mouse ⓡ over **Close** and then press the left mouse button.

■ The footnote text disappears from the screen.

■ To redisplay the footnote text so you can edit the footnote, move the mouse I over the number of the footnote and then quickly press the left mouse button twice.

DELETE A FOOTNOTE

1 Select the number of the footnote in the document. To select text, refer to page 20.

2 Press Delete on your keyboard.

ADD A HEADER AND FOOTER

You can add a header and footer to each page of your document.

■ A header appears at the top of each page.

2 November 1996

■ A footer appears at the bottom of each page.

ADD A HEADER AND FOOTER

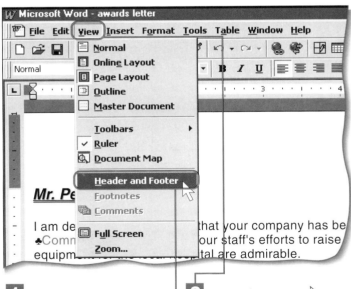

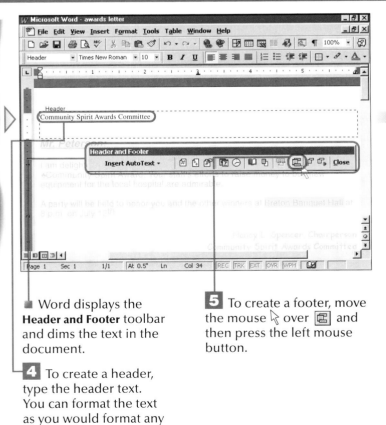

1 Display the document in the Page Layout view. To change the view, refer to page 36.

Note: Word does not display headers and footers in the Normal view.

2 Move the mouse over **View** and then press the left mouse button.

3 Move the mouse over **Header and Footer** and then press the left mouse button.

■ Word displays the **Header and Footer** toolbar and dims the text in the document.

4 To create a header, type the header text. You can format the text as you would format any text in a document.

5 To create a footer, move the mouse over 📃 and then press the left mouse button.

What information can a header or footer contain?

A header or footer can contain information such as the company name, author's name, chapter title or date.

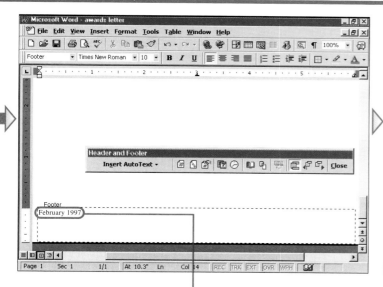

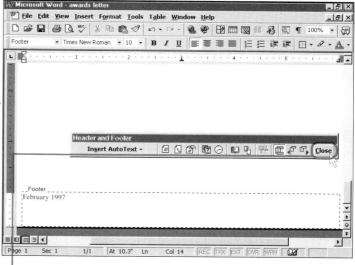

■ The **Footer** area appears.

Note: To return to the header area at any time, repeat step 5.

6 Type the footer text. You can format the text as you would format any text in a document.

Note: To format text, refer to pages 60 to 81.

7 When you have finished creating the header and footer, move the mouse ⇖ over **Close** and then press the left mouse button.

EDIT A HEADER OR FOOTER

1 To edit a header or footer, repeat steps 1 to 7.

INSERT A PAGE BREAK

If you want to start a new page at a specific place in your document, you can insert a page break. A page break shows where one page ends and another begins.

INSERT A PAGE BREAK

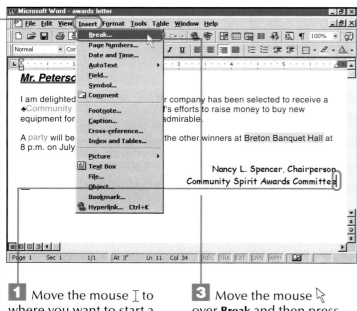

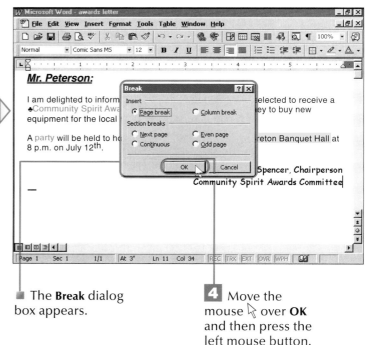

1 Move the mouse I to where you want to start a new page and then press the left mouse button.

2 Move the mouse ⇗ over **Insert** and then press the left mouse button.

3 Move the mouse ⇗ over **Break** and then press the left mouse button.

■ The **Break** dialog box appears.

4 Move the mouse ⇗ over **OK** and then press the left mouse button.

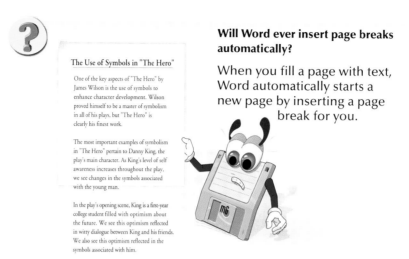

Will Word ever insert page breaks automatically?

When you fill a page with text, Word automatically starts a new page by inserting a page break for you.

REMOVE A PAGE BREAK

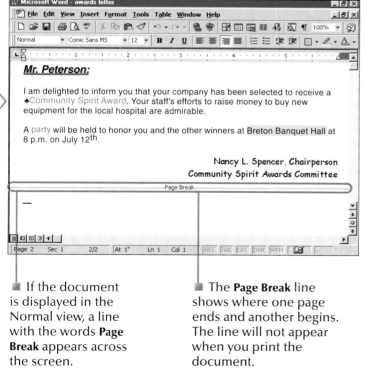

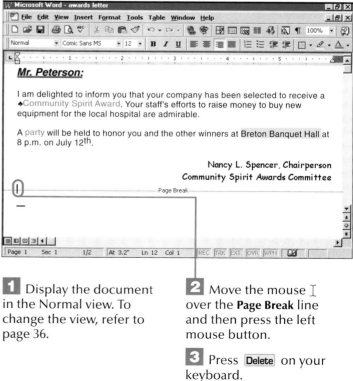

■ If the document is displayed in the Normal view, a line with the words **Page Break** appears across the screen.

■ The **Page Break** line shows where one page ends and another begins. The line will not appear when you print the document.

1 Display the document in the Normal view. To change the view, refer to page 36.

2 Move the mouse I over the **Page Break** line and then press the left mouse button.

3 Press Delete on your keyboard.

You can divide your document into sections so you can format each section separately.

You need to divide a document into sections to change margins, create columns or vertically center text for only part of your document.

INSERT A SECTION BREAK

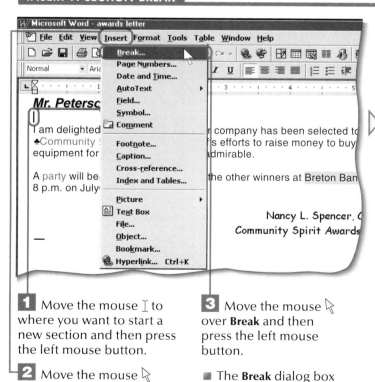

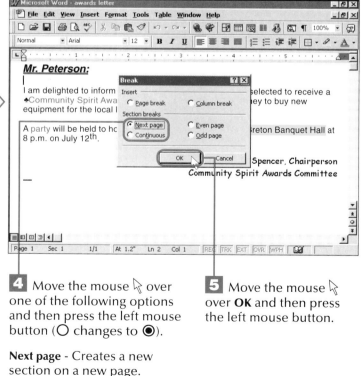

1 Move the mouse I to where you want to start a new section and then press the left mouse button.

2 Move the mouse ↕ over **Insert** and then press the left mouse button.

3 Move the mouse ↕ over **Break** and then press the left mouse button.

■ The **Break** dialog box appears.

4 Move the mouse ↕ over one of the following options and then press the left mouse button (○ changes to ●).

Next page - Creates a new section on a new page.

Continuous - Creates a new section on the current page.

5 Move the mouse ↕ over **OK** and then press the left mouse button.

If I remove a section break will my document change?

When you remove a section break, the text above the break assumes the appearance of the following section.

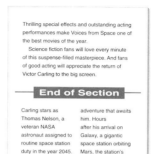

REMOVE A SECTION BREAK

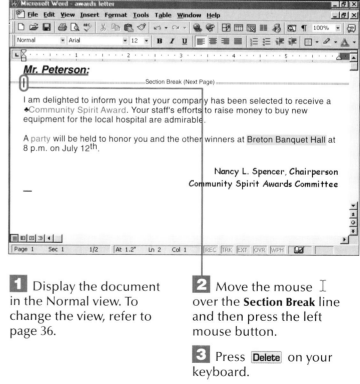

■ If the document is displayed in the Normal view, a double line with the words **Section Break** appears across the screen.

■ The **Section Break** line shows where one section ends and another begins. The line will not appear when you print the document.

1 Display the document in the Normal view. To change the view, refer to page 36.

2 Move the mouse I over the **Section Break** line and then press the left mouse button.

3 Press **Delete** on your keyboard.

CENTER TEXT ON A PAGE

You can vertically center text on each page of a document. This is useful for creating title pages or short memos.

GLOBAL REPORT
Helping the Third World Countries

By: Brad Hilderley, MBA
University of Washington

CENTER TEXT ON A PAGE

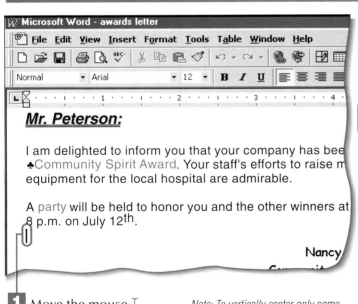

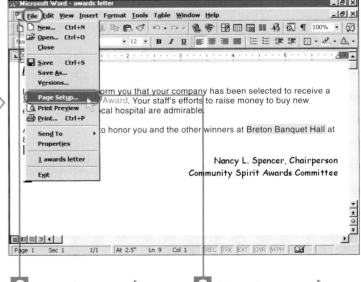

1 Move the mouse I anywhere over the document or section you want to vertically center and then press the left mouse button.

Note: To vertically center only some of the text in a document, you must divide the document into sections. To divide a document into sections, refer to page 90.

2 Move the mouse ⬉ over **File** and then press the left mouse button.

3 Move the mouse ⬉ over **Page Setup** and then press the left mouse button.

■ The **Page Setup** dialog box appears.

How can I see what text centered on a page will look like when printed?

You can use the Print Preview feature to display a page on your screen. This lets you see how the page will look when printed.

Note: For information on using Print Preview, refer to page 26.

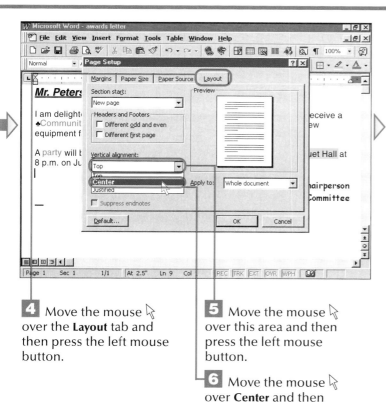

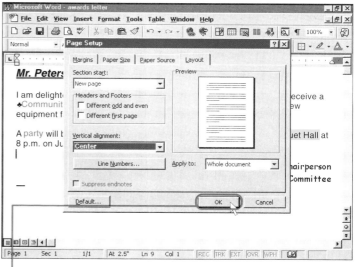

4 Move the mouse over the **Layout** tab and then press the left mouse button.

5 Move the mouse over this area and then press the left mouse button.

6 Move the mouse over **Center** and then press the left mouse button.

7 Move the mouse over **OK** and then press the left mouse button.

REMOVE CENTERING

Perform steps 1 to 7, selecting **Top** in step 6.

CHANGE MARGINS

A margin is the amount of space between text and an edge of your paper. You can easily change the margins to suit your document.

Changing margins lets you accommodate letterhead and other specialty paper.

CHANGE MARGINS

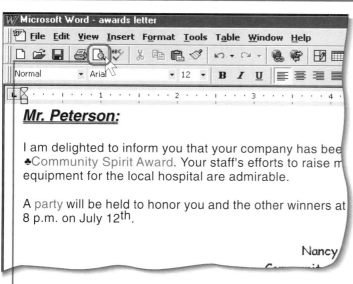

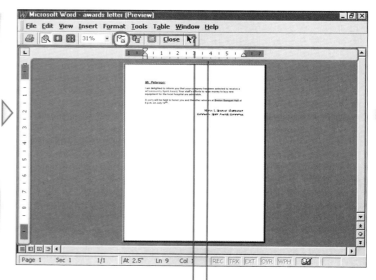

1 To change the margins for the entire document, move the mouse ⬚ over 🔍 and then press the left mouse button.

Note: To change the margins for only part of the document, refer to the top of page 95.

■ The document appears in the Print Preview window. For more information on using Print Preview, refer to page 26.

■ This area displays the ruler.

■ If the ruler is not displayed, move the mouse ⬚ over 🔲 and then press the left mouse button.

How can I change the margins for part of my document?

If you want to change the left and right margins for part of your document, change the indentation of paragraphs. To indent paragraphs, refer to page 76.

If you want to change the top and bottom margins for a few pages in your document, you must divide the document into sections. To divide a document into sections, refer to page 90.

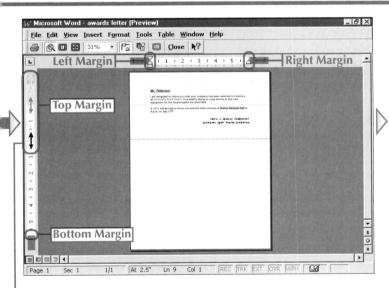

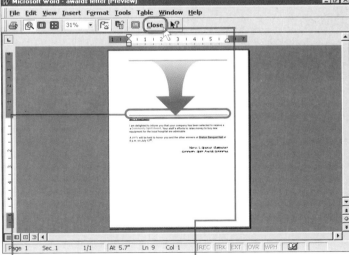

2 Move the mouse ⬉ over the margin you want to move (⬉ changes to ↕ or ↔) and then press and hold down the left mouse button as you move the margin to a new location.

■ A line shows the new location.

Note: To view the exact measurement of a margin from the edge of the page, press and hold down **Alt** *on your keyboard as you perform step* **2**.

3 Release the left mouse button and the margin moves to the new location.

4 Repeat steps 2 and 3 for each margin you want to move.

5 To close the Print Preview window, move the mouse ⬉ over **Close** and then press the left mouse button.

CREATE NEWSPAPER COLUMNS

You can display your text in columns like those found in a newspaper. This is useful for creating documents such as newsletters and brochures.

CREATE NEWSPAPER COLUMNS

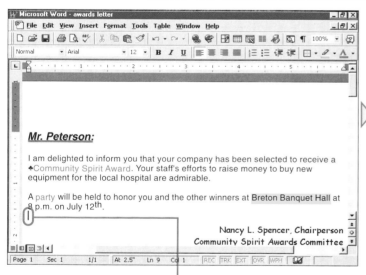

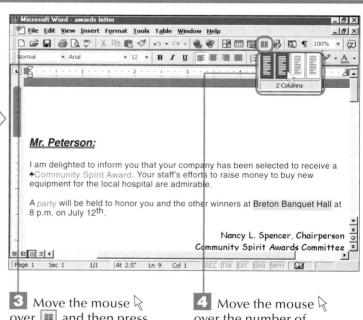

1 Display the document in the Page Layout view. To change the view, refer to page 36.

Note: Word does not display newspaper columns side-by-side in the Normal view.

2 Move the mouse I anywhere over the document or section you want to display in newspaper columns and then press the left mouse button.

Note: To create newspaper columns for only part of the document, you must divide the document into sections. To divide a document into sections, refer to page 90.

3 Move the mouse ⬚ over ▦ and then press the left mouse button.

4 Move the mouse ⬚ over the number of columns you want to display and then press the left mouse button.

Why is there text in only one of my columns?

Word fills one column with text before starting a new column.

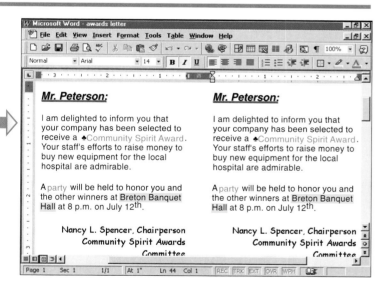

■ The text in the document appears in newspaper columns.

Note: In this example, the existing text was copied to show the newspaper columns. To copy text, refer to page 50.

REMOVE NEWSPAPER COLUMNS

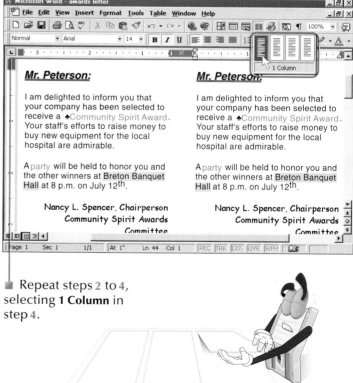

■ Repeat steps 2 to 4, selecting **1 Column** in step 4.

You can create a table to neatly display information in your document.

Word lets you draw a table on the screen as you would draw a table with a pen and paper.

CREATE A TABLE

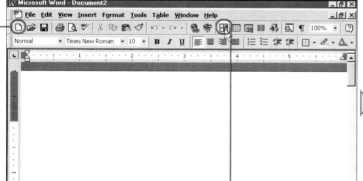

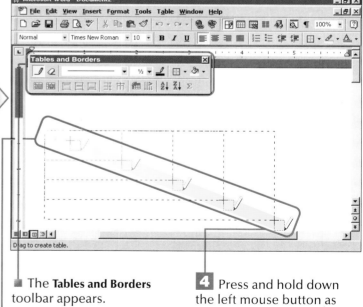

■ In this example, a new document was created. To create a new document, move the mouse ℟ over 🗋 and then press the left mouse button.

1 Display the document in the Page Layout view. To change the view, refer to page 36.

2 To create a table, move the mouse ℟ over 🖽 and then press the left mouse button.

■ The **Tables and Borders** toolbar appears.

3 Move the mouse ⟋ to where you want the top left corner of the table to appear.

4 Press and hold down the left mouse button as you move the mouse ┼⟋ until the outline of the table displays the size you want. Then release the mouse button.

Can I move a toolbar out of the way?

If a toolbar is in the way, you can easily move the toolbar to a new location.

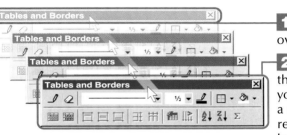

1 Move the mouse ⬉ over the title bar.

2 Press and hold down the left mouse button as you move the toolbar to a new location. Then release the mouse button.

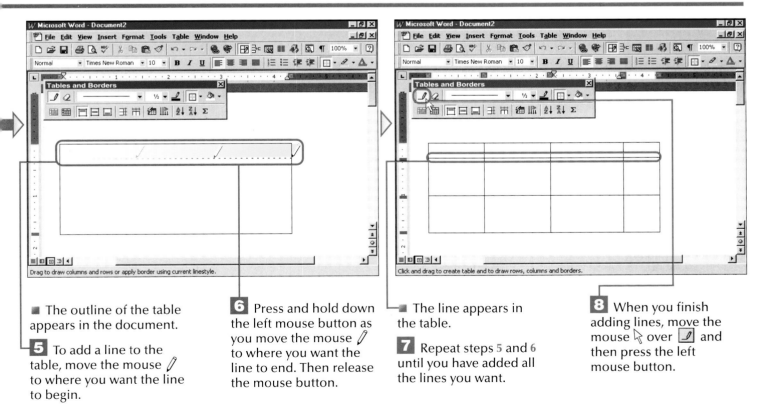

■ The outline of the table appears in the document.

5 To add a line to the table, move the mouse ✐ to where you want the line to begin.

6 Press and hold down the left mouse button as you move the mouse ✐ to where you want the line to end. Then release the mouse button.

■ The line appears in the table.

7 Repeat steps **5** and **6** until you have added all the lines you want.

8 When you finish adding lines, move the mouse ⬉ over ✐ and then press the left mouse button.

CHANGE ROW HEIGHT OR COLUMN WIDTH

After you have created a table, you can change the height of rows or the width of columns.

CHANGE ROW HEIGHT

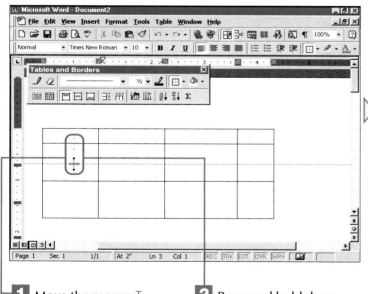

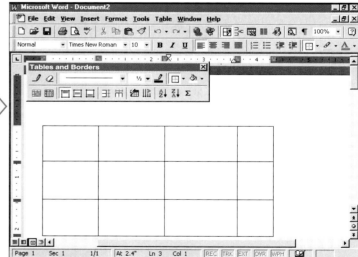

1 Move the mouse I over the bottom edge of the row you want to change (I changes to ÷).

2 Press and hold down the left mouse button as you move the row edge to a new position.

■ A line shows the new position.

3 Release the left mouse button and the row displays the new height.

What are rows, columns and cells?

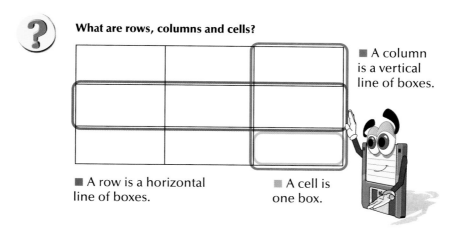

■ A column is a vertical line of boxes.

■ A row is a horizontal line of boxes.

■ A cell is one box.

CHANGE COLUMN WIDTH

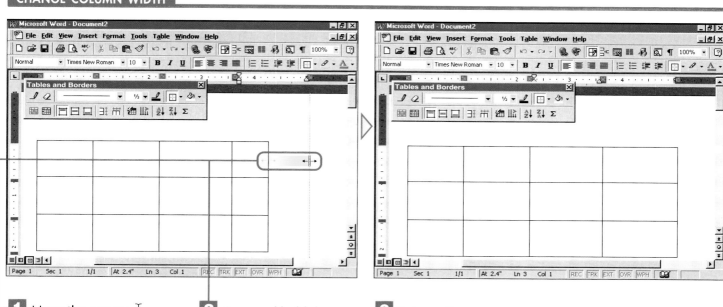

1 Move the mouse I over the right edge of the column you want to change (I changes to ╫).

2 Press and hold down the left mouse button as you move the column edge to a new position.

■ A line shows the new position.

3 Release the mouse button and the column displays the new width.

You can erase lines you do not need in your table.

ERASE LINES

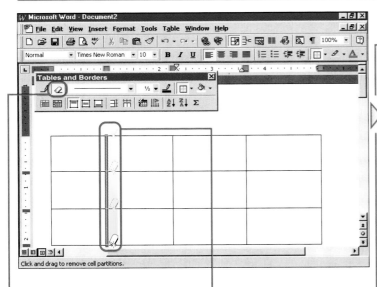

1 Move the mouse ⤣ over 🖉 and then press the left mouse button.

*Note: If the **Tables and Borders** toolbar is not displayed, move the mouse ⤣ over 🔲 and then press the left mouse button to display the toolbar.*

2 Move the mouse 🖉 over the line you want to erase and then press and hold down the left mouse button as you move the mouse 🖉 along the line.

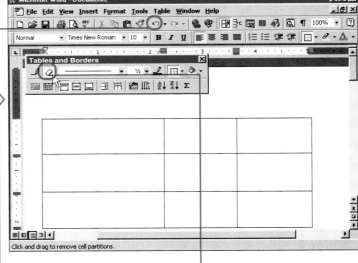

3 Release the left mouse button and the line disappears.

■ To immediately return the line to the table, move the mouse ⤣ over 🔙 and then press the left mouse button.

4 Repeat steps 2 and 3 for all the lines you want to erase.

5 When you finish erasing lines, move the mouse ⤣ over 🖉 and then press the left mouse button.

ENTER TEXT

You can easily enter text into the cells of a table.

ENTER TEXT

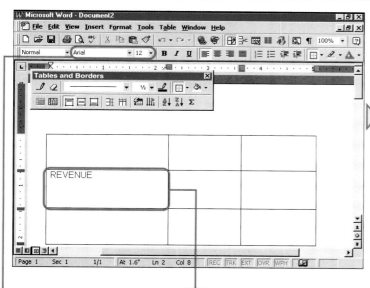

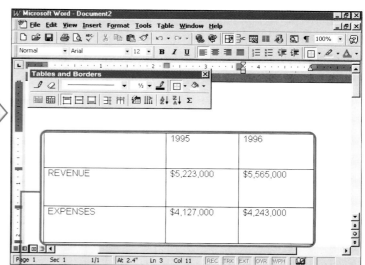

▪ In this example, the design and size of text were changed to make the text easier to read. To change the design and size of text, refer to pages 62 and 63.

1 Move the mouse I over the cell where you want to type text and then press the left mouse button. Then type the text.

Note: To quickly move through the cells in a table, press ← , ↑ , ↓ or → on your keyboard.

2 Repeat step 1 until you have typed all the text.

▪ You can edit and format the text in a table as you would edit and format any text in a document.

ADD A ROW OR COLUMN

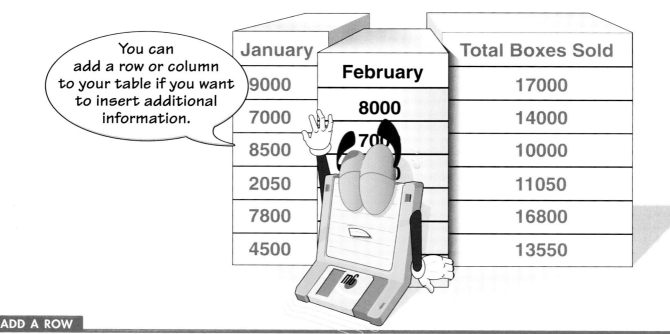

You can add a row or column to your table if you want to insert additional information.

January		Total Boxes Sold
9000	February	17000
7000	8000	14000
8500	700	10000
2050		11050
7800		16800
4500		13550

ADD A ROW

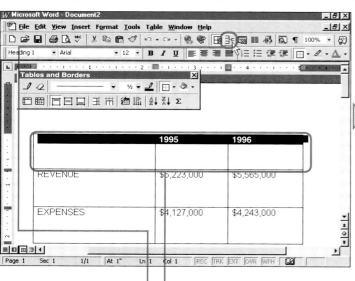

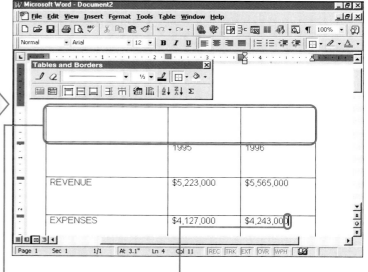

Word will insert a row above the row you select.

1 To select a row, move the mouse I to the left of the row (I changes to ⇗) and then press the left mouse button.

2 Move the mouse ⇗ over ▤ and then press the left mouse button.

■ A new row appears.

ADD A ROW TO THE BOTTOM OF A TABLE

1 Move the mouse I over the bottom right cell in the table and then press the left mouse button.

2 Press **Tab** on your keyboard.

104

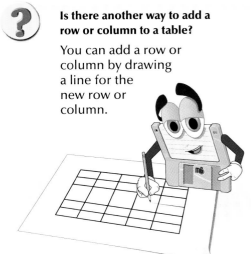

Is there another way to add a row or column to a table?

You can add a row or column by drawing a line for the new row or column.

1 Move the mouse ⬚ over 🖊 on the **Tables and Borders** toolbar and then press the left mouse button.

2 To draw the line in your table, perform steps **5** and **6** on page 99.

ADD A COLUMN

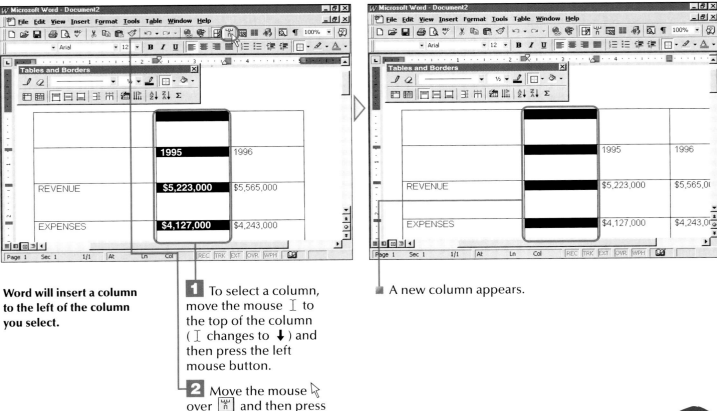

Word will insert a column to the left of the column you select.

1 To select a column, move the mouse I to the top of the column (I changes to ↓) and then press the left mouse button.

2 Move the mouse ⬚ over 🔲 and then press the left mouse button.

■ A new column appears.

DELETE A ROW OR COLUMN

You can delete a row or column you no longer need.

DELETE A ROW OR COLUMN

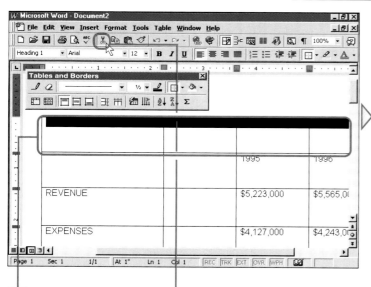

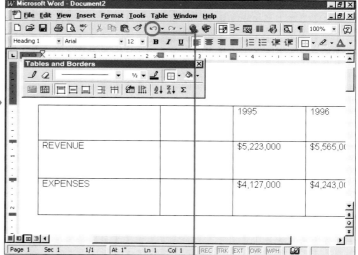

1 To select the row you want to delete, move the mouse I to the left of the row (I changes to ⬧) and then press the left mouse button.

■ To select the column you want to delete, move the mouse I to the top of the column (I changes to ↓) and then press the left mouse button.

2 Move the mouse ⬧ over ✂ and then press the left mouse button.

■ The row or column disappears.

■ To immediately return the row or column to the table, move the mouse ⬧ over ↶ and then press the left mouse button.

106

DELETE A TABLE

You can quickly remove an entire table from your document.

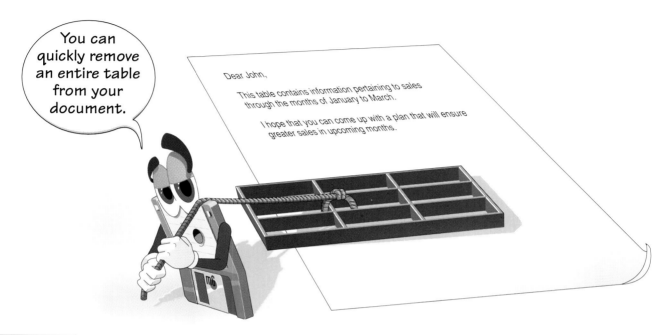

Dear John,

This table contains information pertaining to sales through the months of January to March.

I hope that you can come up with a plan that will ensure greater sales in upcoming months.

DELETE A TABLE

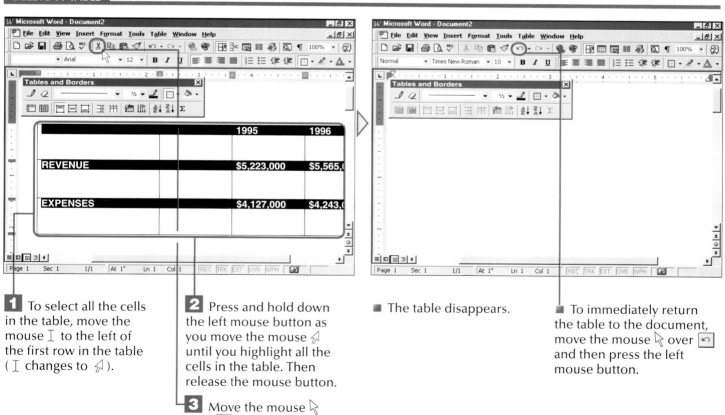

1 To select all the cells in the table, move the mouse I to the left of the first row in the table (I changes to ⇗).

2 Press and hold down the left mouse button as you move the mouse ⇗ until you highlight all the cells in the table. Then release the mouse button.

3 Move the mouse ⇖ over ✂ and then press the left mouse button.

■ The table disappears.

■ To immediately return the table to the document, move the mouse ⇖ over ↺ and then press the left mouse button.

> Word offers many ready-to-use designs that you can choose from to give your table a new appearance.

FORMAT A TABLE

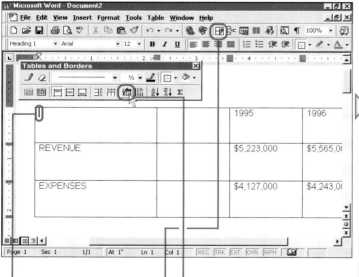

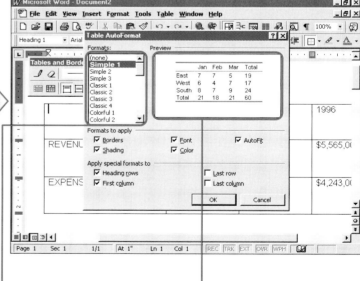

1 Move the mouse I anywhere over the table you want to change and then press the left mouse button.

2 Move the mouse ⇗ over 🖾 and then press the left mouse button.

■ If the **Tables and Borders** toolbar is not displayed, move the mouse ⇗ over 🖽 and then press the left mouse button to display the toolbar.

■ The **Table AutoFormat** dialog box appears.

■ This area displays a list of the available table designs.

■ This area displays a sample of the highlighted table design.

3 Press ↓ or ↑ on your keyboard until a design you like appears.

What are some table designs offered by Word?

	Jan	Feb	Mar	Total
East	7	7	5	19
West	6	4	7	17
South	8	7	9	24
Total	21	18	21	60

Colorful 1

	Jan	Feb	Mar	Total
East	7	7	5	19
West	6	4	7	17
South	8	7	9	24
Total	21	18	21	60

Grid 8

	Jan	Feb	Mar	Total
East	7	7	5	19
West	6	4	7	17
South	8	7	9	24
Total	21	18	21	60

Classic 3

	Jan	Feb	Mar	Total
East	7	7	5	19
West	6	4	7	17
South	8	7	9	24
Total	21	18	21	60

Columns 5

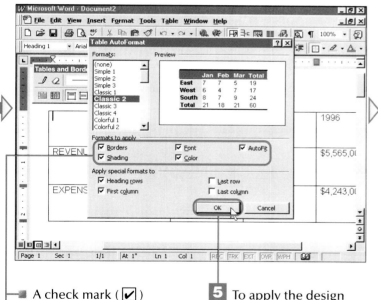

■ A check mark (☑) beside an option tells you that Word will apply the option to the table.

4 To add or remove a check mark (☑) for an option, move the mouse ▯ over the check box beside the option and then press the left mouse button.

5 To apply the design to the table, move the mouse ▯ over **OK** and then press the left mouse button.

■ The table displays the design you selected.

REMOVE AUTOFORMAT

■ Perform steps 1 to 3, selecting **Grid 1** in step 3. Then press **Enter** on your keyboard.

Microsoft Excel is a spreadsheet program that lets you organize, analyze and present data easily and efficiently.

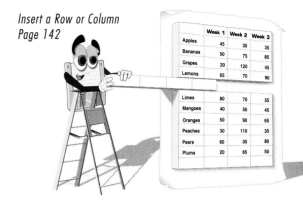

Insert a Row or Column
Page 142

Start Excel
Page 113

Introduction to Excel
Page 112

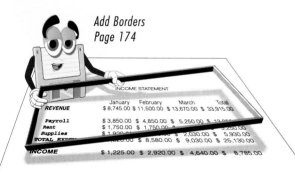

Add Borders
Page 174

Enter a Function
Page 150

EXCEL

1   Getting Started
Pages 112-125

2   Save and Open a Workbook
Pages 126-133

3   Edit a Worksheet
Pages 134-145

4   Using Formulas and Functions
Pages 146-165

5   Format a Worksheet
Pages 166-181

6   Print a Worksheet
Pages 182-193

7   Using Multiple Worksheets
Pages 194-199

8   Working With Charts
Pages 200-209

Insert a Worksheet
Page 196

Copy Data
Page 140

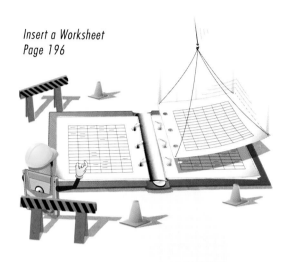

INTRODUCTION TO EXCEL

Excel helps you organize, analyze and attractively present data.

Formulas and Functions

Excel provides powerful tools to calculate and analyze data in your worksheets.

Edit and Format Data

Excel lets you efficiently enter, edit and change the appearance of data in your worksheets.

Charts

Excel helps you create colorful charts using your worksheet data.

When you start Excel, a blank worksheet appears. You can enter data into this worksheet.

START EXCEL

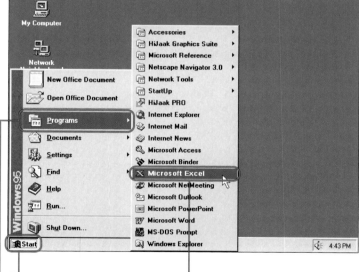

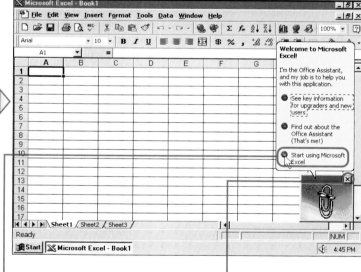

1 Move the mouse � over **Start** and then press the left mouse button.

2 Move the mouse � over **Programs**.

3 Move the mouse � over **Microsoft Excel** and then press the left mouse button.

■ The Microsoft Excel window appears, displaying a blank worksheet.

■ If you are starting Excel for the first time, the Office Assistant welcome appears.

4 To start using Excel, move the mouse � over this option and then press the left mouse button.

■ To hide the Office Assistant, move the mouse � over ☒ and then press the left mouse button.

Note: For more information on the Office Assistant, refer to page 12.

A worksheet consists of rows, columns and cells.

Row

A horizontal line of boxes. A number identifies each row.

Column

A vertical line of boxes. A letter identifies each column.

Cell

One box in a worksheet.

Cell Reference

A cell reference defines the location of each cell in a worksheet. A cell reference consists of a column letter followed by a row number (example: B3).

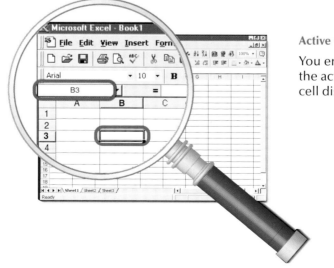

Active Cell

You enter information into the active cell. The active cell displays a thick border.

THE EXCEL SCREEN

The Excel screen displays several items to help you perform tasks efficiently.

Menu Bar

Contains commands that let you perform tasks.

Toolbars

Contain buttons to help you quickly select common commands.

Formula Bar

Displays the cell reference and contents of the active cell.

Status Bar

Displays information about the task you are performing.

Worksheet Tabs

An Excel file is called a workbook. Each workbook is divided into several worksheets. Excel displays a tab for each worksheet.

A workbook is similar to a three-ring binder that contains several sheets of paper.

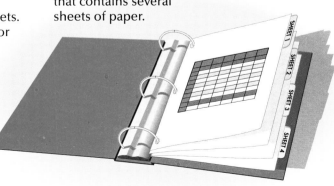

ENTER DATA

You can enter data into your worksheet quickly and easily.

ENTER DATA

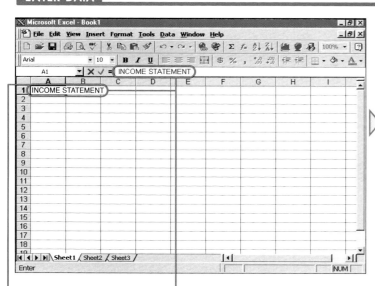

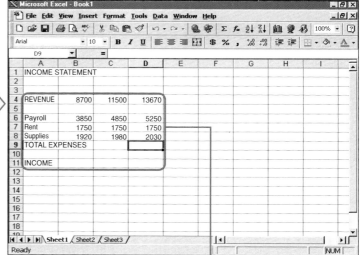

1 Move the mouse ⊕ over the cell where you want to enter data and then press the left mouse button. Then type the data.

■ If you make a typing mistake, press **◆Backspace** on your keyboard to remove the incorrect data and then type the correct data.

■ The data you type appears in the active cell and in the formula bar.

2 To enter the data and move down one cell, press **Enter** on your keyboard.

Note: To enter the data and move one cell in any direction, press ↑, ↓, ← or → on your keyboard.

3 Repeat steps 1 and 2 until you finish entering all the data.

How do I use the number keys on the right side of my keyboard?

When **NUM** appears at the bottom of your screen, you can use the number keys on the right side of your keyboard to enter numbers.

■ To turn on or off the display of **NUM** on your screen, press **Num Lock** on your keyboard.

4	TOTAL EXPENSES
5	
6	

4	TOTAL EX	227
5		
6		

Long Words

If text is too long to fit in a cell, the text will spill into the neighboring cell.

If the neighboring cell contains data, Excel will display as much of the text as the column width will allow. To change the column width, refer to page 166.

4	1.22E+10
5	
6	

4	#####
5	
6	

Long Numbers

If a number is too long to fit in a cell, Excel will display the number in scientific form or as number signs (#). To change the column width, refer to page 166.

Microsoft Excel - Book1

File Edit View Insert Format Tools Data Window Help

Arial ▾ 10 ▾ **B** *I* U $ % , ⁺⁰ ⁰⁺

A12 ▾ X ✓ = INCOME

	A	B	C	D	E	F	G	H	I
1	INCOME STATEMENT								
2									
3									
4	REVENUE	8700	11500	13670					
5									
6	Payroll	3850	4850	5250					
7	Rent	1750	1750	1750					
8	Supplies	1920	1980	2030					
9	TOTAL EXPENSES								
10									
11	INCOME								
12	INCOME								
13									
14									
15									
16									
17									
18									

Sheet1 / Sheet2 / Sheet3

Enter | NUM

AUTOCOMPLETE

If the first few letters you type match another cell in the column, Excel will complete the text for you.

■ To keep the text Excel provides, press **Enter** on your keyboard.

■ To enter different text, continue typing.

COMPLETE A SERIES

Excel can save you time by completing a text or number series for you.

COMPLETE A SERIES

Text Series

Mon	Tue	Wed	Thu
Product 1	Product 2	Product 3	Product 4
1st Quarter	2nd Quarter	3rd Quarter	4th Quarter

■ Excel completes a text series based on the text in the first cell.

Number Series

1995	1996	1997	1998
5	10	15	20
202	204	206	208

■ Excel completes a number series based on the numbers in the first two cells.

These numbers tell Excel how much to add to each number to complete the series.

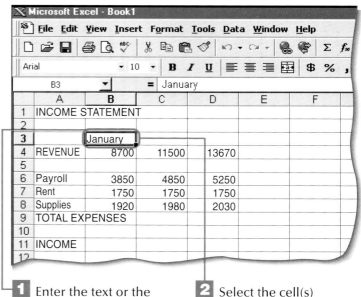

1 Enter the text or the first two numbers you want to start the series.

2 Select the cell(s) containing the text or numbers you entered. To select cells, refer to page 120.

Can I change the color of data in my worksheet?

You can easily change the color of data to make your worksheet more attractive. To do so, refer to page 176.

INCOME STATEMENT

	January	February	March
REVENUE	8700	11500	13670
Payroll	3850	4850	5250
Rent	1750	1750	1750
Supplies	1920	1980	2030
TOTAL EXPENSES			
INCOME			

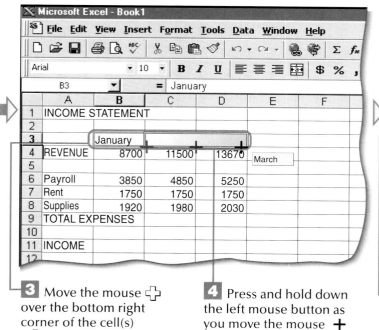

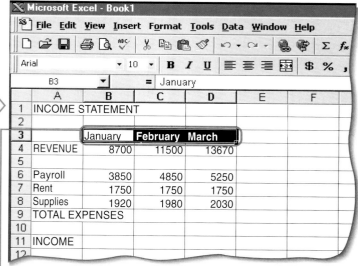

3 Move the mouse ⊕ over the bottom right corner of the cell(s) (⊕ changes to +).

4 Press and hold down the left mouse button as you move the mouse + over the cells you want to include in the series. Then release the mouse button.

◄ The cells display the series.

Note: You can also perform steps 1 to 4 to complete a series in a column.

SELECT CELLS

Before performing many tasks in Excel, you must select the cells you want to work with. Selected cells appear highlighted on your screen.

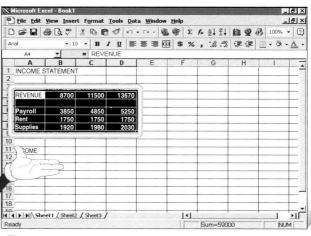

SELECT ONE CELL

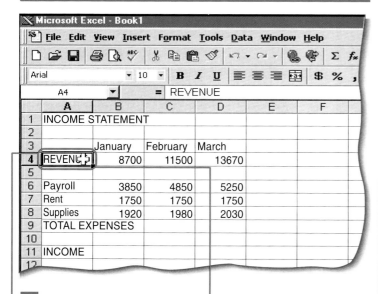

1 Move the mouse ⊕ over the cell you want to select and then press the left mouse button.

■ The cell becomes the active cell and displays a thick border.

SELECT GROUPS OF CELLS

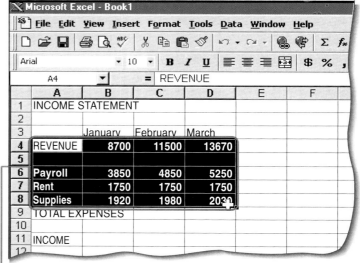

1 Move the mouse ⊕ over the first cell you want to select.

2 Press and hold down the left mouse button as you move the mouse ⊕ to highlight all the cells you want to select. Then release the mouse button.

■ To select multiple groups of cells, press and hold down **Ctrl** on your keyboard as you repeat steps **1** and **2** for each group.

■ To deselect cells, move the mouse ⊕ over any cell and then press the left mouse button.

120

How do I select all the cells in my worksheet?

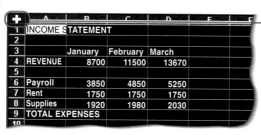

■ To select all the cells in your worksheet, move the mouse ✛ over the area where the row and column headings meet and then press the left mouse button.

SELECT A ROW

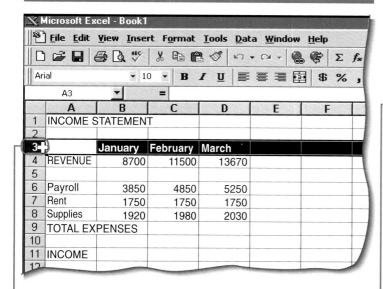

1 Move the mouse ✛ over the number of the row you want to select and then press the left mouse button.

SELECT A COLUMN

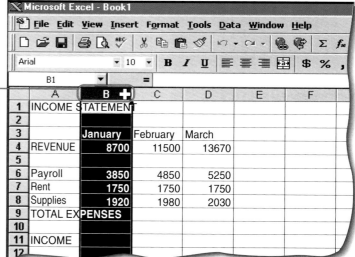

1 Move the mouse ✛ over the letter of the column you want to select and then press the left mouse button.

SCROLL THROUGH A WORKSHEET

If your worksheet contains a lot of data, your computer screen cannot display all the data at once. You must scroll through the worksheet to view other areas.

SCROLL UP OR DOWN

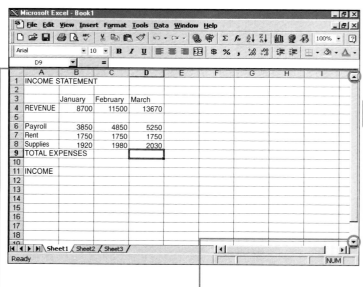

■ To scroll up one row, move the mouse � over ▲ and then press the left mouse button.

■ To scroll down one row, move the mouse � over ▼ and then press the left mouse button.

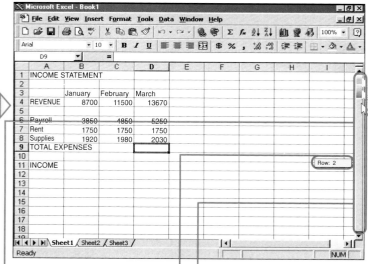

QUICKLY SCROLL

1 To quickly scroll to any row in the worksheet, move the mouse � over the scroll box.

2 Press and hold down the left mouse button as you move the mouse � up or down the scroll bar.

3 When this box displays the number of the row you want to view, release the mouse button.

122

How do I use the new Microsoft IntelliMouse to scroll through a worksheet?

The Microsoft IntelliMouse has a wheel between the left and right mouse buttons. Moving this wheel lets you quickly scroll up and down through a worksheet.

SCROLL LEFT OR RIGHT

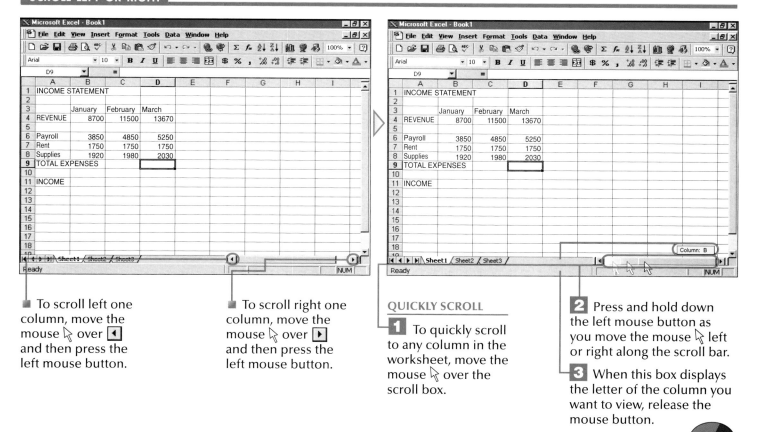

■ To scroll left one column, move the mouse ⬎ over ◀ and then press the left mouse button.

■ To scroll right one column, move the mouse ⬎ over ▶ and then press the left mouse button.

QUICKLY SCROLL

1 To quickly scroll to any column in the worksheet, move the mouse ⬎ over the scroll box.

2 Press and hold down the left mouse button as you move the mouse ⬎ left or right along the scroll bar.

3 When this box displays the letter of the column you want to view, release the mouse button.

Excel lets you enlarge or reduce the display of data on your screen.

Changing the zoom setting will not affect the way data appears on a printed page.

ZOOM IN OR OUT

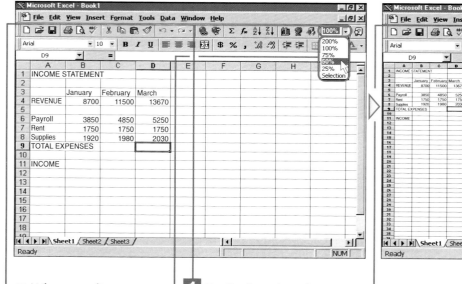

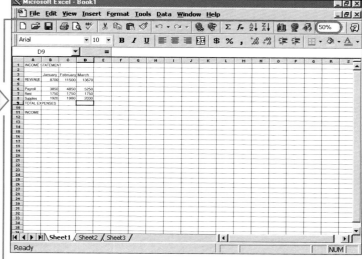

■ When you first start Excel, the worksheet appears in the 100% zoom setting.

1 To display a list of zoom settings, move the mouse over ▾ in this area and then press the left mouse button.

2 Move the mouse over the zoom setting you want to use and then press the left mouse button.

■ The worksheet appears in the new zoom setting. You can edit your worksheet as usual.

■ To return to the normal zoom setting, repeat steps **1** and **2**, selecting **100%** in step **2**.

124

DISPLAY TOOLBARS

Excel offers several toolbars that you can hide or display at any time. Each toolbar contains a series of buttons that help you quickly perform tasks.

Standard
Formatting

When you first start Excel, the Standard and Formatting toolbars appear on your screen.

DISPLAY TOOLBARS

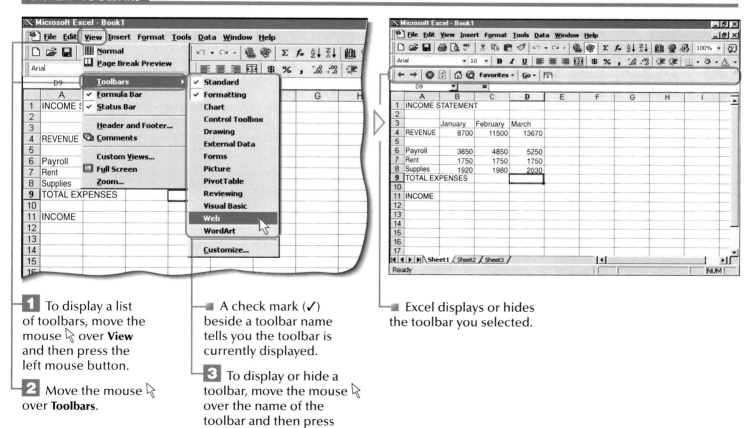

1 To display a list of toolbars, move the mouse ᐟᐟ over **View** and then press the left mouse button.

2 Move the mouse ᐟᐟ over **Toolbars**.

■ A check mark (✓) beside a toolbar name tells you the toolbar is currently displayed.

3 To display or hide a toolbar, move the mouse ᐟᐟ over the name of the toolbar and then press the left mouse button.

■ Excel displays or hides the toolbar you selected.

SAVE A WORKBOOK

You should save your workbook to store it for future use. This lets you later review and make changes to the workbook.

SAVE A WORKBOOK

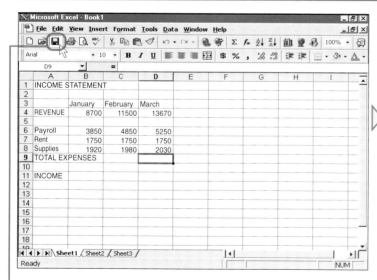

1 Move the mouse ⟋ over 🖫 and then press the left mouse button.

■ The **Save As** dialog box appears.

*Note: If you previously saved the workbook, the **Save As** dialog box will not appear since you have already named the workbook.*

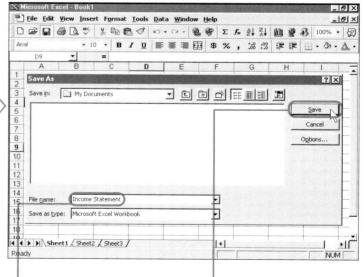

2 Type a name for the workbook.

Note: You can use up to 218 characters, including spaces, to name a workbook.

3 Move the mouse ⟋ over **Save** and then press the left mouse button.

What is the difference between a workbook and a worksheet?

An Excel file is called a workbook. Each workbook is divided into several worksheets. A workbook is similar to a three-ring binder that contains several sheets of paper.

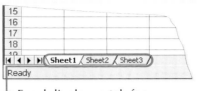

■ Excel displays a tab for each worksheet in your workbook.

Note: To use multiple worksheets in a workbook, refer to pages 194 to 199.

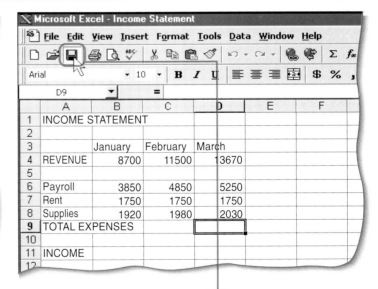

■ Excel saves the workbook and displays the name at the top of the screen.

SAVE CHANGES

To avoid losing your work, you should regularly save changes you make to a workbook.

1 Move the mouse ⟍ over 🔲 and then press the left mouse button.

CREATE A NEW WORKBOOK

You can easily create another workbook to store new data.

CREATE A NEW WORKBOOK

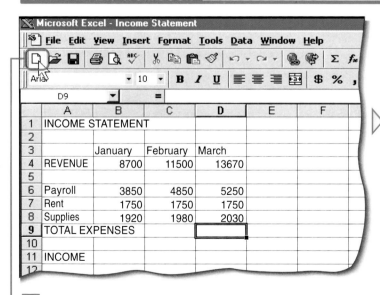

1 Move the mouse ⬚ over ☐ and then press the left mouse button.

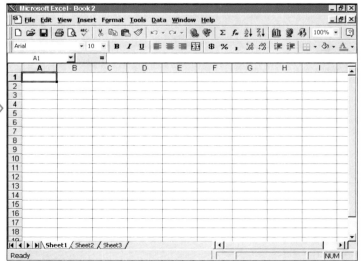

■ A new workbook appears. The previous workbook is now hidden behind the new workbook.

SWITCH BETWEEN WORKBOOKS

Excel lets you have many workbooks open at once. You can easily switch between all of your open workbooks.

SWITCH BETWEEN WORKBOOKS

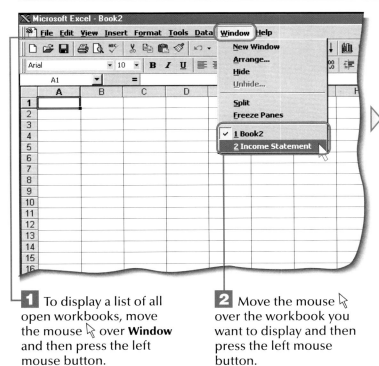

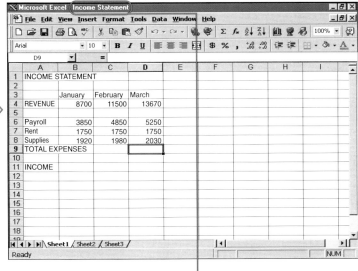

1 To display a list of all open workbooks, move the mouse over **Window** and then press the left mouse button.

2 Move the mouse over the workbook you want to display and then press the left mouse button.

■ The workbook appears.

■ Excel displays the name of the workbook at the top of the screen.

When you finish using a workbook, you can close the workbook to remove it from your screen.

When you close a workbook, you do not exit the Excel program. You can continue to work on other workbooks.

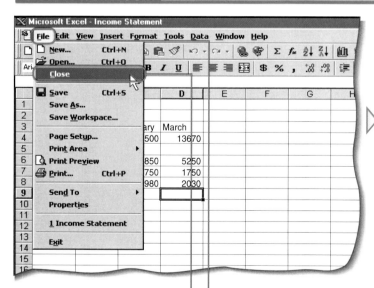

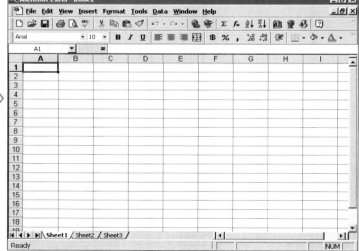

■ To save the workbook before closing, refer to page 126.

1 To close the workbook, move the mouse ⍾ over **File** and then press the left mouse button.

2 Move the mouse ⍾ over **Close** and then press the left mouse button.

■ Excel removes the workbook from the screen.

■ If you had more than one workbook open, the second last workbook you worked on appears on the screen.

EXIT EXCEL

When you finish using Excel, you can exit the program.

You should exit all programs before turning off your computer.

EXIT EXCEL

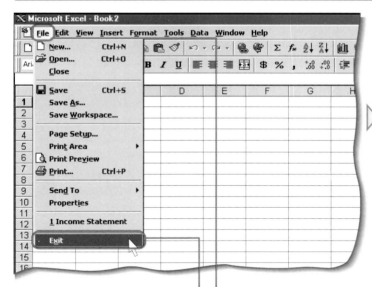

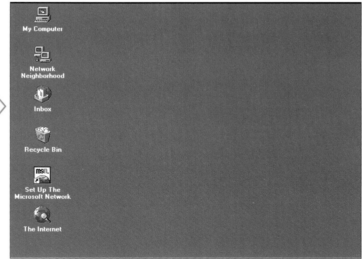

■ Save all open workbooks before exiting Excel. To save a workbook, refer to page 126.

1 Move the mouse ⃕ over **File** and then press the left mouse button.

2 Move the mouse ⃕ over **Exit** and then press the left mouse button.

■ The Excel window disappears from the screen.

Note: To restart Excel, refer to page 113.

OPEN A WORKBOOK

You can open a saved workbook and display it on your screen. This lets you review and make changes to the workbook.

OPEN A WORKBOOK

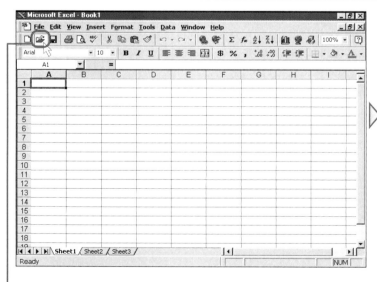

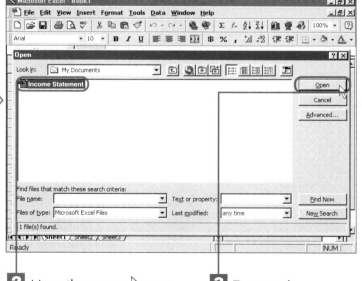

1 Move the mouse ⟩ over 📂 and then press the left mouse button.

■ The **Open** dialog box appears.

2 Move the mouse ⟩ over the name of the workbook you want to open and then press the left mouse button.

3 To open the workbook, move the mouse ⟩ over **Open** and then press the left mouse button.

Excel remembers the names of the last four workbooks you opened. You can quickly open any of these workbooks.

QUICKLY OPEN A WORKBOOK

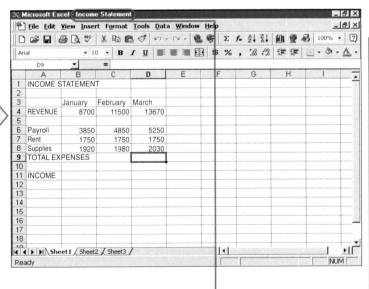

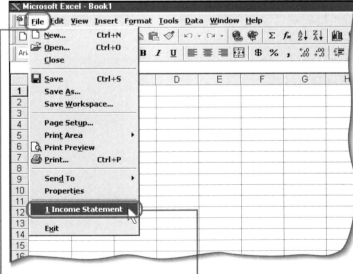

■ Excel opens the workbook and displays it on the screen. You can now review and make changes to the workbook.

■ The name of the workbook appears at the top of the screen.

1 Move the mouse � over **File** and then press the left mouse button.

2 Move the mouse � over the name of the workbook you want to open and then press the left mouse button.

EDIT DATA

After you enter data into your worksheet, you can change the data to correct a mistake or update the data.

EDIT DATA

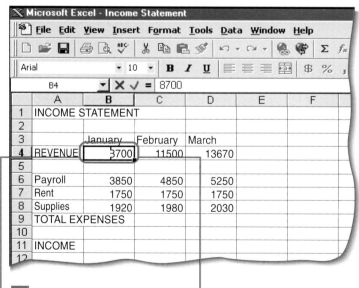

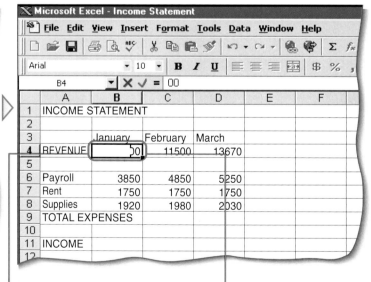

1 Move the mouse ⊕ over the cell containing the data you want to edit and then quickly press the left mouse button twice.

■ A flashing insertion point appears in the cell.

2 Press ← or → on your keyboard to move the insertion point to where you want to add or remove characters.

3 To remove the character to the left of the insertion point, press **←Backspace** on your keyboard.

Can Excel automatically correct my typing mistakes?

Excel automatically corrects common spelling errors as you type.

adn	➞	and
alot	➞	a lot
comittee	➞	committee
don;t	➞	don't
nwe	➞	new
occurence	➞	occurrence
recieve	➞	receive
seperate	➞	separate
teh	➞	the

REPLACE ALL DATA IN A CELL

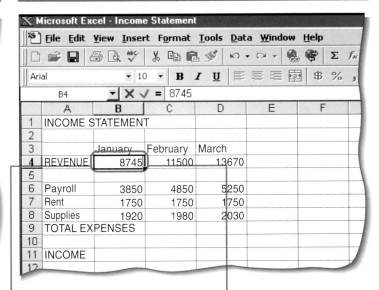

4 To insert data where the insertion point flashes on the screen, type the data.

5 When you finish making changes to the data, press **Enter** on your keyboard.

1 Move the mouse ⊹ over the cell containing the data you want to replace with new data and then press the left mouse button.

2 Type the new data and then press **Enter** on your keyboard.

You can easily remove data you no longer need from cells in your worksheet.

DELETE DATA

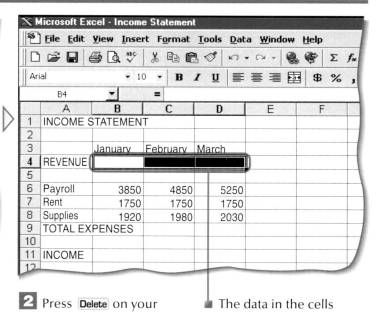

1 Select the cell(s) containing the data you want to delete. To select cells, refer to page 120.

2 Press Delete on your keyboard.

■ The data in the cells you selected disappears.

UNDO LAST CHANGE

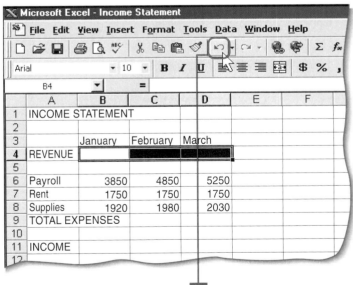

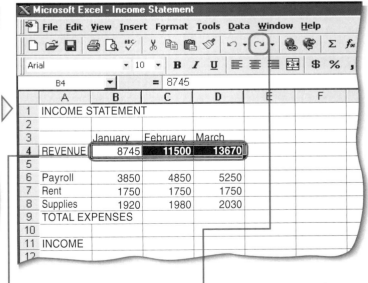

The Undo feature can cancel your last editing and formatting changes.

1 To undo your last change, move the mouse ⌖ over 🔙 and then press the left mouse button.

■ Excel cancels the last change you made to the worksheet.

■ You can repeat step 1 to cancel previous changes you made.

■ To reverse the results of using the Undo feature, move the mouse ⌖ over 🔜 and then press the left mouse button.

MOVE DATA

You can reorganize the data in your worksheet by moving data from one location to another.

MOVE DATA

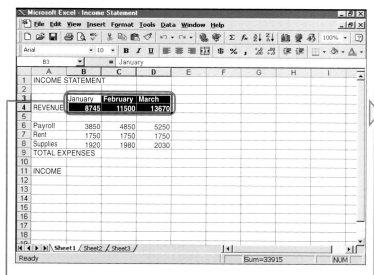

1 Select the cells containing the data you want to move. To select cells, refer to page 120.

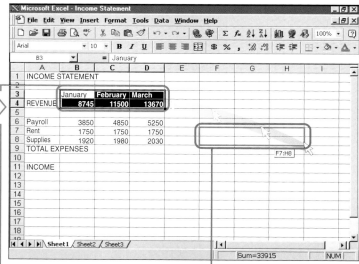

2 Move the mouse ⊹ over a border of the selected cells (⊹ changes to ⇖).

3 Press and hold down the left mouse button as you move the mouse ⇖ to where you want to place the data.

Why does this message appear when I try to move data?

This message may appear when you try to move data to a location that already contains data.

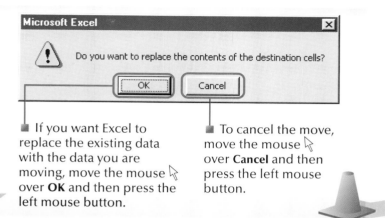

■ If you want Excel to replace the existing data with the data you are moving, move the mouse ⌖ over **OK** and then press the left mouse button.

■ To cancel the move, move the mouse ⌖ over **Cancel** and then press the left mouse button.

MOVE DATA USING TOOLBAR

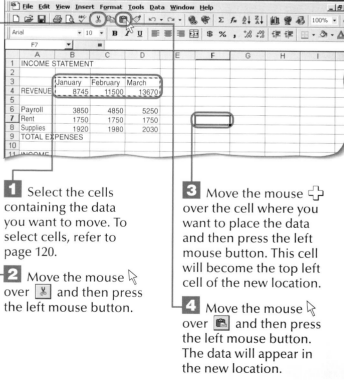

4 Release the mouse button and the data moves to the new location.

UNDO THE MOVE

■ To immediately move the data back, move the mouse ⌖ over ⟲ and then press the left mouse button.

1 Select the cells containing the data you want to move. To select cells, refer to page 120.

2 Move the mouse ⌖ over ✂ and then press the left mouse button.

3 Move the mouse ⌖ over the cell where you want to place the data and then press the left mouse button. This cell will become the top left cell of the new location.

4 Move the mouse ⌖ over 📋 and then press the left mouse button. The data will appear in the new location.

COPY DATA

You can place a copy of data in a different location in your worksheet. This will save you time since you do not have to retype the data.

COPY DATA

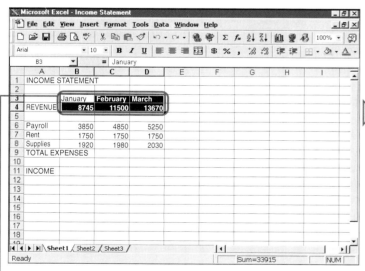

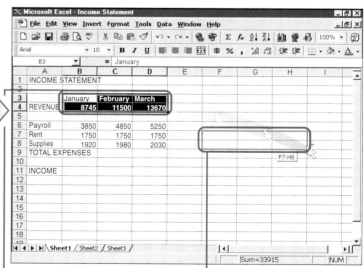

1 Select the cells containing the data you want to copy. To select cells, refer to page 120.

2 Move the mouse ⊕ over a border of the selected cells (⊕ changes to ⟋).

3 Press and hold down **Ctrl** on your keyboard.

4 Still holding down **Ctrl**, press and hold down the left mouse button as you move the mouse ⟋ to where you want to place the copy.

How can I quickly copy data to the active cell?

$9300 | $9300

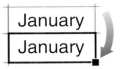

January
January

■ To quickly copy the contents of the cell on the left of the active cell, press and hold down **Ctrl** as you press **R** on your keyboard.

■ To quickly copy the contents of the cell above the active cell, press and hold down **Ctrl** as you press **D** on your keyboard.

COPY DATA USING TOOLBAR

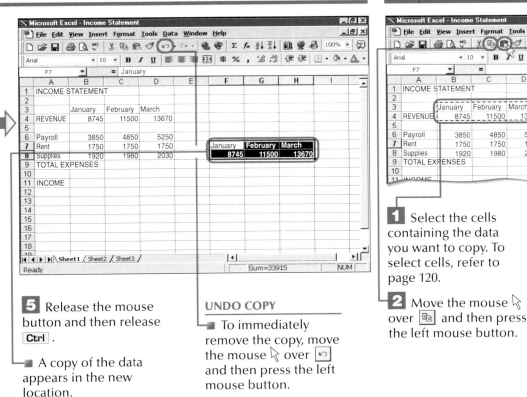

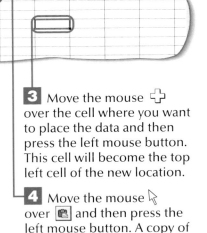

5 Release the mouse button and then release **Ctrl**.

■ A copy of the data appears in the new location.

UNDO COPY

■ To immediately remove the copy, move the mouse over and then press the left mouse button.

1 Select the cells containing the data you want to copy. To select cells, refer to page 120.

2 Move the mouse over and then press the left mouse button.

3 Move the mouse over the cell where you want to place the data and then press the left mouse button. This cell will become the top left cell of the new location.

4 Move the mouse over and then press the left mouse button. A copy of the data will appear in the new location.

INSERT A ROW OR COLUMN

You can add a row or column to your worksheet when you want to insert additional data.

INSERT A ROW

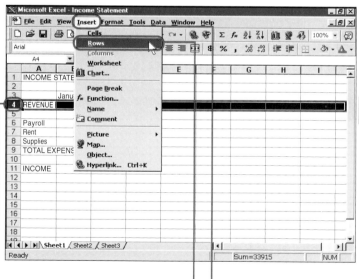

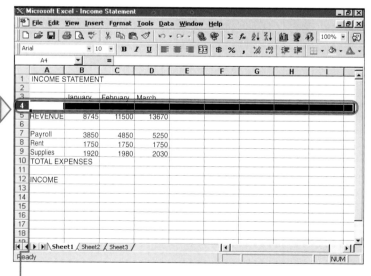

Excel will insert a row above the row you select.

1 To select a row, move the mouse ⊕ over the row number and then press the left mouse button.

2 Move the mouse ⅄ over **Insert** and then press the left mouse button.

3 Move the mouse ⅄ over **Rows** and then press the left mouse button.

◼ The new row appears and all the rows that follow shift downward.

Do I need to adjust my formulas when I insert a row or column?

When you insert a row or column, Excel updates any formulas affected by the insertion.

Note: For information on formulas, refer to page 146.

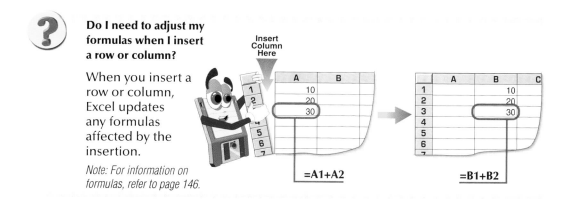

INSERT A COLUMN

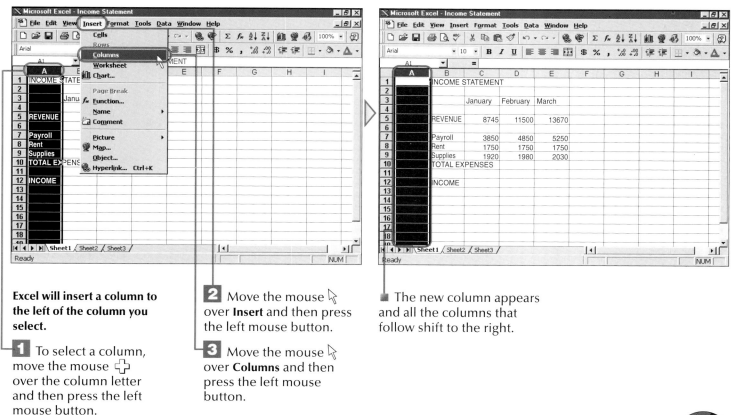

Excel will insert a column to the left of the column you select.

1 To select a column, move the mouse ⇩ over the column letter and then press the left mouse button.

2 Move the mouse ⇩ over **Insert** and then press the left mouse button.

3 Move the mouse ⇩ over **Columns** and then press the left mouse button.

■ The new column appears and all the columns that follow shift to the right.

DELETE A ROW OR COLUMN

You can delete a row or column from your worksheet to remove cells you no longer need.

DELETE A ROW

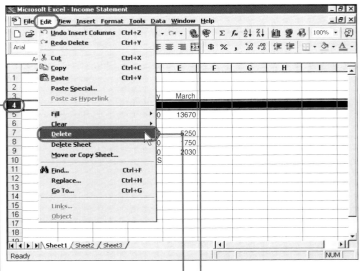

1 To select the row you want to delete, move the mouse ⊹ over the row number and then press the left mouse button.

2 Move the mouse ⧖ over **Edit** and then press the left mouse button.

3 Move the mouse ⧖ over **Delete** and then press the left mouse button.

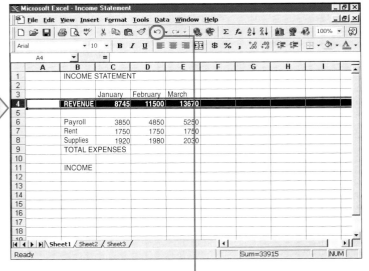

■ The row disappears and all the rows that follow shift upward.

■ To immediately return the row to the worksheet, move the mouse ⧖ over 🔄 and then press the left mouse button.

Why did #REF! appear in a cell after I deleted a row or column?

If **#REF!** appears in a cell in your worksheet, you deleted data needed to calculate a formula.

Note: For information on formulas, refer to page 146.

DELETE A COLUMN

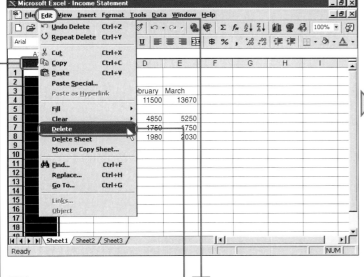

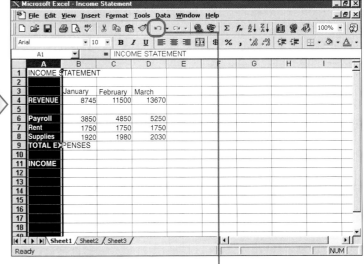

1 To select the column you want to delete, move the mouse ⊕ over the column letter and then press the left mouse button.

2 Move the mouse ↘ over **Edit** and then press the left mouse button.

3 Move the mouse ↘ over **Delete** and then press the left mouse button.

■ The column disappears and all the columns that follow shift to the left.

■ To immediately return the column to the worksheet, move the mouse ↘ over ⟲ and then press the left mouse button.

ENTER A FORMULA

A formula always begins with an equal sign (=).

A formula helps you calculate and analyze data in your worksheet.

INTRODUCTION TO FORMULAS

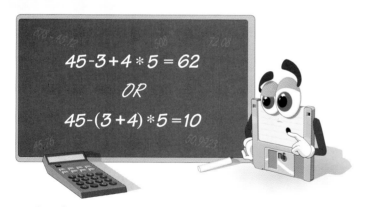

$$45-3+4*5 = 62$$
OR
$$45-(3+4)*5 =10$$

Order of Calculations

Excel performs calculations in the following order:

1 Exponents (^)

2 Multiplication (*) and Division (/)

3 Addition (+) and Subtraction (-)

You can use parentheses ( ) to change the order that Excel performs calculations. Excel will calculate the data inside the parentheses first.

Cell References

When entering formulas, use cell references (example: **=A1+A2**) instead of actual data (example: **=10+30**) whenever possible. When you use cell references and you change a number used in a formula, Excel will automatically redo the calculations for you.

EXAMPLES OF FORMULAS

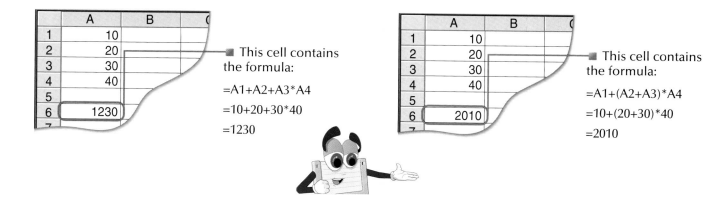

	A	B
1	10	
2	20	
3	30	
4	40	
5		
6	1230	

◼ This cell contains the formula:

=A1+A2+A3*A4

=10+20+30*40

=1230

	A	B
1	10	
2	20	
3	30	
4	40	
5		
6	2010	

◼ This cell contains the formula:

=A1+(A2+A3)*A4

=10+(20+30)*40

=2010

	A	B
1	10	
2	20	
3	30	
4	40	
5		
6	320	

◼ This cell contains the formula:

=A1*A3-A2+A4

=10*30-20+40

=320

	A	B
1	10	
2	20	
3	30	
4	40	
5		
6	140	

◼ This cell contains the formula:

=A1*(A3-A2)+A4

=10*(30-20)+40

=140

	A	B
1	10	
2	20	
3	30	
4	40	
5		
6	63	

◼ This cell contains the formula:

=A3/A1+A2+A4

=30/10+20+40

=63

	A	B
1	10	
2	20	
3	30	
4	40	
5		
6	41	

◼ This cell contains the formula:

=A3/(A1+A2)+A4

=30/(10+20)+40

=41

ENTER A FORMULA

mG's Pizza Parlor

ORDERS

	A	B
1	Pizza	600
2	Spaghetti	200
3	Garlic Bread	400
4	TOTAL	1200

=B1+B2+B3

You can enter a formula into any cell in your worksheet.

ENTER A FORMULA

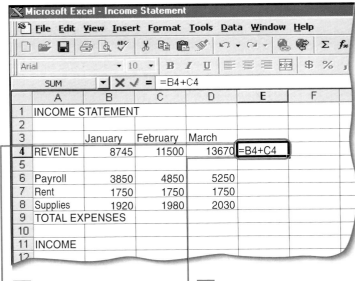

1 Move the mouse ⬦ over the cell where you want to enter a formula and then press the left mouse button.

2 Type an equal sign (=) to begin the formula.

3 Type the formula and then press **Enter** on your keyboard.

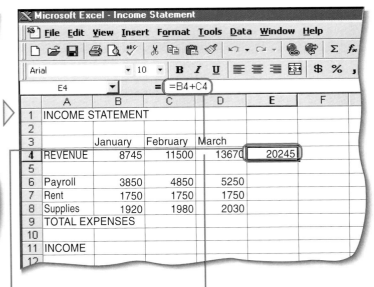

■ The result of the calculation appears in the cell.

4 To view the formula you entered, move the mouse ⬦ over the cell containing the formula and then press the left mouse button.

■ The formula for the cell appears in the formula bar.

What happens if I change a number used in a formula?

If you change a number used in a formula, Excel will automatically calculate a new result.

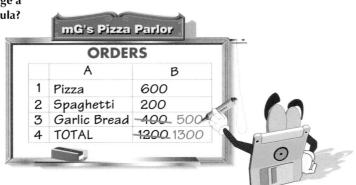

EDIT A FORMULA

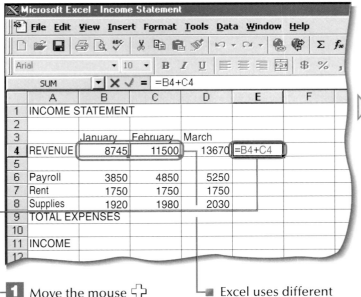

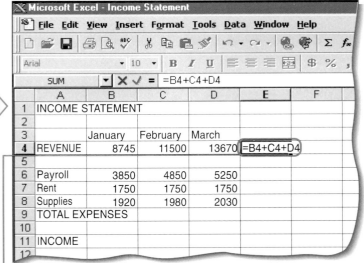

1 Move the mouse ⊕ over the cell containing the formula you want to change and then quickly press the left mouse button twice.

■ The formula appears in the cell.

■ Excel uses different colors to highlight each cell used in the formula.

2 Edit the formula. To edit data in a cell, perform steps 2 to 4 starting on page 134.

3 When you finish making changes to the formula, press **Enter** on your keyboard.

A function is a ready-to-use formula that performs a specialized calculation on your worksheet data.

AVERAGE
MAX
ROUND

INTRODUCTION TO FUNCTIONS

- A function always begins with an equal sign (=).

- The data Excel will use to calculate a function is enclosed in parentheses ( ).

=SUM(A1,A2,A3)

=AVERAGE(C1,C2,C3)

=MAX(B7,C7,D7,E7)

=COUNT(D12,D13,D14)

=SUM(A1:A3)

=AVERAGE(C1:C3)

=MAX(B7:E7)

=COUNT(D12:D14)

Specify Individual Cells

When there is a comma (,) between cell references in a function, Excel uses each cell to perform the calculation.

For example, =SUM(A1,A2,A3) is the same as the formula =A1+A2+A3.

Specify Group of Cells

When there is a colon (:) between cell references in a function, Excel uses the specified cells and all cells between them to perform the calculation.

For example, =SUM(A1:A3) is the same as the formula =A1+A2+A3.

COMMON FUNCTIONS

	A	B	C
1	10		
2	20		
3	30		
4	40		
5			
6	25		
7			

Average

Calculates the average value of a list of numbers.

■ This cell contains the function:

=AVERAGE(A1:A4)

=(A1+A2+A3+A4)/4

=(10+20+30+40)/4

=25

	A	B	C
1	10		
2	20		
3	30		
4	40		
5			
6	4		
7			

Count

Calculates the number of values in a list.

■ This cell contains the function:

=COUNT(A1:A4)

=4

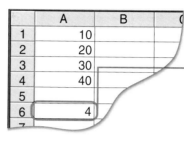

	A	B	C
1	10		
2	20		
3	30		
4	40		
5			
6	40		
7			

Max

Finds the largest value in a list of numbers.

■ This cell contains the function:

=MAX(A1:A4)

=40

	A	B	C
1	10		
2	20		
3	30		
4	40		
5			
6	10		
7			

Min

Finds the smallest value in a list of numbers.

■ This cell contains the function:

=MIN(A1:A4)

=10

	A	B	C
1	10		
2	20		
3	30		
4	40		
5			
6	100		
7			

Sum

Adds a list of numbers.

■ This cell contains the function:

=SUM(A1:A4)

=A1+A2+A3+A4

=10+20+30+40

=100

	A	B	C
1	42.3617		
2			
3			
4			
5			
6	42.36		
7			

Round

Rounds a value to a specific number of digits.

■ This cell contains the function:

=ROUND(A1,2)

=42.36

ENTER A FUNCTION

> Excel helps you enter functions in your worksheet. This lets you perform calculations without typing long, complex formulas.

ENTER A FUNCTION

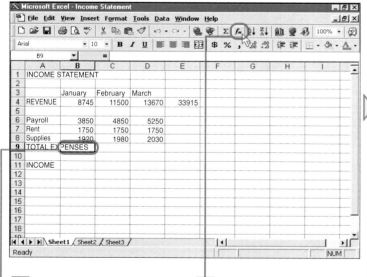

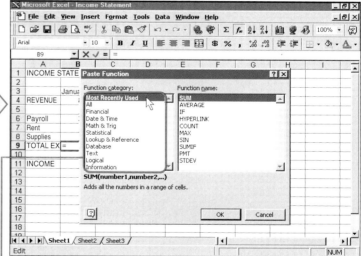

1 Move the mouse ⊕ over the cell where you want to enter a function and then press the left mouse button.

2 Move the mouse ⟍ over ∱ and then press the left mouse button.

■ The **Paste Function** dialog box appears.

3 Move the mouse ⟍ over the category that contains the function you want to use and then press the left mouse button.

*Note: If you do not know which category contains the function you want to use, select **All** to display a list of all the functions.*

How many functions does Excel offer?

Excel offers over 200 functions to help you analyze data in your worksheet. There are financial functions, math and trigonometry functions, date and time functions, statistical functions and many more.

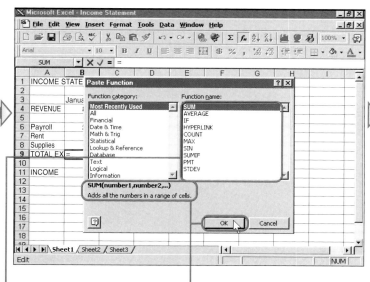

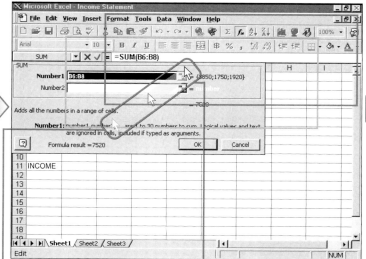

■ This area displays the functions in the category you selected.

4 Move the mouse ⊳ over a function of interest and then press the left mouse button.

■ This area describes the function you selected.

5 To enter the function in the worksheet, move the mouse ⊳ over **OK** and then press the left mouse button.

■ A dialog box appears. If the dialog box covers data you want to use in the calculation, you can move it to a new location.

6 To move the dialog box, position the mouse ⊳ over a blank area in the dialog box.

7 Press and hold down the left mouse button as you move the dialog box to a new location. Then release the mouse button.

CONTINUED➡

When entering a function, you must specify which numbers you want to use in the calculation.

ENTER A FUNCTION (CONTINUED)

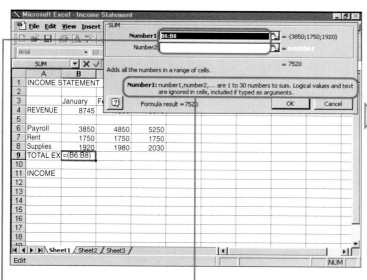

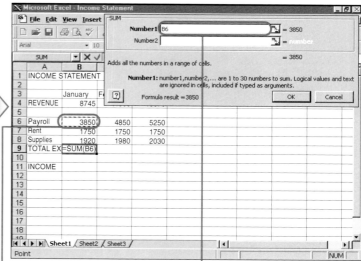

■ This area displays boxes where you enter the numbers you want to use in the calculation.

■ This area describes the number you need to enter.

8 To enter a number, move the mouse ⊡ over the cell in the worksheet that contains the number and then press the left mouse button.

Note: If the number you want to enter does not appear in the worksheet, type the number.

■ The area now displays the cell you selected.

Can I enter a function by myself?

You can easily enter a function yourself by typing the entire function into a cell.

=COUNT(D1:D

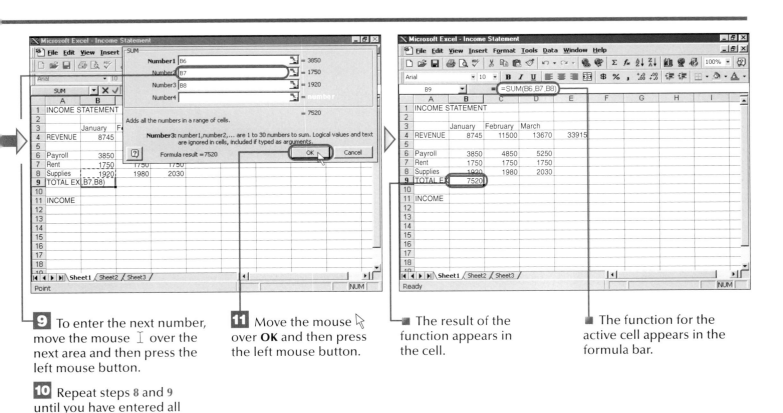

9 To enter the next number, move the mouse I over the next area and then press the left mouse button.

10 Repeat steps **8** and **9** until you have entered all the numbers you want to use in the calculation.

11 Move the mouse over **OK** and then press the left mouse button.

■ The result of the function appears in the cell.

■ The function for the active cell appears in the formula bar.

USING AUTOCALCULATE

You can quickly view the results of common calculations without entering a formula into your worksheet.

USING AUTOCALCULATE

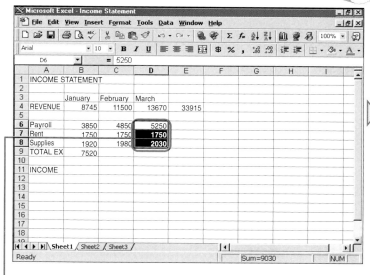

1 Select the cells you want to include in the calculation. To select cells, refer to page 120.

■ This area displays the sum of the cells you selected.

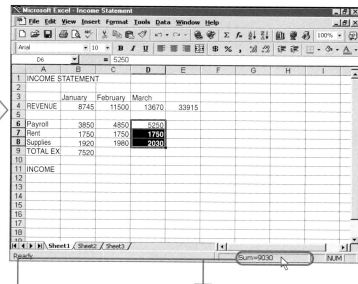

2 To display the result for a different calculation, move the mouse ⇧ over this area and then press the **right** mouse button.

156

What calculations can AutoCalculate perform?

Average
Calculates the average value of a list of numbers.

Count
Calculates the number of items in a list, including text.

Count Nums
Calculates the number of values in a list.

Max
Finds the largest value in a list.

Min
Finds the smallest value in a list.

Sum
Adds a list of numbers.

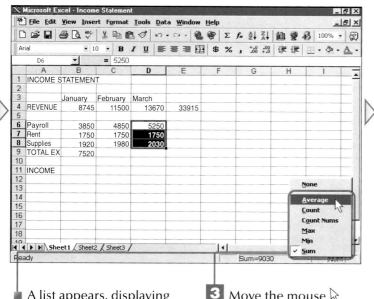

■ A list appears, displaying the calculations you can perform.

3 Move the mouse over the calculation you want to perform and then press the left mouse button.

■ This area displays the result for the new calculation.

ADD NUMBERS

You can quickly add a list of numbers in your worksheet.

ADD NUMBERS

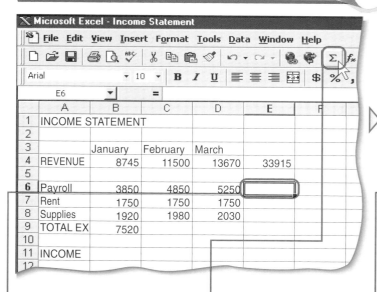

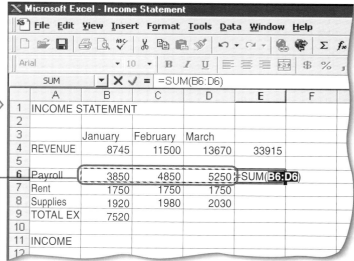

1 Move the mouse ⊕ over the cell below or to the right of the cells you want to add and then press the left mouse button.

2 Move the mouse ⌖ over ∑ and then press the left mouse button.

■ Excel outlines the cells it will use in the calculation with a dotted line.

■ If Excel does not outline the correct cells, select the cells containing the numbers you want to add. To select cells, refer to page 120.

Why did number signs (#) appear in a cell?

If number signs (#) appear in a cell, the result of a calculation is too long to fit in the cell. To display the result, you need to change the column width. To do so, refer to page 166.

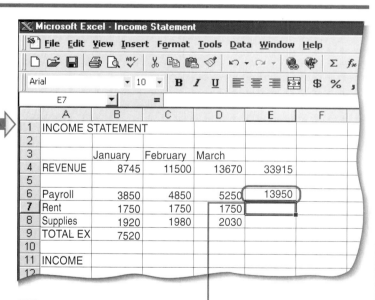

3 Press **Enter** on your keyboard to perform the calculation.

■ The result appears.

CALCULATE A GRAND TOTAL

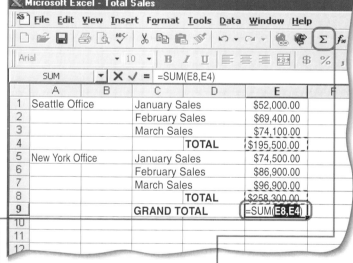

■ If the worksheet contains several subtotals, you can quickly calculate a grand total.

1 Move the mouse ⊹ over the cell below or to the right of the cells that contain the subtotals and then press the left mouse button.

2 Move the mouse ⍩ over Σ and then press the left mouse button.

3 Press **Enter** on your keyboard.

ERRORS IN FORMULAS

An error message appears when Excel cannot properly calculate a formula.

Errors in formulas are often the result of typing mistakes. You can correct an error by editing the cell containing the error. To edit data in a cell, refer to page 134.

#####

The column is too narrow to display the result of the calculation. To display the result, refer to page 166 to change the column width.

	A	B	C
1	9924		
2	5521		
3			
4	#####		
5			
6			

■ This cell contains the formula:

=A1*A2

#DIV/0!

The formula divides a number by zero (0). Excel considers a blank cell to contain a value of zero.

	A	B	C
1	50		
2			
3			
4	#DIV/0!		
5			
6			

■ This cell contains the formula:

=A1/A2

=50/0

#NAME?

The formula contains a function name or cell reference Excel does not recognize.

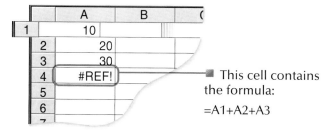

■ This cell contains the formula:

=SUMM(A1:A3)

In this example, the name of the SUM function was misspelled.

#REF!

The formula refers to a cell that is not valid.

■ This cell contains the formula:

=A1+A2+A3

In this example, a row containing a cell used in the formula was deleted.

#VALUE!

The formula refers to a cell that Excel cannot use in a calculation.

■ This cell contains the formula:

=A1+A2+A3

In this example, a cell used in the formula contains text.

Circular Reference

A warning message appears when a formula refers to the cell that contains the formula. This is called a circular reference.

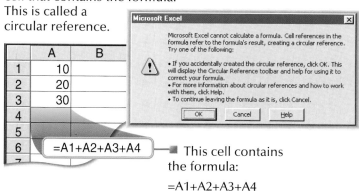

Microsoft Excel cannot calculate a formula. Cell references in the formula refer to the formula's result, creating a circular reference. Try one of the following:

• If you accidentally created the circular reference, click OK. This will display the Circular Reference toolbar and help for using it to correct your formula.
• For more information about circular references and how to work with them, click Help.
• To continue leaving the formula as it is, click Cancel.

■ This cell contains the formula:

=A1+A2+A3+A4

COPY A FORMULA

If you want to use the same formula several times in your worksheet, you can save time by copying the formula.

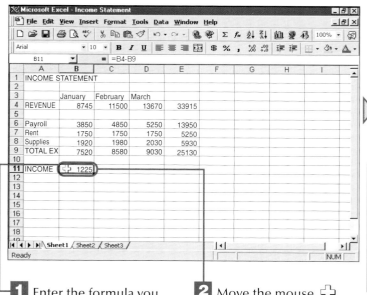

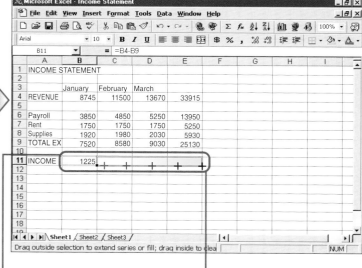

1 Enter the formula you want to copy to other cells. To enter a formula, refer to page 148.

Note: In this example, enter the formula =B4-B9 in cell B11 to calculate INCOME.

2 Move the mouse ⊕ over the cell containing the formula you want to copy and then press the left mouse button.

3 Move the mouse ⊕ over the bottom right corner of the cell (⊕ changes to ✛).

4 Press and hold down the left mouse button as you move the mouse ✛ over the cells you want to receive a copy of the formula. Then release the mouse button.

What is a relative reference?

A relative reference changes when you copy a formula.

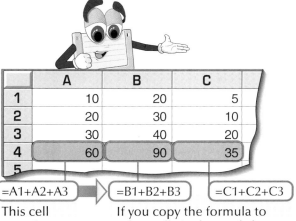

	A	B	C
1	10	20	5
2	20	30	10
3	30	40	20
4	60	90	35
5			

=A1+A2+A3   =B1+B2+B3   =C1+C2+C3

This cell contains the formula =A1+A2+A3

If you copy the formula to other cells in the worksheet, Excel automatically changes the cell references in the new formulas.

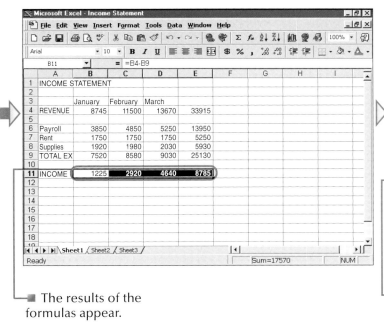

■ The results of the formulas appear.

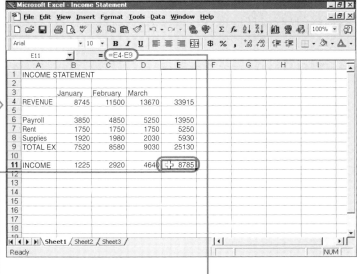

5 To see the new formulas, move the mouse ⊕ over a cell that received a copy of the formula and then press the left mouse button.

■ The formula bar displays the formula with the new cell references.

COPY A FORMULA

You can copy a formula to other cells in your worksheet to save time. If you do not want Excel to change a cell reference when you copy a formula, you can use an absolute reference.

COPY A FORMULA—USING ABSOLUTE REFERENCES

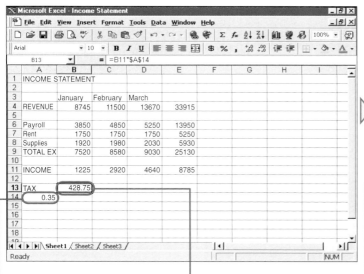

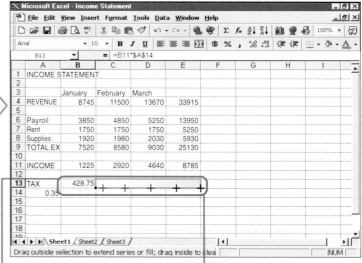

1 Enter the data you want to remain the same in all the formulas.

2 Enter the formula you want to copy to other cells. To enter a formula, refer to page 146.

Note: In this example, enter the formula =B11*$A$14 in cell B13 to calculate TAX. For information on absolute references, refer to the top of page 165.

3 Move the mouse ⇦ over the cell containing the formula you want to copy and then press the left mouse button.

4 Move the mouse ⇦ over the bottom right corner of the cell (⇦ changes to ✛).

5 Press and hold down the left mouse button as you move the mouse ✛ over the cells you want to receive a copy of the formula. Then release the mouse button.

What is an absolute reference?

An absolute reference does not change when you copy a formula. To make a cell reference absolute, type a dollar sign ($) before both the column letter and row number (example: $A$7).

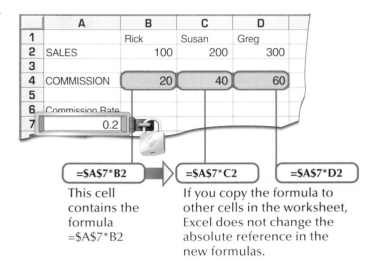

	A	B	C	D
1		Rick	Susan	Greg
2	SALES	100	200	300
3				
4	COMMISSION	20	40	60
5				
6	Commission Rate			
7	0.2			

=$A$7*B2

=$A$7*C2

=$A$7*D2

This cell contains the formula =$A$7*B2

If you copy the formula to other cells in the worksheet, Excel does not change the absolute reference in the new formulas.

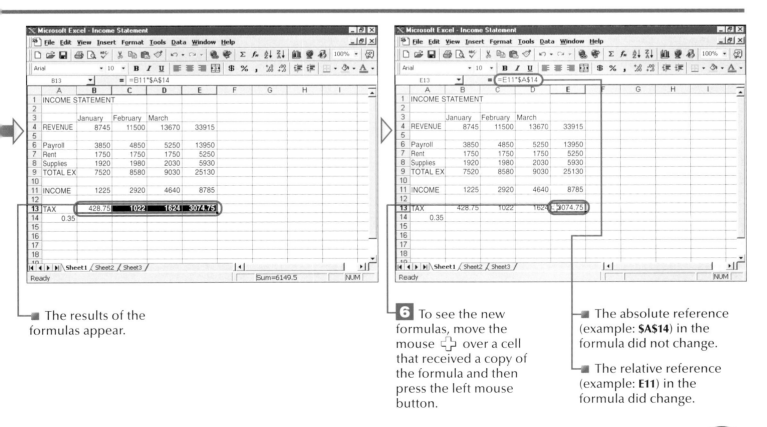

■ The results of the formulas appear.

6 To see the new formulas, move the mouse ⊕ over a cell that received a copy of the formula and then press the left mouse button.

■ The absolute reference (example: **$A$14**) in the formula did not change.

■ The relative reference (example: **E11**) in the formula did change.

CHANGE COLUMN WIDTH

You can improve the appearance of your worksheet and display hidden data by changing the width of columns.

FRUIT SALES		
Fruit	Jan	Feb
Waterme	100	180
Apples	120	150
Bananas	200	220
Cherries	300	200
Strawberr	100	150
Mangoes	110	110

CHANGE COLUMN WIDTH

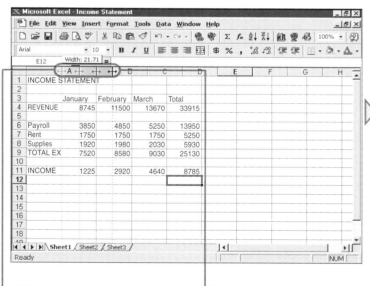

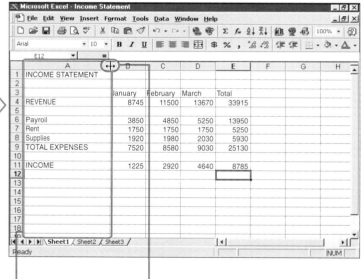

1 To change the width of a column, move the mouse ⬥ over the right edge of the column heading (⬥ changes to ↔).

2 Press and hold down the left mouse button as you move the column edge until the dotted line displays the column width you want. Then release the mouse button.

■ The column displays the new width.

FIT LONGEST ITEM

You can have Excel change a column width to fit the longest item in the column.

■ Move the mouse ⬥ over the right edge of the column heading (⬥ changes to ↔) and then quickly press the left mouse button twice.

CHANGE ROW HEIGHT

You can change the height of rows to add space between the rows of data in your worksheet.

FRUIT SALES

Fruit	Jan	Feb
Watermelon	100	180
Apples	120	150
Bananas	200	220
Cherries	300	200
Strawberries	100	150
Mangoes	110	110

CHANGE ROW HEIGHT

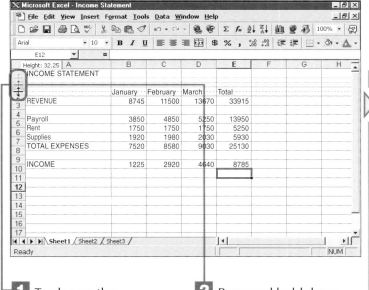

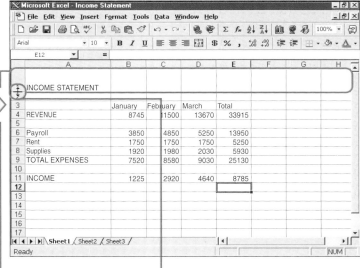

1 To change the height of a row, move the mouse ⬚ over the bottom edge of the row heading (⬚ changes to ✛).

2 Press and hold down the left mouse button as you move the row edge until the dotted line displays the row height you want. Then release the mouse button.

■ The row displays the new height.

FIT TALLEST ITEM

You can have Excel change a row height to fit the tallest item in the row.

■ Move the mouse ⬚ over the bottom edge of the row heading (⬚ changes to ✛) and then quickly press the left mouse button twice.

You can quickly change the appearance of numbers in your worksheet without retyping the numbers.

Option		Example
$	Change to dollar value	10 → $10.00
%	Change to percentage	0.15 → 15%
,	Add comma and display two decimal places	1000 → 1,000.00
+.0 .00	Add decimal place	10.19 → 10.190
.00 +.0	Remove decimal place	10.19 → 10.2

When you change the appearance of numbers, you do not change the value of the numbers.

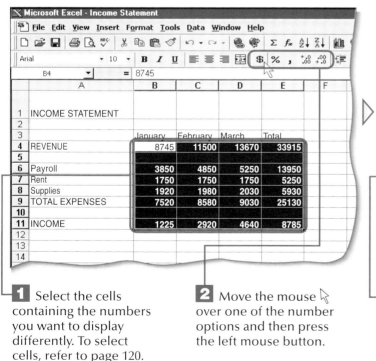

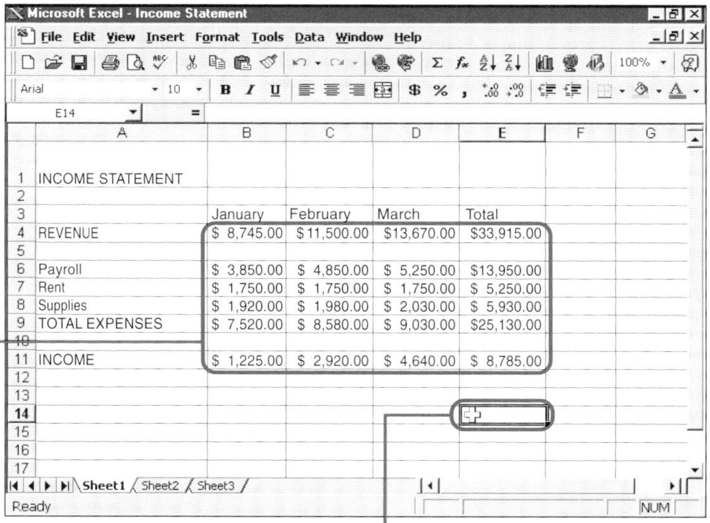

1 Select the cells containing the numbers you want to display differently. To select cells, refer to page 120.

2 Move the mouse � over one of the number options and then press the left mouse button.

■ The numbers display the appearance you selected.

■ To deselect cells, move the mouse ⬚ over any cell and then press the left mouse button.

Note: If number signs (#) appear in a cell, the column is not wide enough to display the entire number. To change the column width, refer to page 166.

You can use the bold, italic and underline styles to emphasize data in your worksheet.

Bold   *Italic*   <u>Underline</u>

BOLD, ITALIC AND UNDERLINE

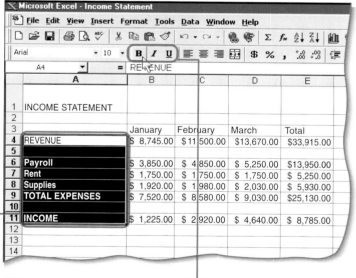

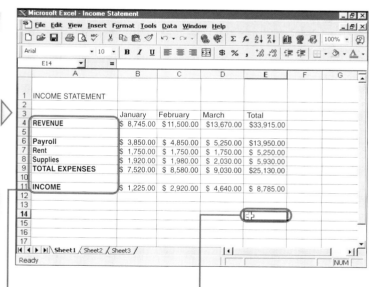

1 Select the cells containing the data you want to emphasize. To select cells, refer to page 120.

2 Move the mouse ⬚ over one of the following options and then press the left mouse button.

B	Bold
I	Italic
<u>U</u>	Underline

■ The data displays the style you selected.

■ To deselect cells, move the mouse ⬚ over any cell and then press the left mouse button.

■ To remove a bold, italic or underline style, repeat steps 1 and 2.

169

CHANGE FONT OF DATA

You can enhance the appearance of your worksheet by changing the font of data.

CHANGE FONT OF DATA

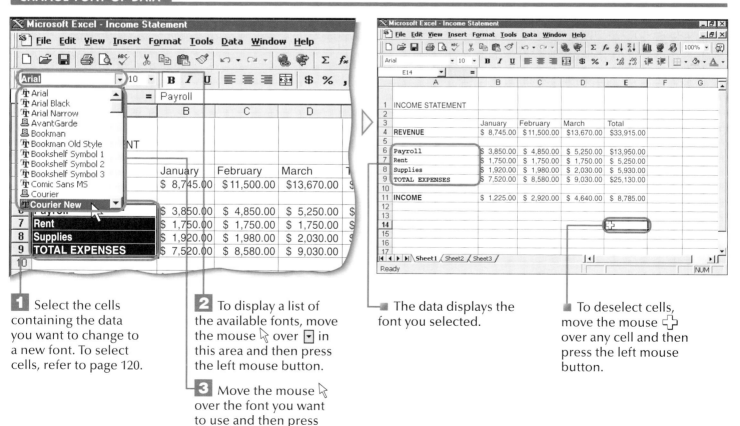

1 Select the cells containing the data you want to change to a new font. To select cells, refer to page 120.

2 To display a list of the available fonts, move the mouse ⌀ over ⏷ in this area and then press the left mouse button.

3 Move the mouse ⌀ over the font you want to use and then press the left mouse button.

■ The data displays the font you selected.

■ To deselect cells, move the mouse ⌗ over any cell and then press the left mouse button.

You can increase or decrease the size of data in your worksheet.

8 point
12 point
14 point
18 point
24 point

CHANGE SIZE OF DATA

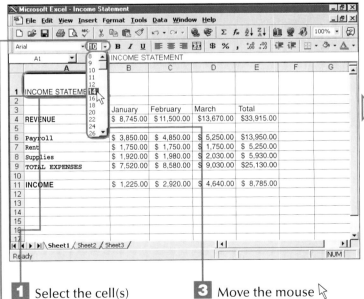

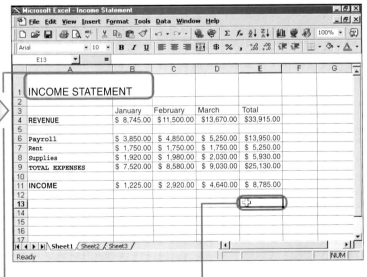

1 Select the cell(s) containing the data you want to change to a new size. To select cells, refer to page 120.

2 To display a list of the available sizes, move the mouse ⬚ over ▾ in this area and then press the left mouse button.

3 Move the mouse ⬚ over the size you want to use and then press the left mouse button.

◼ The data displays the size you selected.

◼ To deselect cells, move the mouse ⬚ over any cell and then press the left mouse button.

You can change the position of data in each cell of your worksheet.

CHANGE ALIGNMENT OF DATA

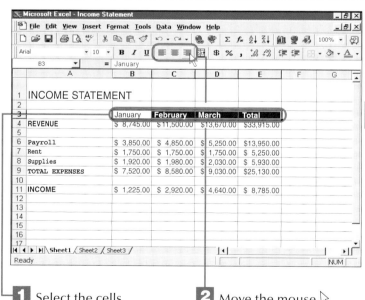

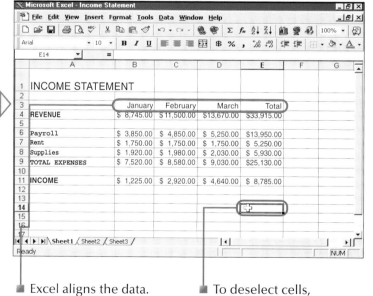

1 Select the cells containing the data you want to align differently. To select cells, refer to page 120.

2 Move the mouse ⟍ over one of the following options and then press the left mouse button.

≡ Left align

≡ Center

≡ Right align

■ Excel aligns the data.

■ To deselect cells, move the mouse ✛ over any cell and then press the left mouse button.

You can use the Indent feature to move data away from the left edge of a cell.

INDENT DATA

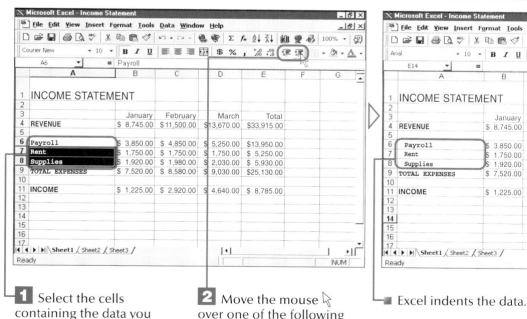

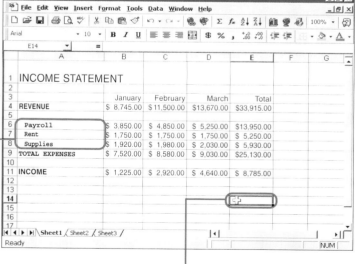

1 Select the cells containing the data you want to indent. To select cells, refer to page 120.

2 Move the mouse ↖ over one of the following options and then press the left mouse button.

⏪ Move data to the left

⏩ Move data to the right

■ Excel indents the data.

■ To deselect cells, move the mouse ✛ over any cell and then press the left mouse button.

ADD BORDERS

You can add borders to enhance the appearance of your worksheet.

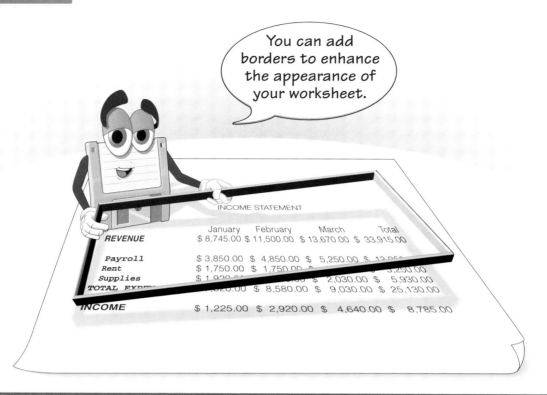

ADD BORDERS

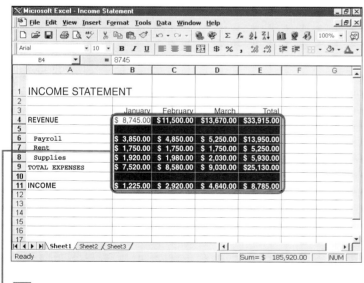

1 Select the cells you want to display borders. To select cells, refer to page 120.

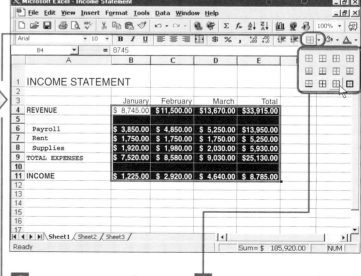

2 Move the mouse over ▾ in this area and then press the left mouse button.

3 Move the mouse over the type of border you want to add and then press the left mouse button.

Can I print lines in my worksheet without adding borders?

Instead of adding borders to your worksheet, you can have Excel automatically print light lines, called gridlines, around each cell. To print gridlines, refer to page 190.

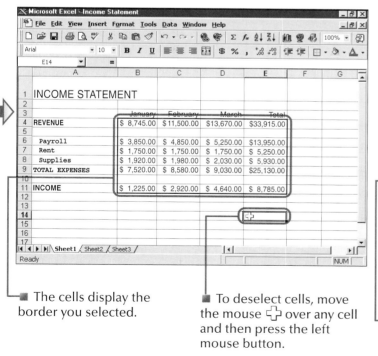

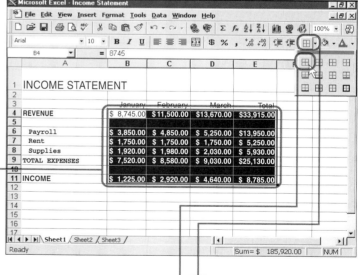

■ The cells display the border you selected.

■ To deselect cells, move the mouse ⊹ over any cell and then press the left mouse button.

REMOVE BORDERS

1 Select the cells you no longer want to display borders. To select cells, refer to page 120.

2 Move the mouse ⟋ over ▾ in this area and then press the left mouse button.

3 Move the mouse ⟋ over ▦ and then press the left mouse button.

CHANGE COLOR

You can make your worksheet more attractive by adding color.

CHANGE CELL COLOR

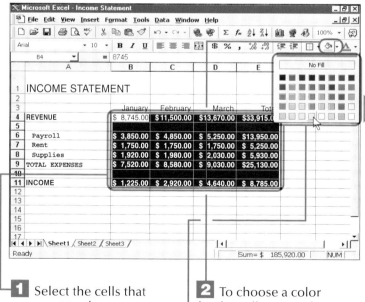

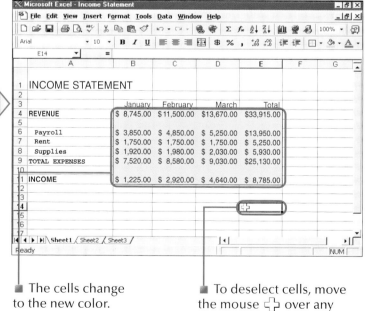

1 Select the cells that you want to change to a different color. To select cells, refer to page 120.

2 To choose a color for the cells, move the mouse ⟍ over ▾ in this area and then press the left mouse button.

3 Move the mouse ⟍ over the color you want to use and then press the left mouse button.

■ The cells change to the new color.

■ To deselect cells, move the mouse ⊹ over any cell and then press the left mouse button.

REMOVE CELL COLOR

■ Perform steps 1 to 3, selecting **No Fill** in step 3.

What colors should I choose?

When adding color to a worksheet, make sure you choose cell and data colors that work well together. For example, red text on a blue background is difficult to read. To choose from many ready-to-use designs offered by Excel, refer to page 180.

CHANGE DATA COLOR

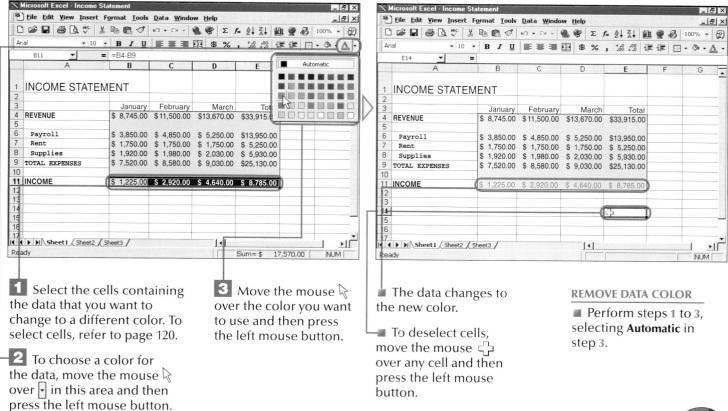

1 Select the cells containing the data that you want to change to a different color. To select cells, refer to page 120.

2 To choose a color for the data, move the mouse ↖ over ▾ in this area and then press the left mouse button.

3 Move the mouse ↖ over the color you want to use and then press the left mouse button.

■ The data changes to the new color.

■ To deselect cells, move the mouse ⇧ over any cell and then press the left mouse button.

REMOVE DATA COLOR

■ Perform steps **1** to **3**, selecting **Automatic** in step **3**.

COPY FORMATTING

If you like the appearance of a cell in your worksheet, you can make other cells look exactly the same.

Sales		
	1995	1996
Product A	3180	3210
Product B	3180	2740
Product C	3240	3140
Product D	2610	2750

COPY FORMATTING

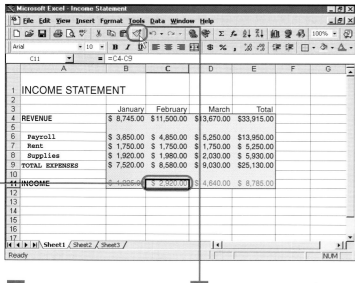

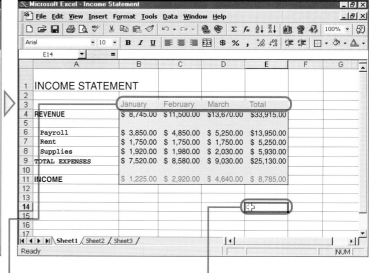

1 Move the mouse ⊕ over a cell displaying the formats you like and then press the left mouse button.

2 Move the mouse ⇖ over 🖌 and then press the left mouse button (⇖ changes to ⊕🖌 when over the worksheet).

3 Select the cells you want to display the same formats. To select cells, refer to page 120.

◾ When you release the mouse button, the cells display the formats.

◾ To deselect cells, move the mouse ⊕ over any cell and then press the left mouse button.

Note: If number signs (#) appear in a cell, the column is too narrow to fit the data. To change the column width, refer to page 166.

178

You can center data across several columns in your worksheet. This is useful for centering titles over your data.

CENTER DATA ACROSS COLUMNS

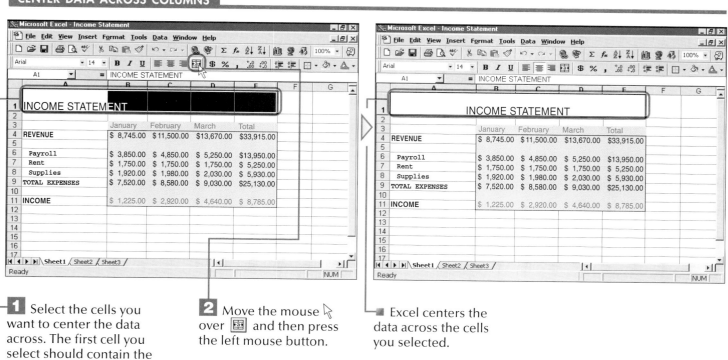

■1■ Select the cells you want to center the data across. The first cell you select should contain the data you want to center.

■2■ Move the mouse ⊠ over 🔳 and then press the left mouse button.

■ Excel centers the data across the cells you selected.

Excel offers many ready-to-use designs that you can choose from to give your worksheet a new appearance.

QUICKLY APPLY A DESIGN

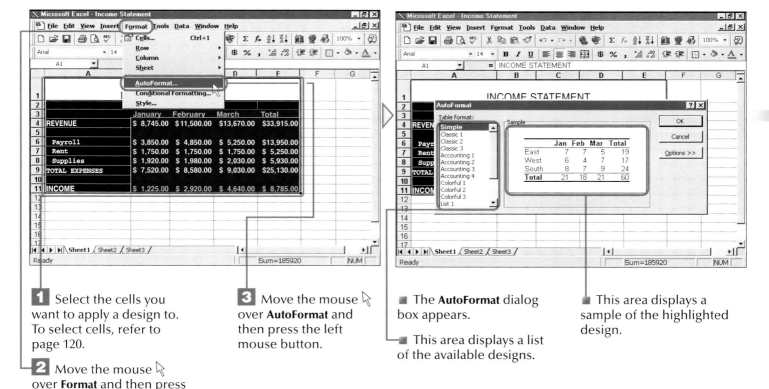

1 Select the cells you want to apply a design to. To select cells, refer to page 120.

2 Move the mouse ⌖ over **Format** and then press the left mouse button.

3 Move the mouse ⌖ over **AutoFormat** and then press the left mouse button.

■ The **AutoFormat** dialog box appears.

■ This area displays a list of the available designs.

■ This area displays a sample of the highlighted design.

What are some designs offered by Excel?

	Jan	Feb	Mar	Total
East	7	7	5	19
West	6	4	7	17
South	8	7	9	24
Total	21	18	21	60

List 2

		Jan		Feb		Mar		Total
East	$	7	$	7	$	5	$	19
West		6		4		7		17
South		8		7		9		24
Total	$	21	$	18	$	21	$	60

Accounting 2

	Jan	Feb	Mar	Total
East	7	7	5	19
West	6	4	7	17
South	8	7	9	24
Total	21	18	21	60

Classic 2

	Jan	Feb	Mar	Total
East	7	7	5	19
West	6	4	7	17
South	8	7	9	24
Total	21	18	21	60

3D Effects 1

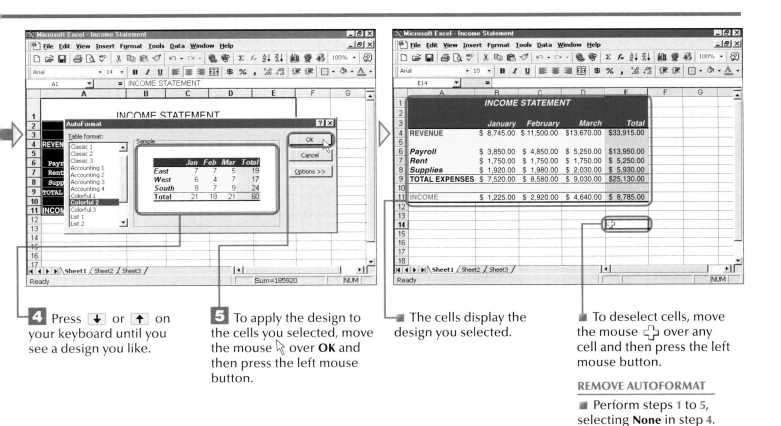

4 Press ↓ or ↑ on your keyboard until you see a design you like.

5 To apply the design to the cells you selected, move the mouse ⊗ over **OK** and then press the left mouse button.

■ The cells display the design you selected.

■ To deselect cells, move the mouse ⊕ over any cell and then press the left mouse button.

REMOVE AUTOFORMAT

■ Perform steps **1** to **5**, selecting **None** in step **4**.

PREVIEW A WORKSHEET

You can see on the screen how your worksheet will look when printed.

PREVIEW A WORKSHEET

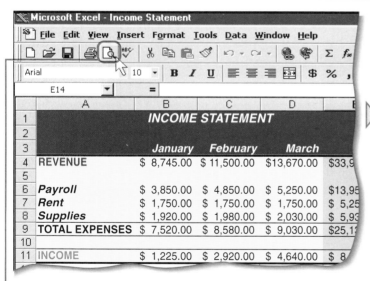

1 Move the mouse ⬚ over 🔍 and then press the left mouse button.

■ The Print Preview window appears.

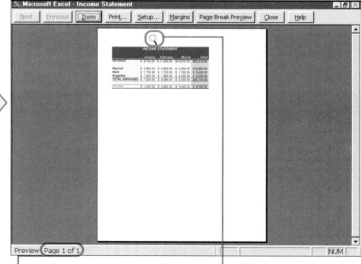

■ This area tells you which page is displayed and the total number of pages in the worksheet.

Note: If you have a black-and-white printer, Excel displays the page in black and white.

2 To magnify an area of the page, move the mouse ⬚ over the area (⬚ changes to 🔍) and then press the left mouse button.

What should I do before printing my worksheet?

Before printing your worksheet, preview the worksheet to ensure it will print the way you want. Also make sure the printer is turned on and contains paper.

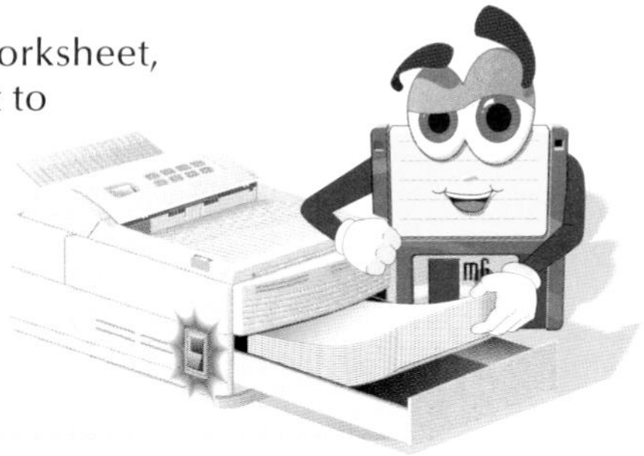

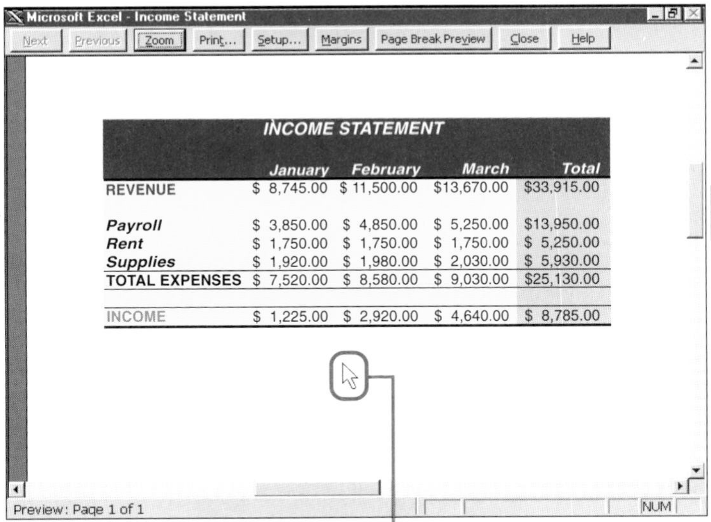

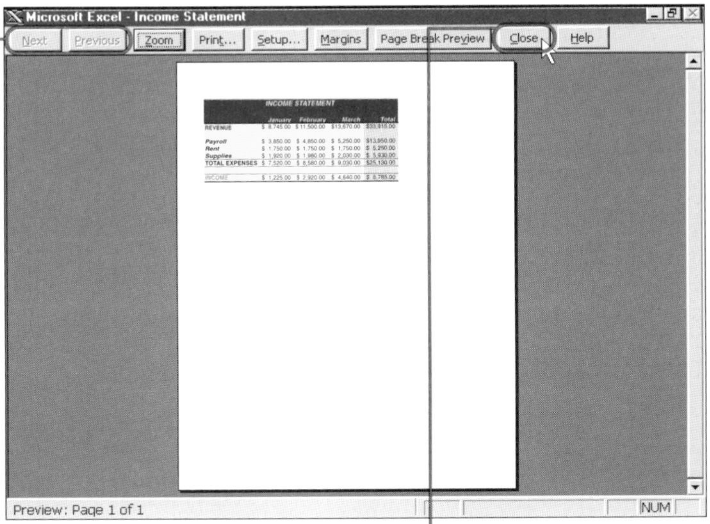

■ A magnified view of the area appears.

3 To display the entire page again, move the mouse anywhere over the page and then press the left mouse button.

■ If the worksheet contains more than one page, move the mouse over one of these options and then press the left mouse button to view the next or previous page.

4 To close the Print Preview window, move the mouse over **Close** and then press the left mouse button.

A margin is the amount of space between data and an edge of your paper. You can easily change the margins.

CHANGE MARGINS

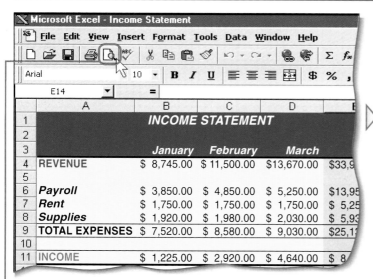

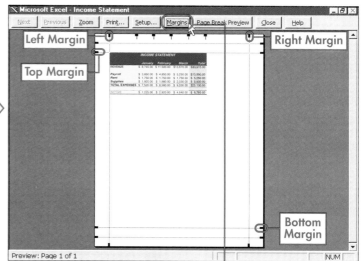

1 To display the worksheet in the Print Preview window, move the mouse ⬉ over 🔍 and then press the left mouse button.

■ The worksheet appears in the Print Preview window. For information on previewing a worksheet, refer to page 182.

2 If the margins are not displayed, move the mouse ⬉ over **Margins** and then press the left mouse button.

Why would I change the margins?

Changing margins lets you accommodate letterhead and other specialty paper.

You can also change the margins to fit more or less information on a page.

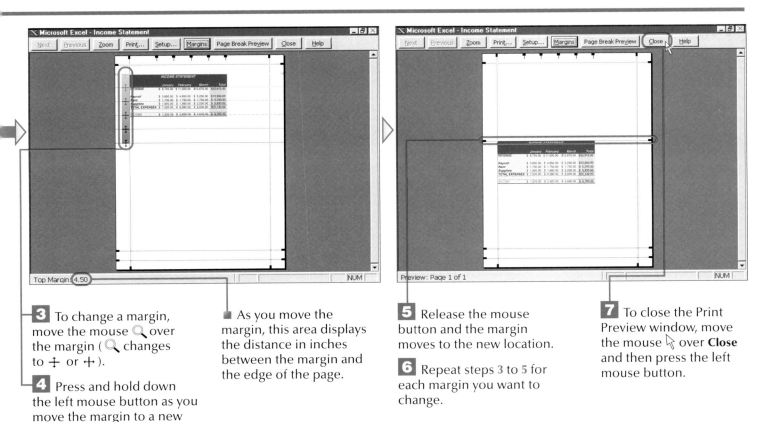

3 To change a margin, move the mouse ⌕ over the margin (⌕ changes to ╪ or ╫).

4 Press and hold down the left mouse button as you move the margin to a new location. A line shows the new location.

■ As you move the margin, this area displays the distance in inches between the margin and the edge of the page.

5 Release the mouse button and the margin moves to the new location.

6 Repeat steps 3 to 5 for each margin you want to change.

7 To close the Print Preview window, move the mouse ⌖ over **Close** and then press the left mouse button.

PRINT A WORKSHEET

You can produce a paper copy of the worksheet displayed on your screen.

PRINT A WORKSHEET

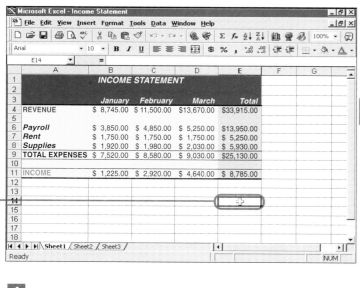

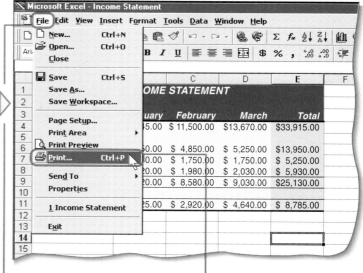

1 To print a worksheet, move the mouse ⊕ over any cell in the worksheet and then press the left mouse button.

■ To print only part of the worksheet, select the cells you want to print. To select cells, refer to page 120.

2 Move the mouse ⊱ over **File** and then press the left mouse button.

3 Move the mouse ⊱ over **Print** and then press the left mouse button.

■ The **Print** dialog box appears.

186

6
EXCEL

PRINT A WORKSHEET

What can I print?

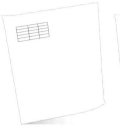

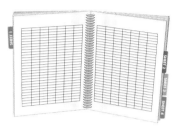

For information
on using multiple
worksheets in a
workbook, refer to
pages 194 to 199.

Selection
Print the cells
you selected.

Active sheet(s)
Print the entire
worksheet.

Entire workbook
Print every worksheet
in the workbook.

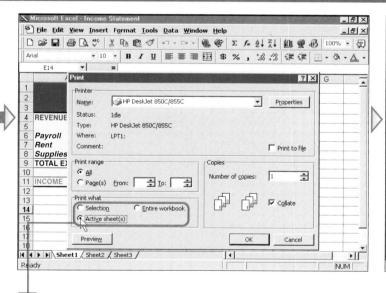

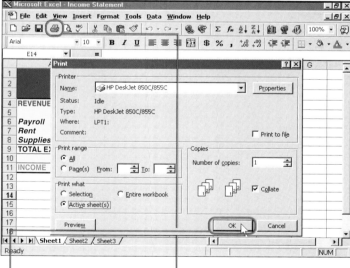

4 Move the mouse ▷
over what you want to
print and then press
the left mouse button
(○ changes to ⊙).

*Note: For information on what
you can print, refer to the top
of this page.*

5 Move the mouse ▷
over **OK** and then press
the left mouse button.

**QUICKLY PRINT ENTIRE
WORKSHEET**

◼ To quickly print the
worksheet displayed on
your screen, move the
mouse ▷ over 🖨 and
then press the left
mouse button.

187

CENTER DATA ON A PAGE

You can center data horizontally and vertically between the margins on a page.

CENTER DATA ON A PAGE

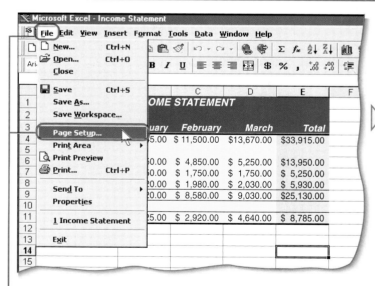

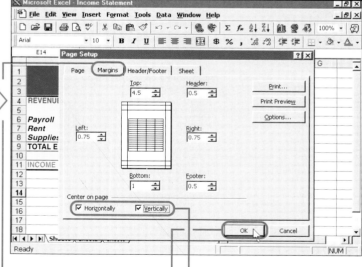

1 Move the mouse ⬚ over **File** and then press the left mouse button.

2 Move the mouse ⬚ over **Page Setup** and then press the left mouse button.

■ The **Page Setup** dialog box appears.

3 Move the mouse ⬚ over the **Margins** tab and then press the left mouse button.

4 Move the mouse ⬚ over the way you want to center the data and then press the left mouse button (☐ changes to ☑). You can select both center options if you wish.

5 Move the mouse ⬚ over **OK** and then press the left mouse button.

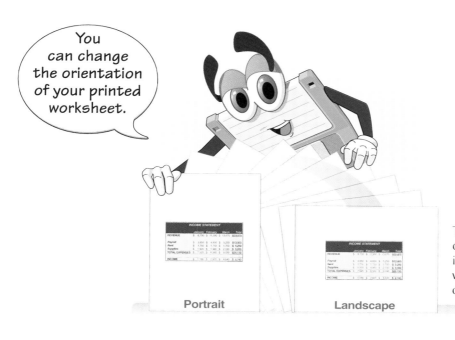

You can change the orientation of your printed worksheet.

Portrait Landscape

The landscape orientation is ideal if you want a wide worksheet to fit on one page.

CHANGE PAGE ORIENTATION

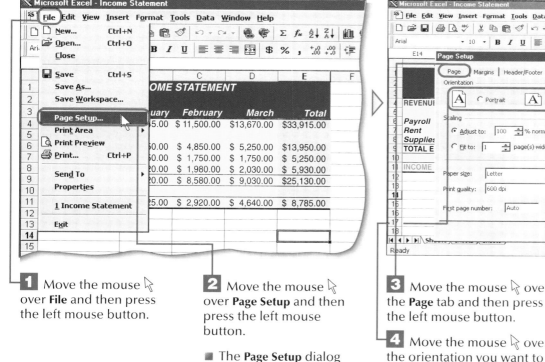

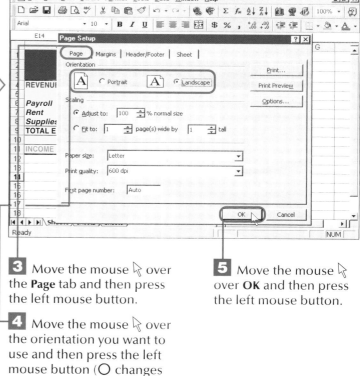

1 Move the mouse ⌖ over **File** and then press the left mouse button.

2 Move the mouse ⌖ over **Page Setup** and then press the left mouse button.

■ The **Page Setup** dialog box appears.

3 Move the mouse ⌖ over the **Page** tab and then press the left mouse button.

4 Move the mouse ⌖ over the orientation you want to use and then press the left mouse button (O changes to ●).

5 Move the mouse ⌖ over **OK** and then press the left mouse button.

CHANGE PRINT OPTIONS

You can change the way your worksheet appears on a printed page.

CHANGE PRINT OPTIONS

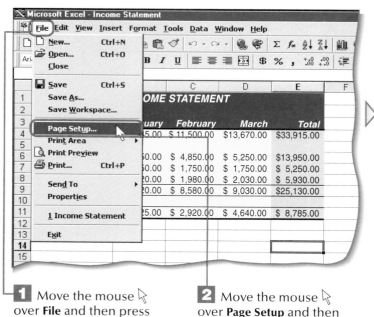

1 Move the mouse ⟨ over **File** and then press the left mouse button.

2 Move the mouse ⟨ over **Page Setup** and then press the left mouse button.

■ The **Page Setup** dialog box appears.

3 Move the mouse ⟨ over the **Sheet** tab and then press the left mouse button.

190

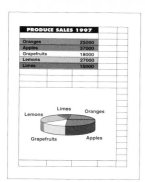

Gridlines

Prints lines around each cell in your worksheet.

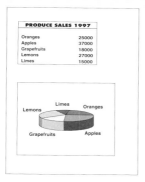

Black and white

Prints the worksheet in black and white. This can make a colored worksheet printed on a black-and-white printer easier to read.

Draft quality

Does not print gridlines or most graphics to reduce printing time.

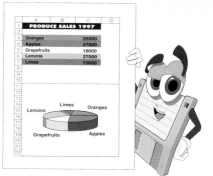

Row and column headings

Prints the row numbers and column letters.

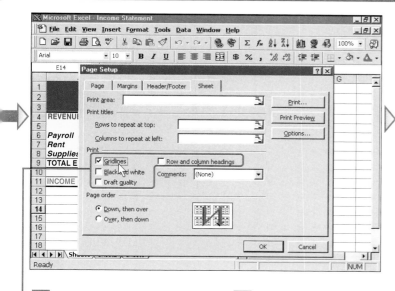

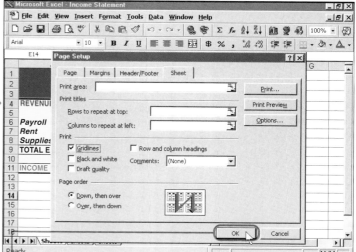

4 Move the mouse ⟍ over the print option you want to select and then press the left mouse button (☐ changes to ✔).

Note: For information on the print options, refer to the top of this page.

5 Repeat step 4 for each print option you want to select.

6 Move the mouse ⟍ over **OK** and then press the left mouse button.

■ The print options you selected only change the way the worksheet appears on a printed page. The print options do not affect the way the worksheet appears on your screen.

INSERT A PAGE BREAK

If you want to start a new page at a specific place in your worksheet, you can add a page break. A page break defines where one page ends and another begins.

When you fill a page with data, Excel automatically starts a new page by inserting a page break for you.

INSERT A PAGE BREAK

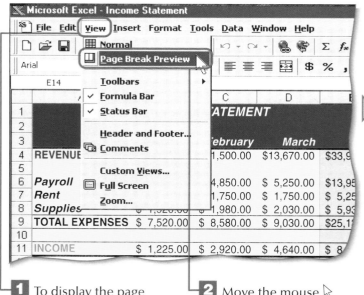

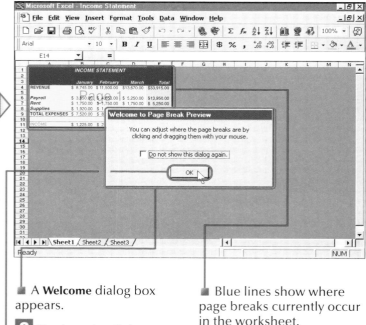

1 To display the page breaks in the worksheet, move the mouse ⌖ over **View** and then press the left mouse button.

2 Move the mouse ⌖ over **Page Break Preview** and then press the left mouse button.

■ A **Welcome** dialog box appears.

3 To close the dialog box, move the mouse ⌖ over **OK** and then press the left mouse button.

■ Blue lines show where page breaks currently occur in the worksheet.

Note: To return to the normal view at any time, repeat steps 1 and 2, selecting Normal in step 2.

How can I move a page break?

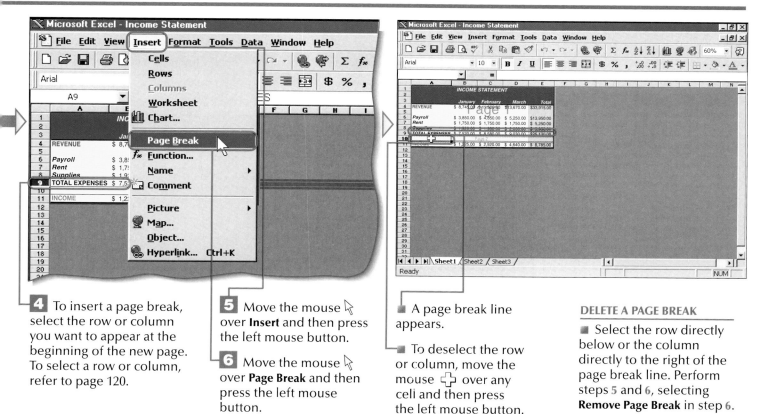

1 To move a page break, move the mouse ⊹ over the page break line (⊹ changes to ↔ or ↕).

2 Press and hold down the left mouse button as you move the page break line to a new location. Then release the mouse button.

4 To insert a page break, select the row or column you want to appear at the beginning of the new page. To select a row or column, refer to page 120.

5 Move the mouse ⌖ over **Insert** and then press the left mouse button.

6 Move the mouse ⌖ over **Page Break** and then press the left mouse button.

■ A page break line appears.

■ To deselect the row or column, move the mouse ⊹ over any cell and then press the left mouse button.

DELETE A PAGE BREAK

■ Select the row directly below or the column directly to the right of the page break line. Perform steps 5 and 6, selecting **Remove Page Break** in step 6.

SWITCH BETWEEN WORKSHEETS

The worksheet displayed on your screen is one of several worksheets in a workbook. You can easily switch between the worksheets.

SWITCH BETWEEN WORKSHEETS

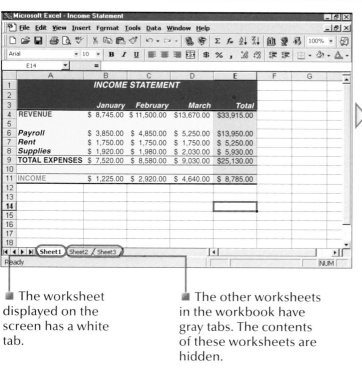

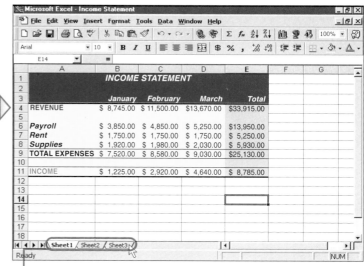

■ The worksheet displayed on the screen has a white tab.

■ The other worksheets in the workbook have gray tabs. The contents of these worksheets are hidden.

1 To display the contents of a worksheet, move the mouse ⌖ over the tab of the worksheet and then press the left mouse button.

Why would I need more than one worksheet?

Worksheets allow you to keep related information in a single file, called a workbook. For example, information for each division of a company can be stored on a separate worksheet in one workbook.

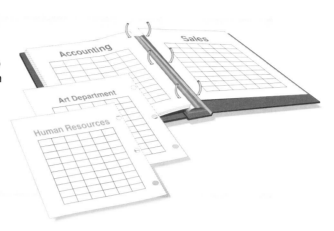

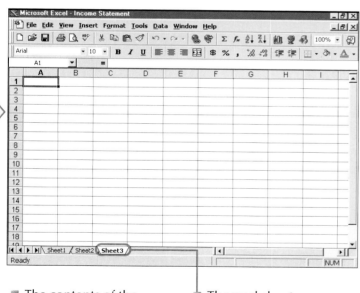

■ The contents of the worksheet appear. The contents of the other worksheets in the workbook are hidden.

■ The worksheet you selected now has a white tab.

BROWSE THROUGH TABS

BROWSE THROUGH TABS

■ If you have many worksheets in your workbook, you may not be able to see all the tabs.

Note: To insert additional worksheets, refer to page 196.

1 To browse through the tabs, move the mouse ⌖ over one of the following options and then press the left mouse button.

|◄| Display first tab

|◄| Display tab to the left

|►| Display tab to the right

|►| Display last tab

INSERT A WORKSHEET

You can easily insert a new worksheet to add related information to a workbook.

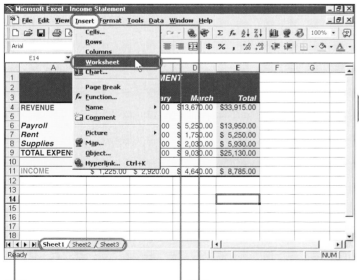

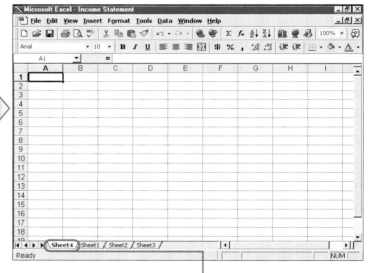

1 Move the mouse over the tab of the worksheet you want to appear after the new worksheet and then press the left mouse button.

2 Move the mouse over **Insert** and then press the left mouse button.

3 Move the mouse over **Worksheet** and then press the left mouse button.

■ The new worksheet appears.

■ This area displays the tab for the new worksheet.

DELETE A WORKSHEET

You can permanently remove a worksheet you no longer need.

DELETE A WORKSHEET

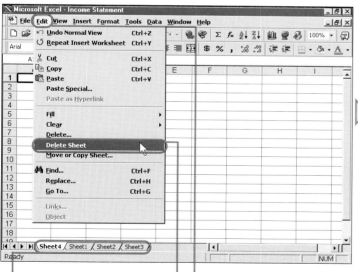

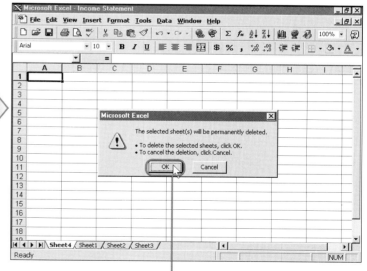

1 Move the mouse ⌖ over the tab of the worksheet you want to delete and then press the left mouse button.

2 Move the mouse ⌖ over **Edit** and then press the left mouse button.

3 Move the mouse ⌖ over **Delete Sheet** and then press the left mouse button.

■ A warning dialog box appears.

4 To permanently delete the worksheet, move the mouse ⌖ over **OK** and then press the left mouse button.

RENAME A WORKSHEET

> You can give each worksheet in a workbook a descriptive name. This helps you remember where you stored your data.

RENAME A WORKSHEET

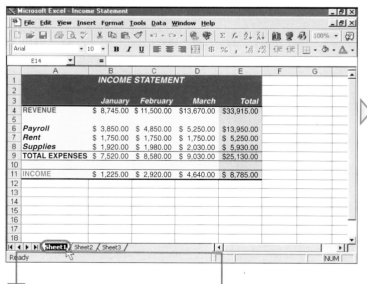

1 Move the mouse ⌖ over the tab of the worksheet you want to rename and then quickly press the left mouse button twice.

■ The current name is highlighted.

2 Type a new name and then press **Enter** on your keyboard. A worksheet name can contain up to 31 characters, including spaces.

MOVE A WORKSHEET

You can reorganize information by moving a worksheet to a new location in a workbook.

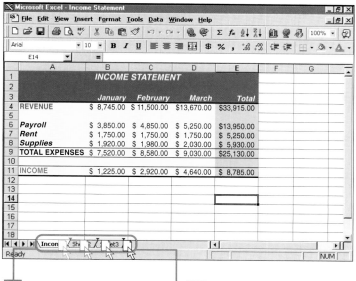

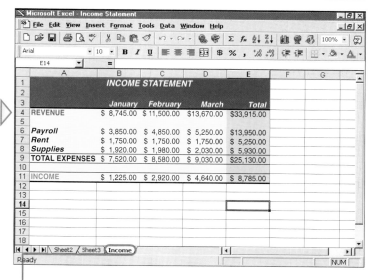

1 Move the mouse ⟍ over the tab of the worksheet you want to move.

2 Press and hold down the left mouse button as you move the worksheet to a new location.

■ An arrow (▾) shows where the worksheet will appear.

3 Release the mouse button and the worksheet appears in the new location.

You can graphically display your worksheet data in a chart.

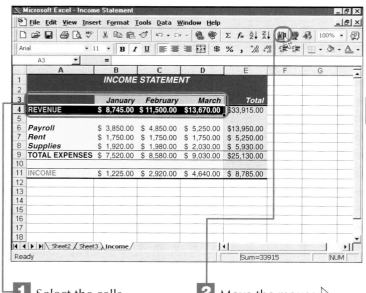

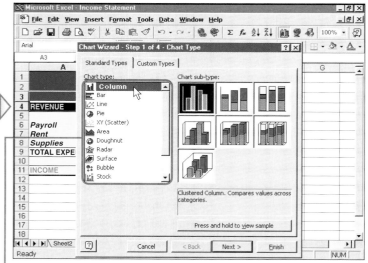

1 Select the cells containing the data you want to display in a chart, including the row and column labels. To select cells, refer to page 120.

2 Move the mouse ⌖ over 🔳 and then press the left mouse button.

■ The **Chart Wizard** dialog box appears.

3 Move the mouse ⌖ over the type of chart you want to create and then press the left mouse button.

Note: You can easily change the type of chart later on. For information, refer to page 204.

Can I change my selections?

While creating a chart, you can return to a previous step at any time to change the choices you made.

■ To do so, move the mouse over **Back** and then press the left mouse button.

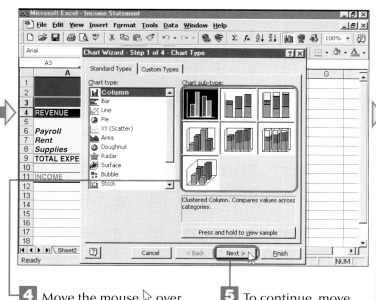

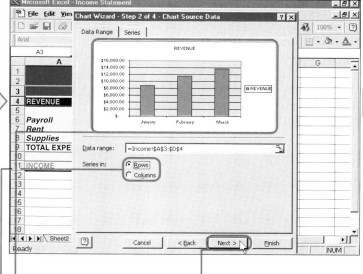

4 Move the mouse over the chart design you want to use and then press the left mouse button.

Note: The available designs depend on the type of chart you selected in step 3.

5 To continue, move the mouse over **Next** and then press the left mouse button.

■ This area displays a sample of the chart.

6 To select the way you want Excel to plot the data from the worksheet, move the mouse over one of these options and then press the left mouse button (○ changes to ◉).

7 To continue, move the mouse over **Next** and then press the left mouse button.

CONT◉NUED➡

CREATE A CHART

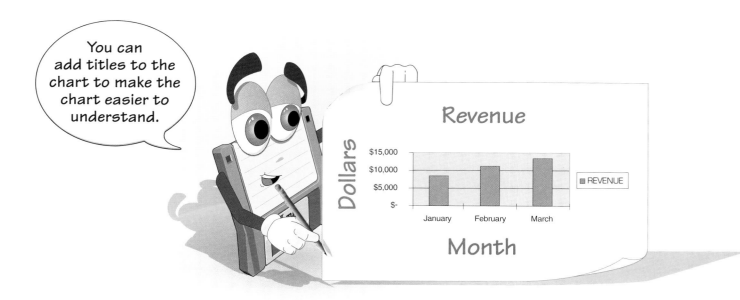

You can add titles to the chart to make the chart easier to understand.

CREATE A CHART (CONTINUED)

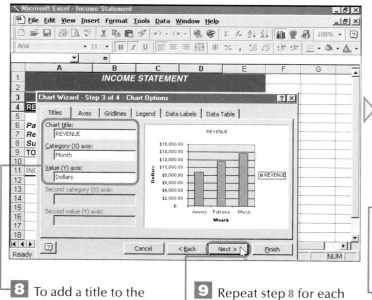

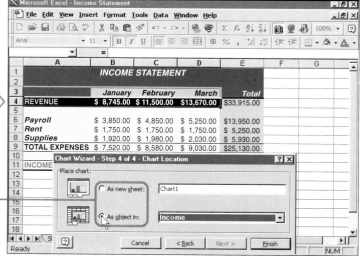

8 To add a title to the chart, move the mouse I over the box for the title you want to add and then press the left mouse button. Then type the title.

9 Repeat step 8 for each title you want to add.

10 To continue, move the mouse ⍈ over **Next** and then press the left mouse button.

11 To choose where you want to display the chart, move the mouse ⍈ over one of these options and then press the left mouse button (O changes to ⦿).

As new sheet

Display chart on its own sheet, called a chart sheet.

As object in

Display chart on the same worksheet as the data.

What happens if I change data used in a chart?

If you change data used in a chart, Excel will automatically update the chart.

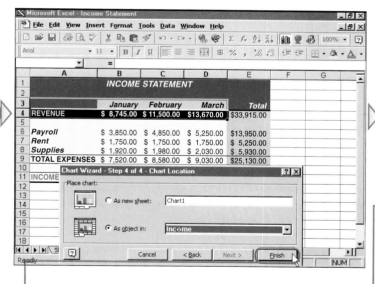

12 To complete the chart, move the mouse ⌖ over **Finish** and then press the left mouse button.

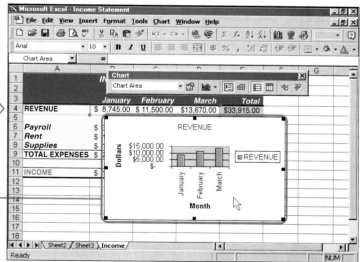

▪ The chart appears.

DELETE A CHART

1 Move the mouse ⌖ over a blank area in the chart and then press the left mouse button. Handles (▪) appear around the chart.

2 Press Delete on your keyboard.

Note: To delete a chart displayed on a chart sheet, follow the steps to delete a worksheet. To delete a worksheet, refer to page 197.

CHANGE CHART TYPE

After you create a chart, you can select a different type of chart that will better suit your data.

CHANGE CHART TYPE

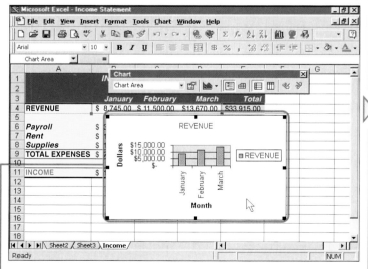

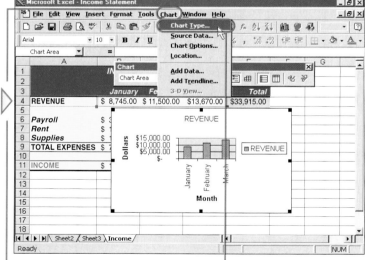

1 To change a chart on a worksheet, move the mouse ⟍ over a blank area in the chart and then press the left mouse button. Handles (■) appear around the chart.

■ To change a chart on a chart sheet, move the mouse ⟍ over the tab for the chart sheet and then press the left mouse button.

2 Move the mouse ⟍ over **Chart** and then press the left mouse button.

3 Move the mouse ⟍ over **Chart Type** and then press the left mouse button.

■ The **Chart Type** dialog box appears.

What type of chart should I choose?

The type of chart you should choose depends on your data. For example, area, column and line charts are ideal for showing changes to values over time, whereas pie charts are ideal for showing percentages.

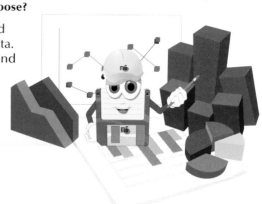

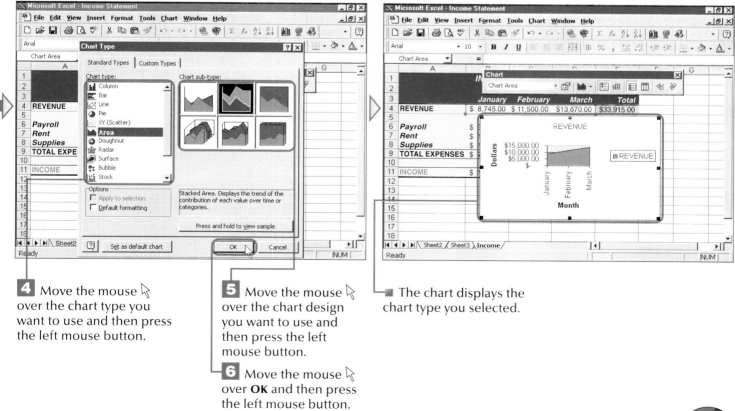

4 Move the mouse ⬚ over the chart type you want to use and then press the left mouse button.

5 Move the mouse ⬚ over the chart design you want to use and then press the left mouse button.

6 Move the mouse ⬚ over **OK** and then press the left mouse button.

■ The chart displays the chart type you selected.

MOVE OR RESIZE A CHART

After you create a chart, you can change the location and size of the chart.

MOVE A CHART

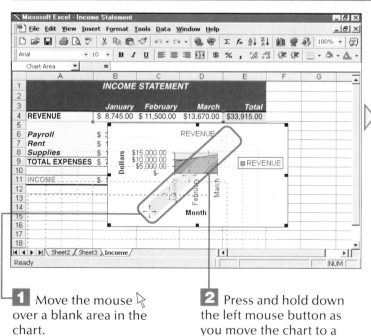

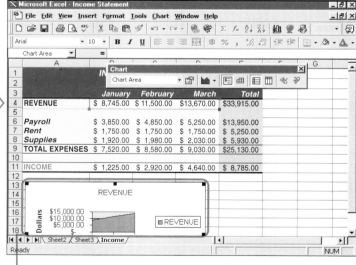

1 Move the mouse ⌖ over a blank area in the chart.

2 Press and hold down the left mouse button as you move the chart to a new location.

■ A dotted line shows the new location.

3 Release the mouse button and the chart appears in the new location.

What are the handles (■) that appear around a chart?

The handles around a chart let you change the size of the chart.

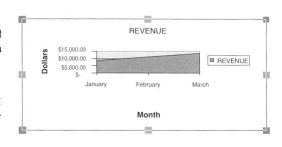

■ Change the height of a chart.

■ Change the width of a chart.

■ Change the height and width of a chart at the same time.

RESIZE A CHART

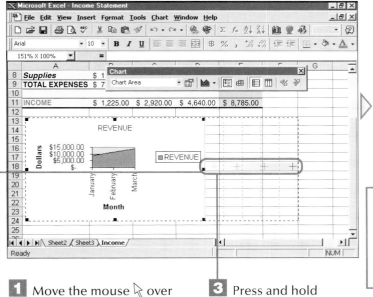

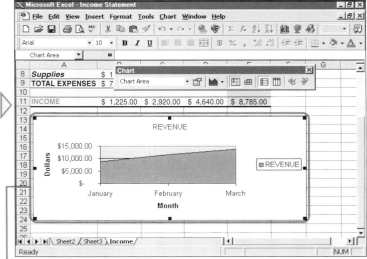

1 Move the mouse ⬚ over a blank area in the chart and then press the left mouse button. Handles (■) appear around the chart.

2 Move the mouse ⬚ over one of the handles (■) (⬚ changes to ↕ or ↔).

3 Press and hold down the left mouse button as you move the edge of the chart until the chart is the size you want.

■ A dotted line shows the new size.

4 Release the mouse button and the chart appears in the new size.

PRINT A CHART

You can print your chart with the worksheet data or on its own page.

PRINT A CHART WITH WORKSHEET DATA

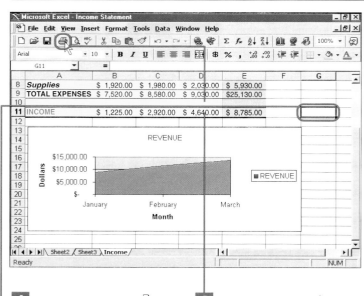

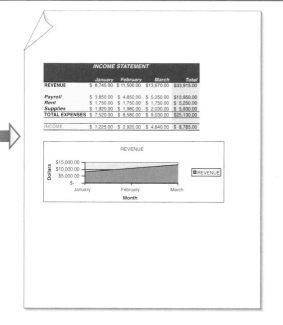

1 Move the mouse ⊹ over any cell outside the chart and then press the left mouse button.

2 Move the mouse ⌖ over 🖨 and then press the left mouse button.

Note: For more information on printing, refer to pages 182 to 193.

Can I see what my chart will look like when printed?

You can preview your chart to see what the chart will look like when printed. To preview a chart, refer to page 182.

PRINT A CHART ON ITS OWN PAGE

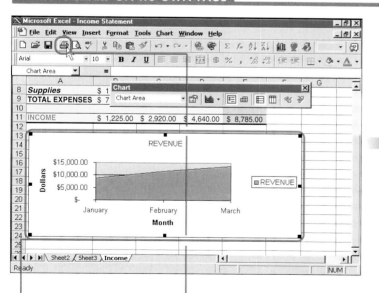

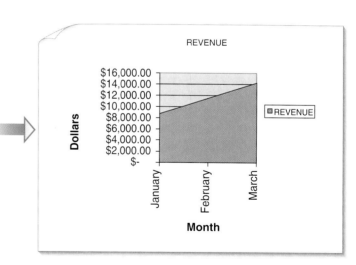

1 To print a chart displayed on a worksheet, move the mouse ⤢ over a blank area in the chart and then press the left mouse button.

◼ To print a chart displayed on a chart sheet, move the mouse ⤢ over the tab for the chart sheet and then press the left mouse button.

2 Move the mouse ⤢ over 🖨 and then press the left mouse button.

Note: When you print a chart on its own page, the chart will expand to fill the page. The printed chart may look different from the chart on the worksheet.

Create a Presentation
Page 218

Add a Chart
Page 246

Microsoft PowerPoint helps you plan, organize and design professional presentations.

Delete Text
Page 234

Change Text Color
Page 262

Save a Presentation
Page 224

POWERPOINT

*Change the Slide Layout
Page 240*

*Change Slide Design
Page 254*

1 Getting Started
Pages 212-227

2 Edit Slides
Pages 228-239

3 Add Objects to Slides
Pages 240-253

4 Enhance a Presentation
Pages 254-267

5 Fine-Tune a Presentation
Pages 268-277

WAYS TO USE POWERPOINT

On-Screen Presentations

You can deliver a colorful, professional presentation on your computer screen.

Handouts

You can print handouts to help the audience follow your presentation. Handouts contain copies of your slides.

35mm Slides or Overheads

You can create 35mm slides or overhead transparencies for presenting your ideas to a large audience.

Speaker Notes

You can create speaker notes to help you deliver your presentation. Speaker notes contain copies of your slides along with all the ideas you want to discuss.

START POWERPOINT

You can start PowerPoint to create a professional presentation.

START POWERPOINT

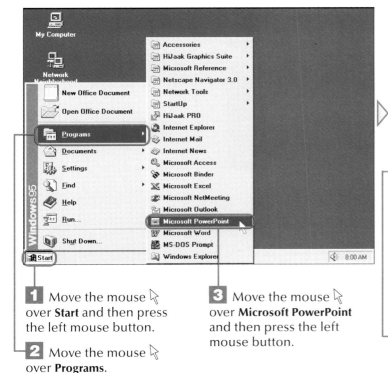

1 Move the mouse ▷ over **Start** and then press the left mouse button.

2 Move the mouse ▷ over **Programs**.

3 Move the mouse ▷ over **Microsoft PowerPoint** and then press the left mouse button.

■ The PowerPoint program opens.

4 To start using PowerPoint, move the mouse ▷ over this option and then press the left mouse button.

■ To hide the Office Assistant, move the mouse ▷ over ⊠ and then press the left mouse button.

You can use the AutoContent wizard to quickly create a presentation.

The wizard will ask you a series of questions and then set up a presentation based on your answers.

■ The **PowerPoint** dialog box appears each time you start PowerPoint.

1 To create a new presentation, move the mouse ⌖ over **AutoContent wizard** and then press the left mouse button (○ changes to ◉).

2 Move the mouse ⌖ over **OK** and then press the left mouse button.

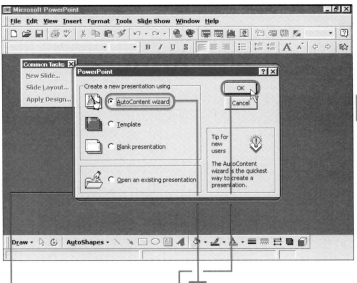

■ The **AutoContent Wizard** dialog box appears.

3 To start creating the presentation, move the mouse ⌖ over **Next** and then press the left mouse button.

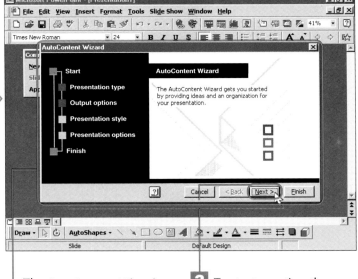

What types of presentations can I create?

The AutoContent wizard provides ideas and an organization for many types of presentations. You can select the type of presentation that best suits your needs.

1) Company Meeting
2) Marketing Plan
3) Motivating A Team
4) Selling Your Ideas
5) Product/Services Overview
6) Introducing A Speaker

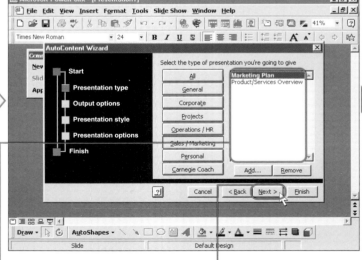

4 Move the mouse over the category that best describes the type of presentation you want to create and then press the left mouse button.

■ If you are not sure which category best describes the presentation, select **All**.

■ This area displays the types of presentations within the category you selected.

5 Move the mouse over the type of presentation that best suits your needs and then press the left mouse button.

6 To continue, move the mouse over **Next** and then press the left mouse button.

CONT🐭NUED➡

You can choose to deliver a presentation to an audience or have people view the presentation on their own.

CREATE A PRESENTATION (CONTINUED)

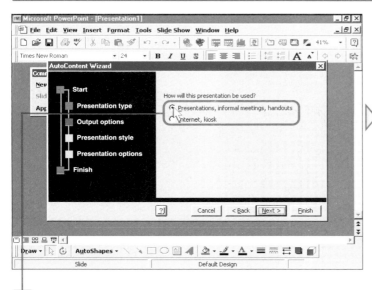

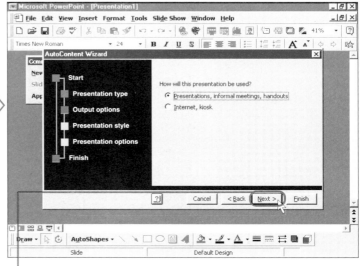

7 Move the mouse over the way you plan to use the presentation and then press the left mouse button (O changes to ⦿).

Presentations
You will deliver the presentation to an audience.

Internet
People will view the presentation on their own.

8 To continue, move the mouse over **Next** and then press the left mouse button.

How can I output my presentation?

There are four ways you can output your presentation.

On-screen presentation

Black and white overheads

Color overheads

35mm slides

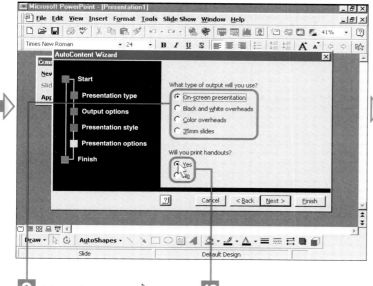
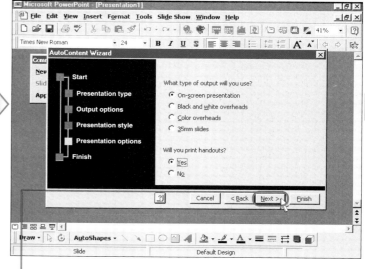

9 Move the mouse ⌖ over the type of output you want to use for the presentation and then press the left mouse button (○ changes to ◉).

10 To choose whether or not you want to print handouts for the audience, move the mouse ⌖ over **Yes** or **No** and then press the left mouse button (○ changes to ◉).

11 To continue, move the mouse ⌖ over **Next** and then press the left mouse button.

CONTINUED➡

The
AutoContent
wizard asks you what
information you want
to appear on your
first slide.

CREATE A PRESENTATION (CONTINUED)

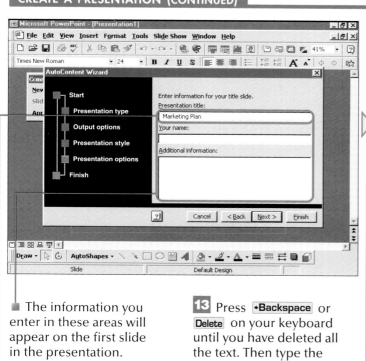

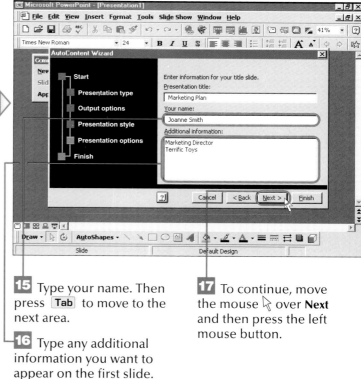

■ The information you enter in these areas will appear on the first slide in the presentation.

12 Move the mouse ⬐ over this area and then press the left mouse button.

13 Press ←Backspace or Delete on your keyboard until you have deleted all the text. Then type the title of the presentation.

14 Press Tab on your keyboard to move to the next area.

15 Type your name. Then press Tab to move to the next area.

16 Type any additional information you want to appear on the first slide.

17 To continue, move the mouse ⬐ over **Next** and then press the left mouse button.

Can I change my answers?

While using the AutoContent
wizard to create a presentation,
you can return at any time to
a previous step to change
your answers.

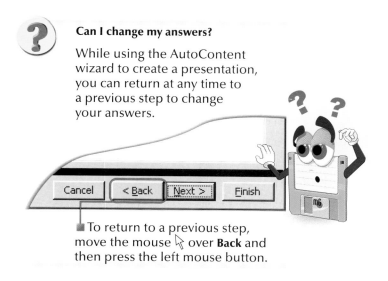

■ To return to a previous step,
move the mouse ↳ over **Back** and
then press the left mouse button.

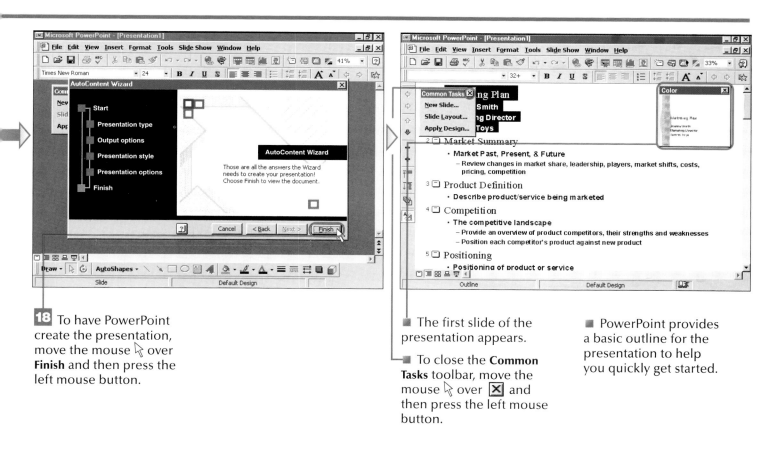

18 To have PowerPoint
create the presentation,
move the mouse ↳ over
Finish and then press the
left mouse button.

■ The first slide of the
presentation appears.

■ To close the **Common
Tasks** toolbar, move the
mouse ↳ over ✕ and
then press the left mouse
button.

■ PowerPoint provides
a basic outline for the
presentation to help
you quickly get started.

PowerPoint offers four different ways that you can view a presentation on your screen.

CHANGE THE VIEW

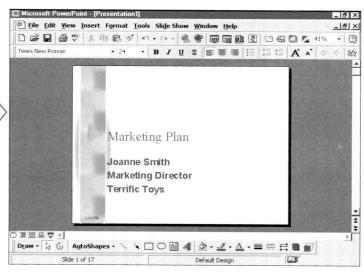

■ When you first create a presentation, PowerPoint displays the presentation in the Outline view.

1 To display the presentation in a different view, move the mouse ⟋ over one of the following options and then press the left mouse button.

▯ Slide
▤ Outline
▦ Slide Sorter
▣ Notes Page

■ PowerPoint displays the presentation in the new view.

■ All views display the same presentation. If you make changes to a slide in one view, the other views will also change.

THE FOUR VIEWS

Slide

The Slide view displays one slide at a time. This view is useful for changing the layout or design of your slides.

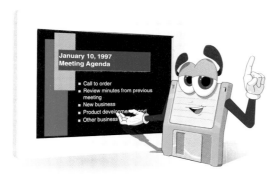

Slide Sorter

The Slide Sorter view displays a miniature version of each slide. This view lets you see a general overview of your presentation.

Outline

The Outline view displays the text on all the slides. This view lets you develop the content and organization of your presentation.

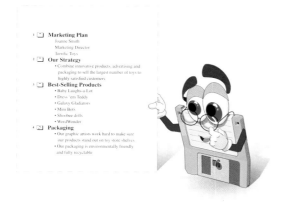

Notes Page

The Notes Page view displays one slide at a time, with space to type comments. You can use these comments as a guide when delivering your presentation.

Your computer screen cannot display your entire presentation at once. You must browse through the presentation to view slides or text not displayed on your screen.

SLIDE OR NOTES PAGE VIEW

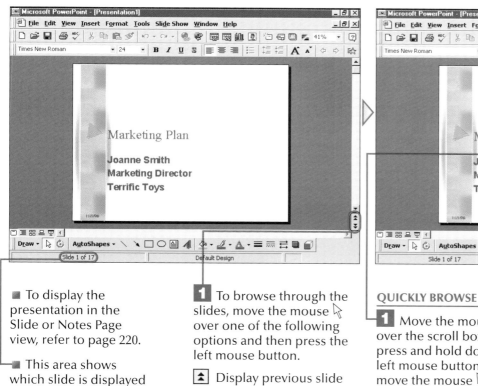

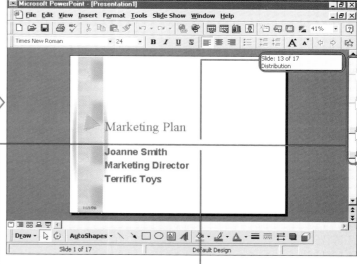

■ To display the presentation in the Slide or Notes Page view, refer to page 220.

■ This area shows which slide is displayed on the screen.

1 To browse through the slides, move the mouse over one of the following options and then press the left mouse button.

⬆ Display previous slide

⬇ Display next slide

QUICKLY BROWSE

1 Move the mouse over the scroll box. Then press and hold down the left mouse button as you move the mouse up or down the scroll bar.

2 When this box displays the number of the slide you want to view, release the mouse button.

Which views let me see more than one slide at a time?

These views display one slide at a time.

Slide   **Notes Page**

These views display more than one slide at a time.

Outline   **Slide Sorter**

OUTLINE OR SLIDE SORTER VIEW

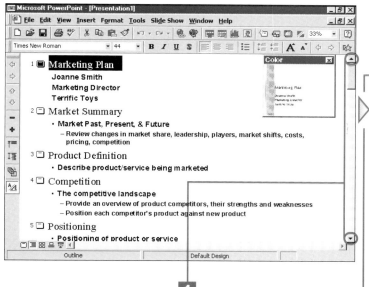

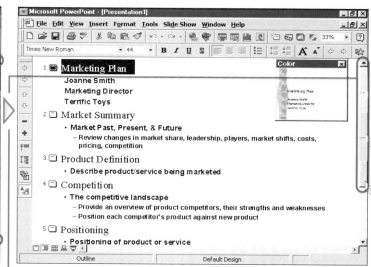

■ To display the presentation in the Outline or Slide Sorter view, refer to page 220.

1 To browse through the slides, move the mouse over one of the following options and then press the left mouse button.

▲ Scroll up

▼ Scroll down

QUICKLY BROWSE

1 Move the mouse over the scroll box. Then press and hold down the left mouse button as you move the mouse up or down the scroll bar.

2 Release the mouse button.

You should save your presentation to store it for future use. This lets you later review and make changes to the presentation.

SAVE A PRESENTATION

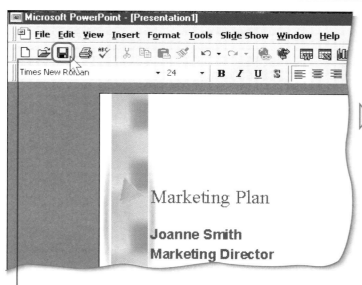

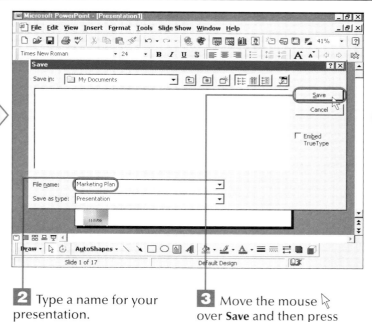

1 Move the mouse ⬡ over 🔲 and then press the left mouse button.

■ The **Save** dialog box appears.

*Note: If you previously saved the presentation, the **Save** dialog box will not appear since you have already named the presentation.*

2 Type a name for your presentation.

Note: You can use up to 255 characters to name a presentation.

3 Move the mouse ⬡ over **Save** and then press the left mouse button.

When you finish using PowerPoint, you can exit the program.

EXIT POWERPOINT

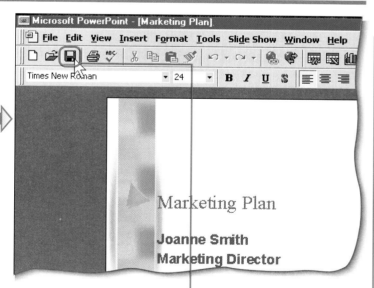

■ PowerPoint saves the presentation and displays the name at the top of the screen.

SAVE CHANGES

To avoid losing your work, you should regularly save changes to the presentation.

1 Move the mouse � over 🖫 and then press the left mouse button.

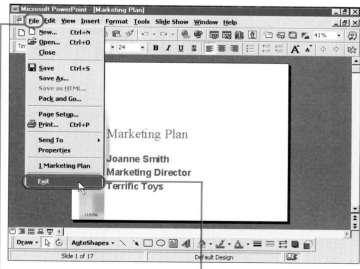

■ Make sure you save the presentation before exiting PowerPoint.

1 Move the mouse � over **File** and then press the left mouse button.

2 Move the mouse � over **Exit** and then press the left mouse button.

Note: To restart PowerPoint, refer to page 213.

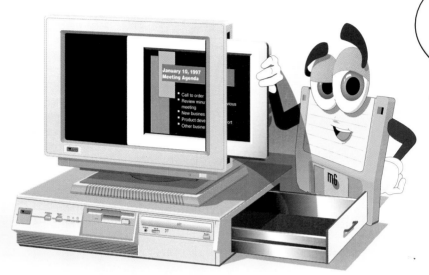

You can open a saved presentation and display it on your screen. This lets you review and make changes to the presentation.

OPEN A PRESENTATION

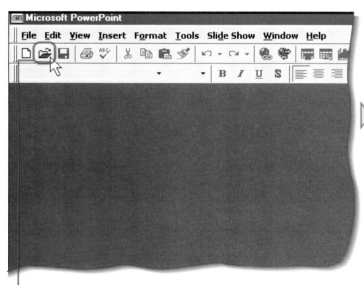

1 Move the mouse ▷ over 🖆 and then press the left mouse button.

■ The **Open** dialog box appears.

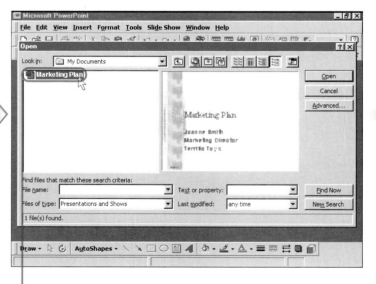

2 Move the mouse ▷ over the name of the presentation you want to open and then press the left mouse button.

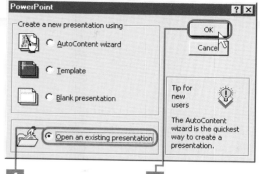

How can I quickly open a presentation when I first start PowerPoint?

The **PowerPoint** dialog box appears when you start PowerPoint.

1 To quickly open a presentation, move the mouse over this option and then press the left mouse button.

2 Move the mouse over **OK** and then press the left mouse button. Then perform steps **2** and **3** starting on page 226.

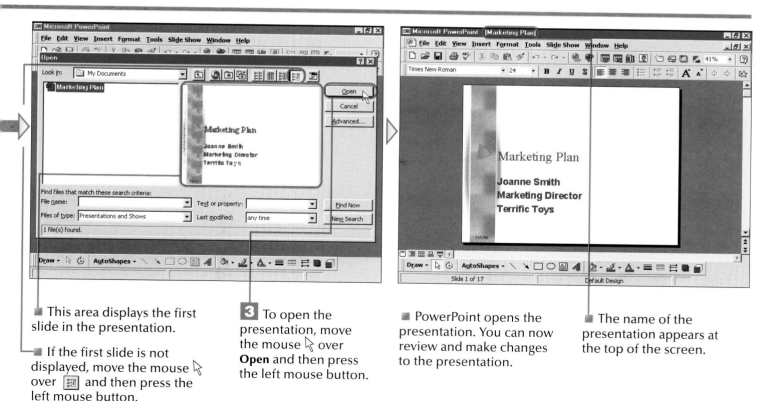

■ This area displays the first slide in the presentation.

■ If the first slide is not displayed, move the mouse over 📇 and then press the left mouse button.

3 To open the presentation, move the mouse over **Open** and then press the left mouse button.

■ PowerPoint opens the presentation. You can now review and make changes to the presentation.

■ The name of the presentation appears at the top of the screen.

Before changing text in a presentation, you must select the text you want to work with. Selected text appears highlighted on your screen.

SELECT TEXT

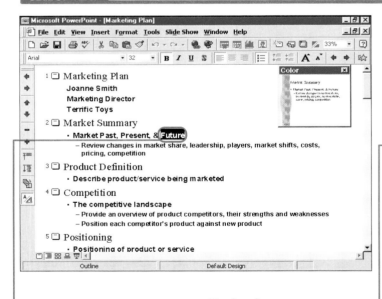

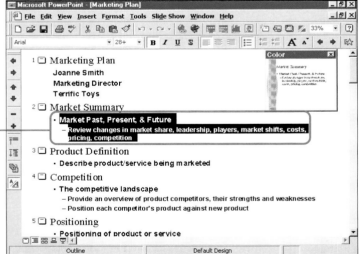

SELECT A WORD

1 Move the mouse I over the word you want to select and then quickly press the left mouse button twice.

■ To deselect text, move the mouse I outside the selected area and then press the left mouse button.

SELECT A POINT

1 Move the mouse I over the bullet (■) beside the point you want to select (I changes to ✛) and then press the left mouse button.

How do I select all the text in my presentation?

To quickly select all the text in your presentation, press and hold down **Ctrl** and then press **A** on your keyboard. Then release both keys.

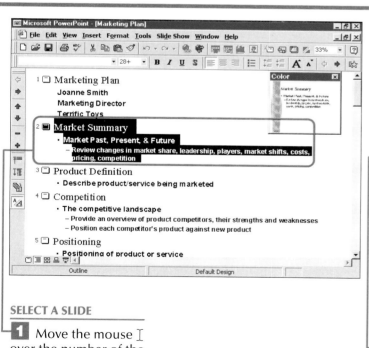

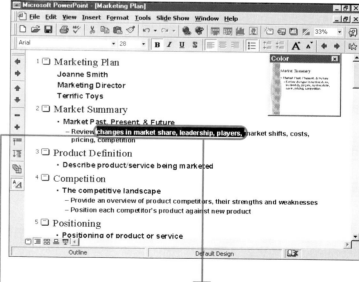

SELECT A SLIDE

1 Move the mouse I over the number of the slide you want to select (I changes to) and then press the left mouse button.

SELECT ANY AMOUNT OF TEXT

1 Move the mouse I over the first word you want to select.

2 Press and hold down the left mouse button as you move the mouse I over the text you want to select. Then release the mouse button.

REPLACE TEXT

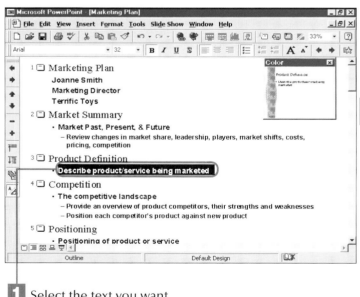

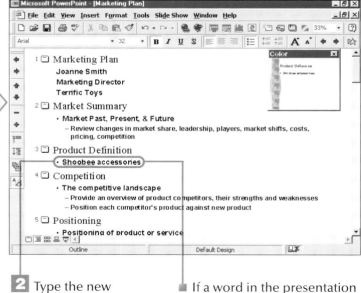

1 Select the text you want to replace with new text. To select text, refer to page 228.

2 Type the new text. The text you type will replace the selected text.

If a word in the presentation appears with a red underline, PowerPoint does not recognize the word and considers it misspelled. To spell check the presentation, refer to page 238.

UNDO LAST CHANGE

PowerPoint remembers the last changes you made to your presentation. If you regret these changes, you can cancel them by using the Undo feature.

UNDO LAST CHANGE

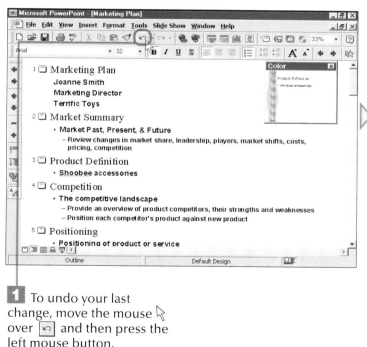

1 To undo your last change, move the mouse over ⬤ and then press the left mouse button.

■ PowerPoint cancels the last change you made to the presentation.

■ You can repeat step **1** to cancel previous changes you made.

■ To reverse the results of using the Undo feature, move the mouse over ⬤ and then press the left mouse button.

You can easily add new text to your presentation.

INSERT CHARACTERS

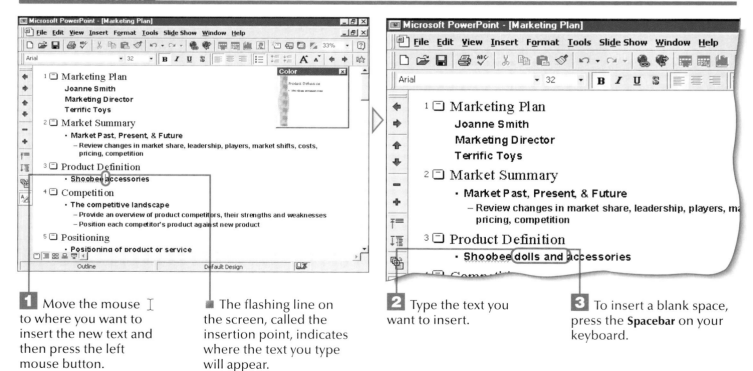

1 Move the mouse I to where you want to insert the new text and then press the left mouse button.

■ The flashing line on the screen, called the insertion point, indicates where the text you type will appear.

Note: You can also use the →, ←, ↑ and ↓ keys on your keyboard to move the insertion point on the screen.

2 Type the text you want to insert.

3 To insert a blank space, press the **Spacebar** on your keyboard.

Why are some words in my presentation underlined with a wavy, red line?

If PowerPoint does not recognize a word in your presentation and considers it misspelled, the word will display a wavy, red underline. To spell check your presentation, refer to page 238.

INSERT A NEW POINT

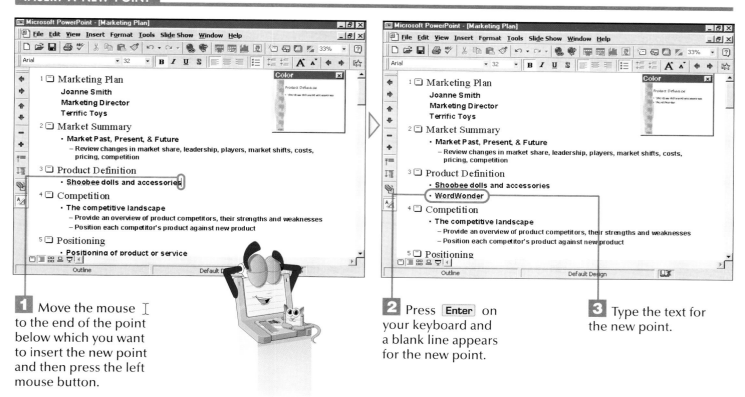

1 Move the mouse I to the end of the point below which you want to insert the new point and then press the left mouse button.

2 Press **Enter** on your keyboard and a blank line appears for the new point.

3 Type the text for the new point.

You can easily remove text you no longer need from your presentation.

DELETE CHARACTERS

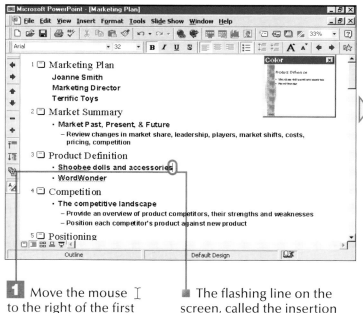

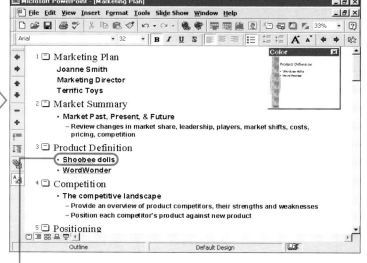

1 Move the mouse I to the right of the first character you want to delete and then press the left mouse button.

■ The flashing line on the screen, called the insertion point, moves to the location you selected.

Note: You can also use the → , ← , ↑ and ↓ keys on your keyboard to move the insertion point on the screen.

2 Press ◆**Backspace** on your keyboard once for each character or space you want to delete.

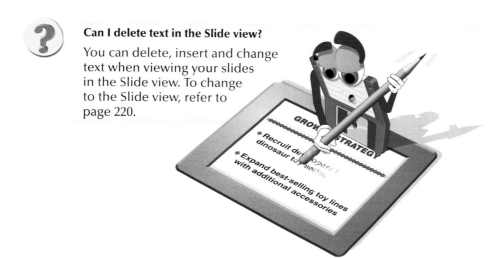

Can I delete text in the Slide view?

You can delete, insert and change text when viewing your slides in the Slide view. To change to the Slide view, refer to page 220.

DELETE SELECTED TEXT

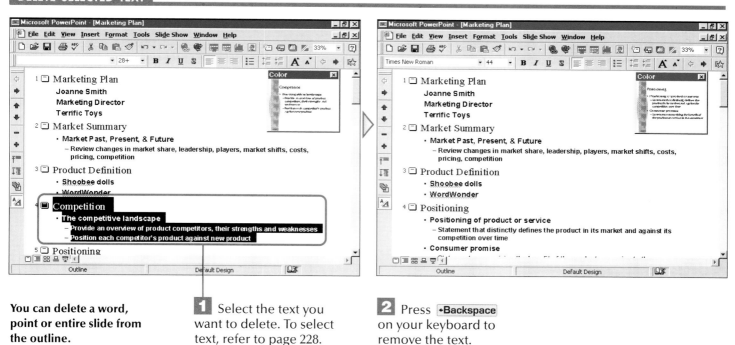

You can delete a word, point or entire slide from the outline.

1 Select the text you want to delete. To select text, refer to page 228.

2 Press **→Backspace** on your keyboard to remove the text.

You can move text in your presentation to reorganize your ideas.

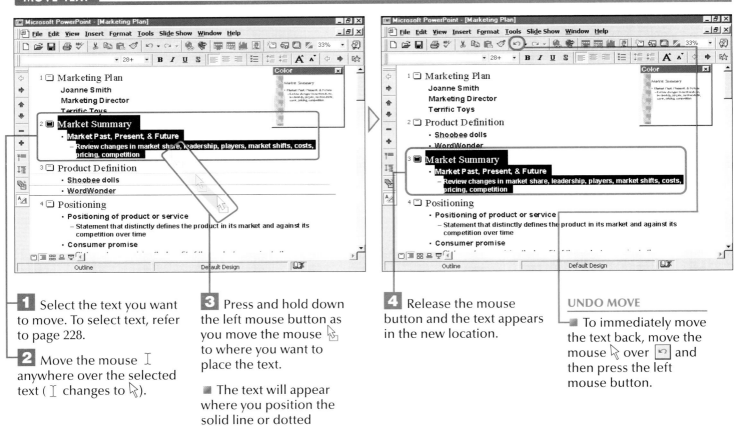

1 Select the text you want to move. To select text, refer to page 228.

2 Move the mouse I anywhere over the selected text (I changes to ⬚).

3 Press and hold down the left mouse button as you move the mouse ⬚ to where you want to place the text.

■ The text will appear where you position the solid line or dotted insertion point on the screen.

4 Release the mouse button and the text appears in the new location.

UNDO MOVE

■ To immediately move the text back, move the mouse ⬚ over ↺ and then press the left mouse button.

You can increase or decrease the importance of text in your presentation.

Marketing Plan ← Most important
- Advertising
  - television ← Least important
  - Internet
- In-store Displays

CHANGE IMPORTANCE OF TEXT

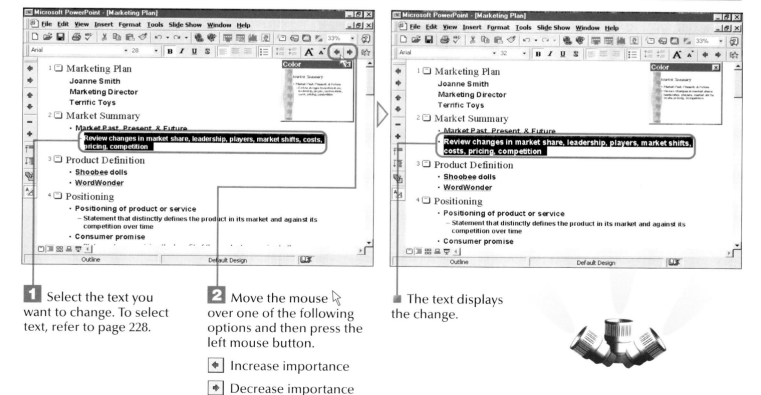

1 Select the text you want to change. To select text, refer to page 228.

2 Move the mouse ⬚ over one of the following options and then press the left mouse button.

◄ Increase importance

► Decrease importance

■ The text displays the change.

237

You can quickly find and correct spelling errors in your presentation.

PowerPoint compares every word in your presentation to words in its dictionary. If a word does not exist in the dictionary, PowerPoint considers it misspelled.

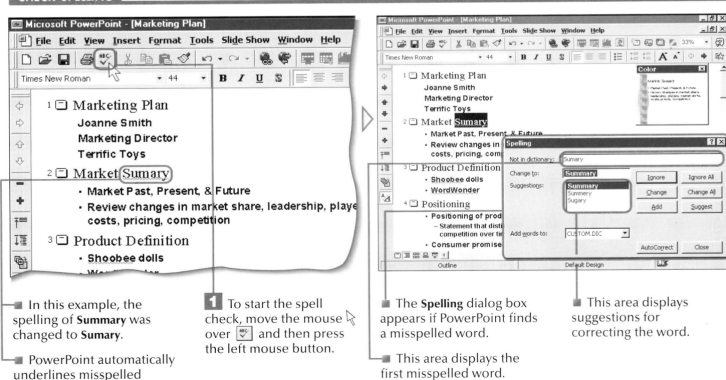

■ In this example, the spelling of **Summary** was changed to **Sumary**.

■ PowerPoint automatically underlines misspelled words in red.

1 To start the spell check, move the mouse over 🔤 and then press the left mouse button.

■ The **Spelling** dialog box appears if PowerPoint finds a misspelled word.

■ This area displays the first misspelled word.

■ This area displays suggestions for correcting the word.

Can PowerPoint automatically correct my typing mistakes?

PowerPoint automatically corrects common spelling errors as you type.

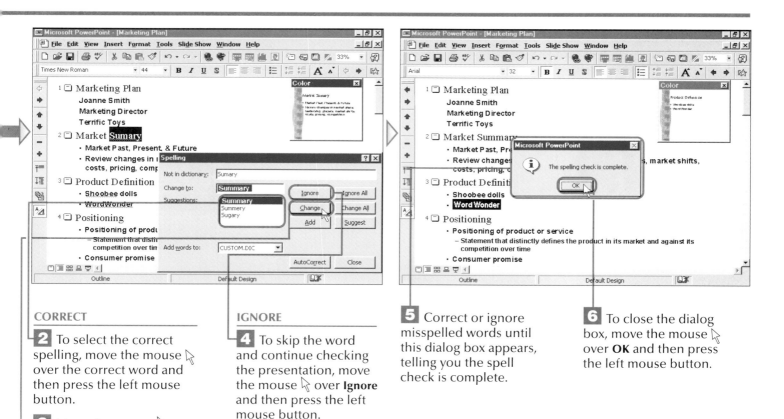

CORRECT

■2 To select the correct spelling, move the mouse ⇗ over the correct word and then press the left mouse button.

■3 Move the mouse ⇗ over **Change** and then press the left mouse button.

IGNORE

■4 To skip the word and continue checking the presentation, move the mouse ⇗ over **Ignore** and then press the left mouse button.

■5 Correct or ignore misspelled words until this dialog box appears, telling you the spell check is complete.

■6 To close the dialog box, move the mouse ⇗ over **OK** and then press the left mouse button.

You can have PowerPoint arrange text and objects on a slide for you.

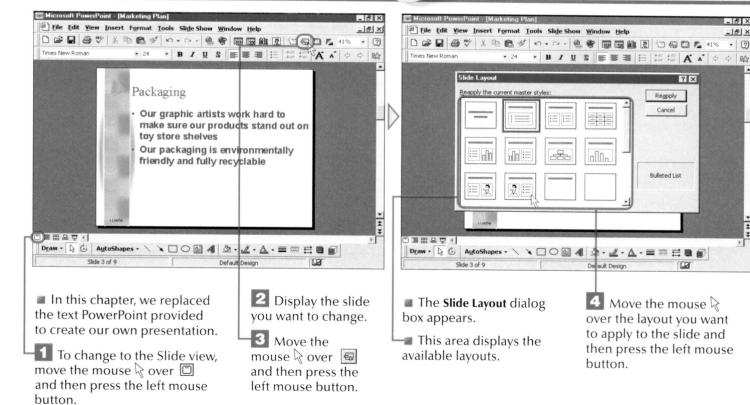

■ In this chapter, we replaced the text PowerPoint provided to create our own presentation.

1 To change to the Slide view, move the mouse ⊾ over 🔲 and then press the left mouse button.

2 Display the slide you want to change.

3 Move the mouse ⊾ over 🗐 and then press the left mouse button.

■ The **Slide Layout** dialog box appears.

■ This area displays the available layouts.

4 Move the mouse ⊾ over the layout you want to apply to the slide and then press the left mouse button.

How can changing the slide layout help me add objects to my slides?

PowerPoint offers slide layouts that allow you to easily add objects such as a bulleted list, a chart or clip art to your slides.

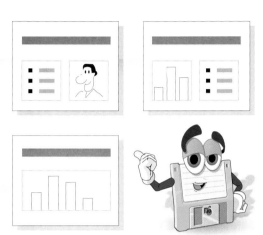

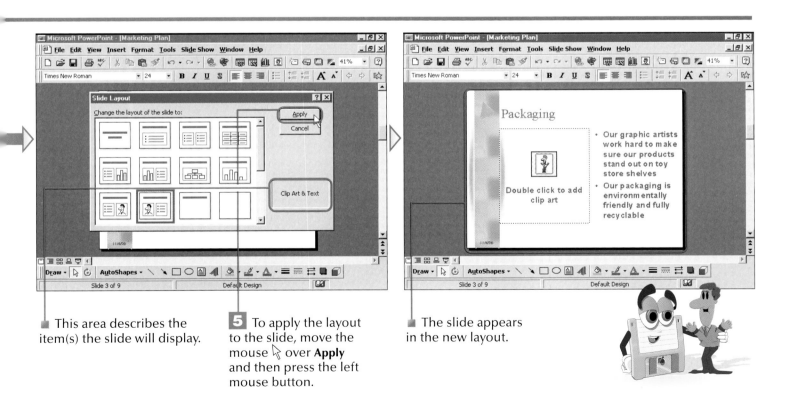

■ This area describes the item(s) the slide will display.

5 To apply the layout to the slide, move the mouse ⌖ over **Apply** and then press the left mouse button.

■ The slide appears in the new layout.

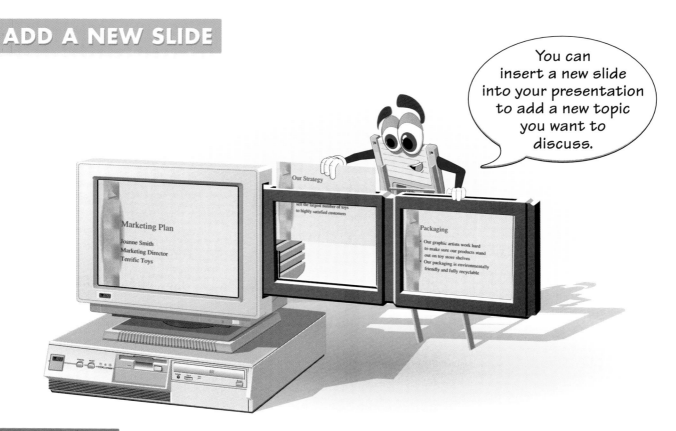

You can insert a new slide into your presentation to add a new topic you want to discuss.

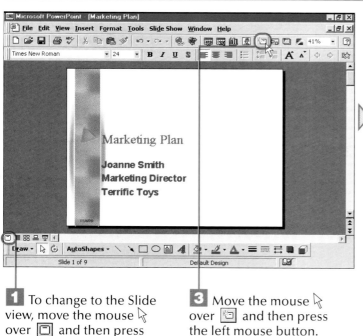

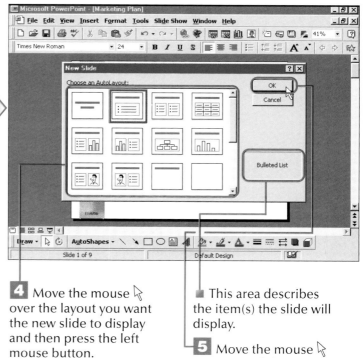

1 To change to the Slide view, move the mouse ⍭ over ▣ and then press the left mouse button.

2 Display the slide you want to appear before the new slide.

3 Move the mouse ⍭ over 🔲 and then press the left mouse button.

■ The **New Slide** dialog box appears.

4 Move the mouse ⍭ over the layout you want the new slide to display and then press the left mouse button.

■ This area describes the item(s) the slide will display.

5 Move the mouse ⍭ over **OK** and then press the left mouse button.

How much text should I display on one slide?

Too many words on a slide can minimize the impact of important ideas. If a slide contains too much text, place the text on two or three slides.

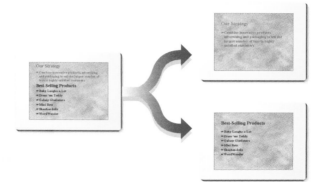

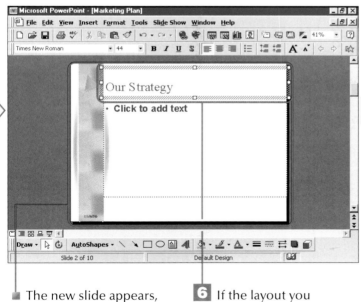

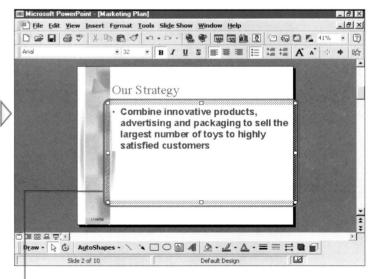

■ The new slide appears, displaying the layout you selected.

Note: You can change the layout at any time. To change the slide layout, refer to page 240.

6 If the layout you selected displays an area for a title, move the mouse I over the title area and then press the left mouse button. Then type the title.

7 If the layout you selected displays an area for text, move the mouse I over the text area and then press the left mouse button. Then type the text.

■ Press **Enter** on your keyboard each time you want to start a new point.

ADD CLIP ART OR PICTURES

You can add images to slides to make your presentation more interesting and entertaining.

ADD CLIP ART OR PICTURES

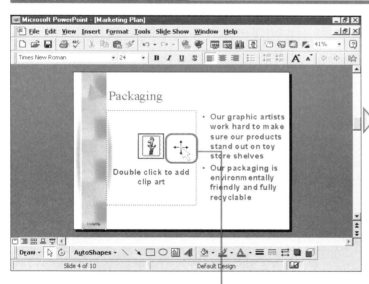

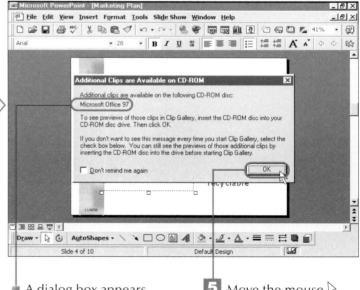

1 Display the slide you want to add an image to.

2 Change the layout of the slide to one that includes space for a clip art image. To change the slide layout, refer to page 240.

3 To add an image, move the mouse ⊹ over the clip art area and then quickly press the left mouse button twice.

■ A dialog box appears if additional images are available on the CD-ROM disc identified in this area.

4 To view the additional images, insert the CD-ROM disc into your CD-ROM drive.

5 Move the mouse ⟍ over **OK** and then press the left mouse button.

■ The **Microsoft Clip Gallery** dialog box appears.

How do I delete an image from a slide?

To delete an image from a slide in your presentation, move the mouse ⊹ over the image and then press the left mouse button. Then press **Delete** on your keyboard.

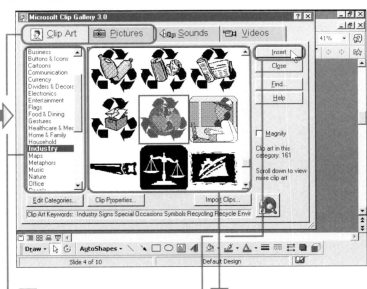

6 Move the mouse ⊳ over the **Clip Art** or **Pictures** tab and then press the left mouse button.

7 Move the mouse ⊳ over the category of images you want to display and then press the left mouse button.

8 Move the mouse ⊳ over the image you want to add to the slide and then press the left mouse button.

9 To add the image to the slide, move the mouse ⊳ over **Insert** and then press the left mouse button.

■ The image appears on the slide. The handles (□) around the image let you change the size of the image. To resize the image, refer to page 253.

■ To close the **Picture** toolbar, move the mouse ⊳ over **X** and then press the left mouse button.

ADD A CHART

You can add a chart to a slide to show trends and compare data.

ADD A CHART

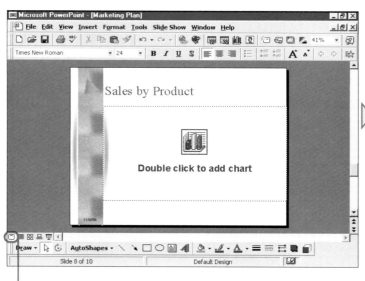

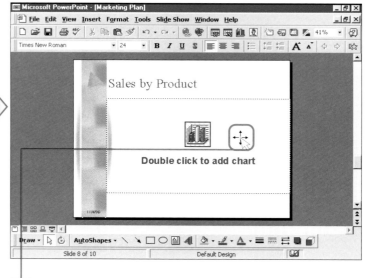

1 To change to the Slide view, move the mouse ⊳ over □ and then press the left mouse button.

2 Display the slide you want to add a chart to.

3 Change the layout of the slide to one that includes space for a chart. To change the slide layout, refer to page 240.

4 To add a chart, move the mouse ⊹ over the chart area and then quickly press the left mouse button twice.

When should I use a chart in my presentation?

A chart is more appealing and often easier to understand than a list of numbers.

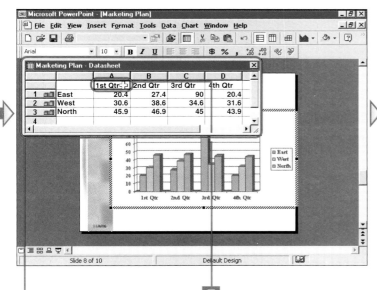

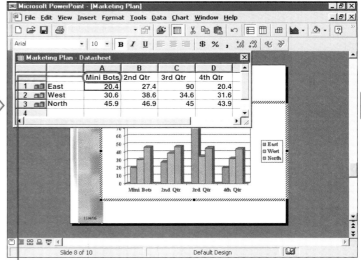

■ A datasheet appears, displaying sample data to show you where to enter your information.

5 To change the data in a cell, move the mouse ⊹ over the cell and then press the left mouse button. A thick border appears around the cell.

6 Type your data and then press **Enter** on your keyboard.

7 Repeat steps 5 and 6 until you finish entering all your data.

CONTINUED➡

ADD A CHART

You can choose the type of chart you want to create.

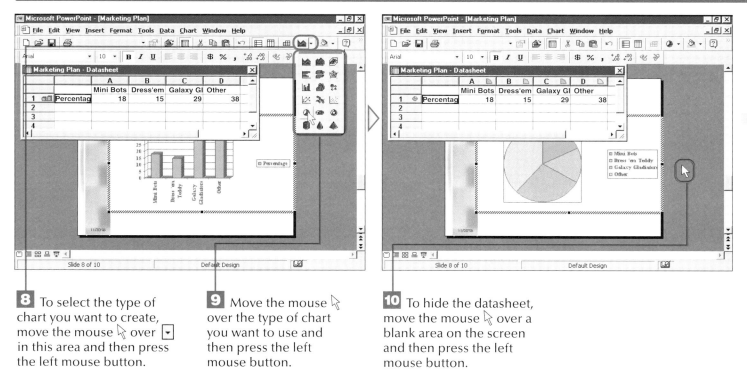

8 To select the type of chart you want to create, move the mouse over ▼ in this area and then press the left mouse button.

9 Move the mouse over the type of chart you want to use and then press the left mouse button.

10 To hide the datasheet, move the mouse over a blank area on the screen and then press the left mouse button.

What type of chart should I choose?

The type of chart you should choose depends on your data. For example, area, column and line charts are ideal for showing changes to values over time, whereas pie charts are ideal for showing percentages.

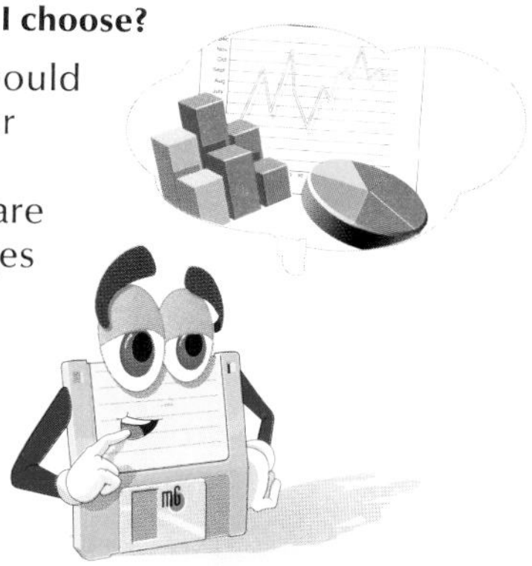

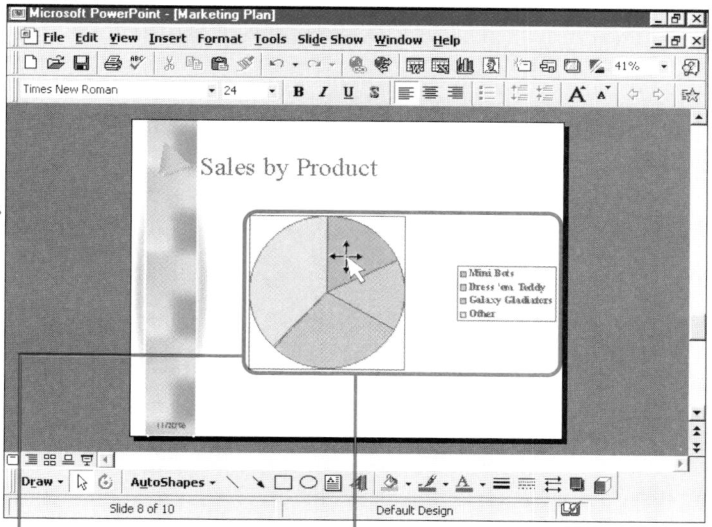

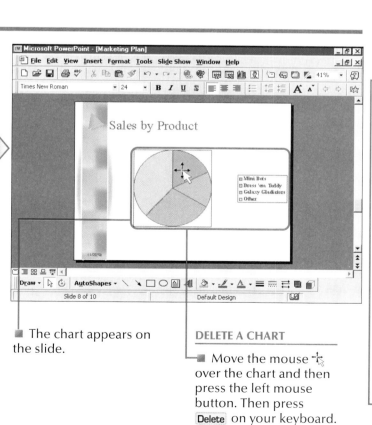

■ The chart appears on the slide.

DELETE A CHART

■ Move the mouse over the chart and then press the left mouse button. Then press Delete on your keyboard.

EDIT A CHART

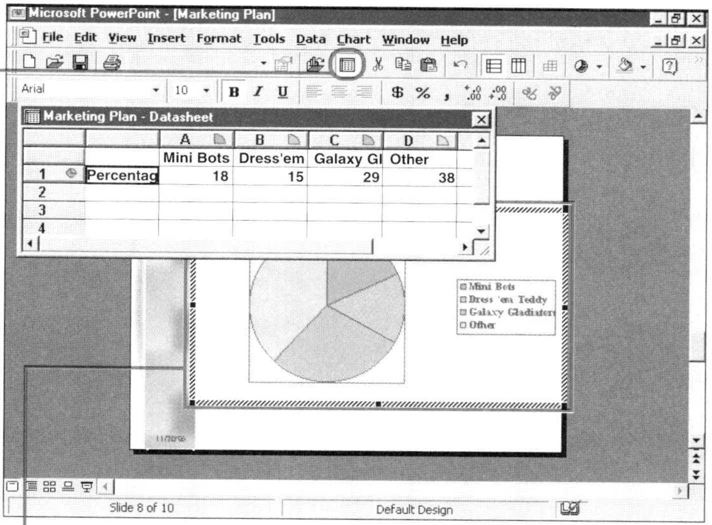

1 Move the mouse over the chart and then quickly press the left mouse button twice.

■ If the datasheet does not appear, move the mouse over and then press the left mouse button to display the datasheet.

2 To make changes to the chart, perform steps **5** to **10** starting on page 247.

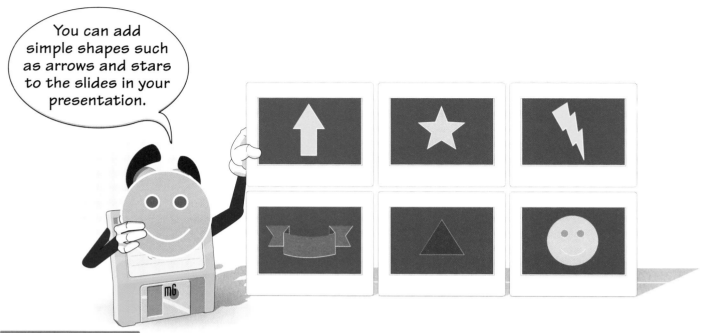

You can add simple shapes such as arrows and stars to the slides in your presentation.

ADD AN AUTOSHAPE

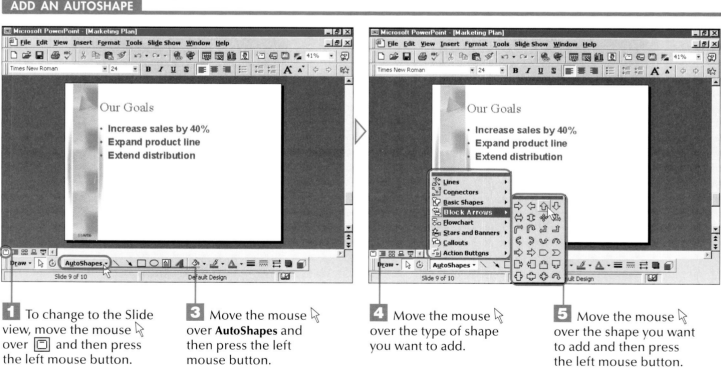

1 To change to the Slide view, move the mouse ☐ over ☐ and then press the left mouse button.

2 Display the slide you want to add a shape to.

3 Move the mouse ☐ over **AutoShapes** and then press the left mouse button.

4 Move the mouse ☐ over the type of shape you want to add.

5 Move the mouse ☐ over the shape you want to add and then press the left mouse button.

Why should I use an AutoShape?

You can use AutoShapes to emphasize important information on your slides.

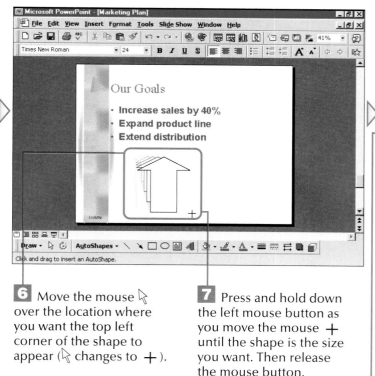

6 Move the mouse ▷ over the location where you want the top left corner of the shape to appear (▷ changes to ＋).

7 Press and hold down the left mouse button as you move the mouse ＋ until the shape is the size you want. Then release the mouse button.

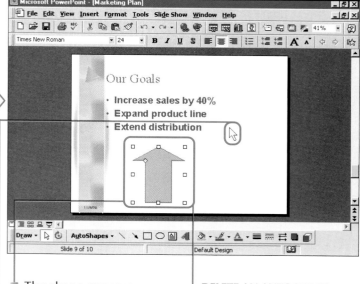

■ The shape appears on the slide. The handles (□) around the shape let you change the size of the shape. To resize the shape, refer to page 253.

8 To hide the handles, move the mouse ▷ outside the shape area and then press the left mouse button.

DELETE AN AUTOSHAPE

■ Move the mouse ⊹ over the shape and then press the left mouse button. Then press Delete on your keyboard.

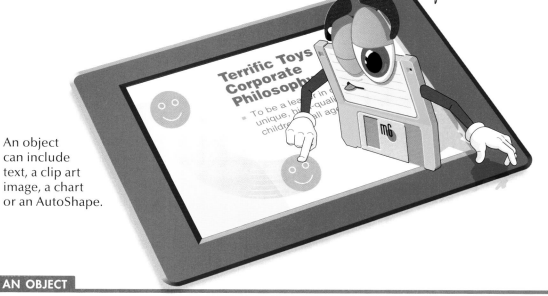

You can easily change the location or size of any object on a slide.

An object can include text, a clip art image, a chart or an AutoShape.

MOVE AN OBJECT

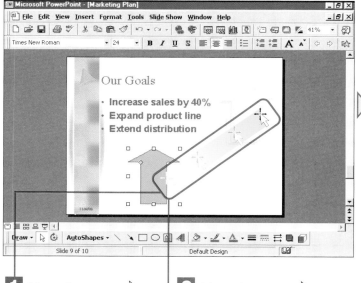

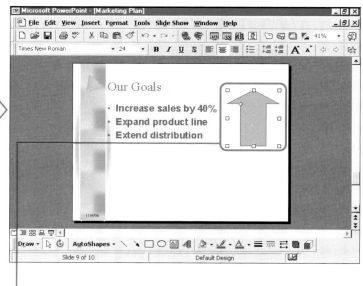

1 Move the mouse ⬚ over the object you want to move and then press the left mouse button.

2 Move the mouse ⬚ over an edge of the object (⬚ changes to ⊹).

3 Press and hold down the left mouse button as you move the object to a new location. Then release the mouse button.

■ The object appears in the new location.

How can I use the handles (□) that appear around a selected object?

The handles around an object let you change the size of the object.

■ Changes the height of an object.

■ Changes the width of an object.

■ Changes the height and width of an object at the same time.

RESIZE AN OBJECT

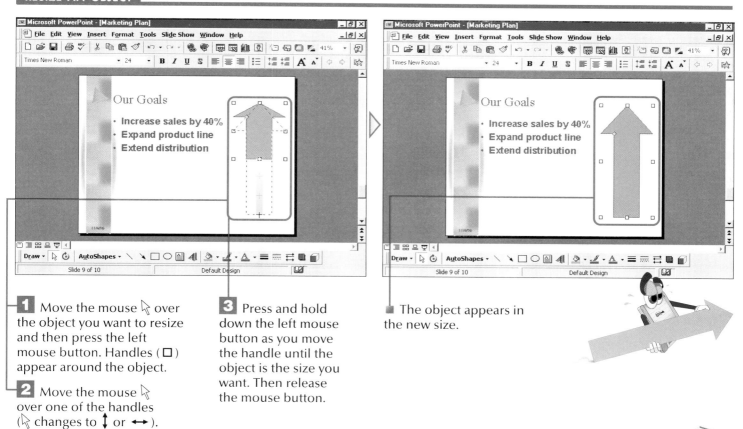

1 Move the mouse ⍉ over the object you want to resize and then press the left mouse button. Handles (□) appear around the object.

2 Move the mouse ⍉ over one of the handles (⍉ changes to ↕ or ↔).

3 Press and hold down the left mouse button as you move the handle until the object is the size you want. Then release the mouse button.

■ The object appears in the new size.

CHANGE SLIDE DESIGN

PowerPoint offers many ready-to-use designs that you can choose from to give the slides in your presentation a new appearance.

CHANGE SLIDE DESIGN

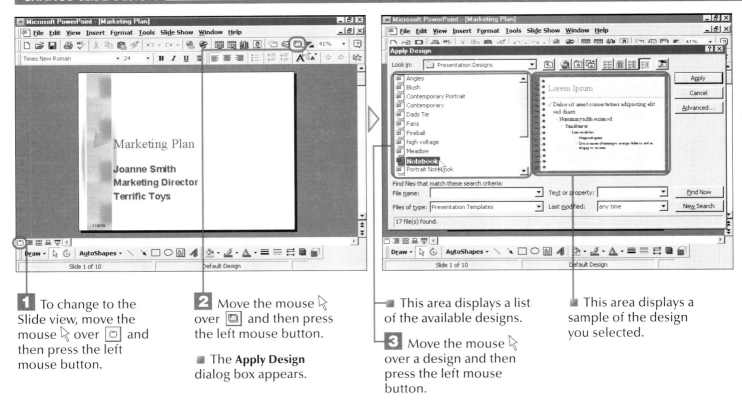

1 To change to the Slide view, move the mouse ⌖ over 🔲 and then press the left mouse button.

2 Move the mouse ⌖ over 🔲 and then press the left mouse button.

■ The **Apply Design** dialog box appears.

■ This area displays a list of the available designs.

3 Move the mouse ⌖ over a design and then press the left mouse button.

■ This area displays a sample of the design you selected.

What slide designs does PowerPoint offer?

Here are some of the designs that PowerPoint offers.

Contemporary

Fans

Professional

Whirlpool

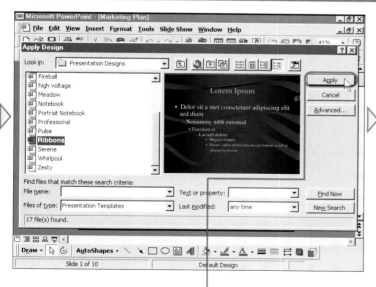

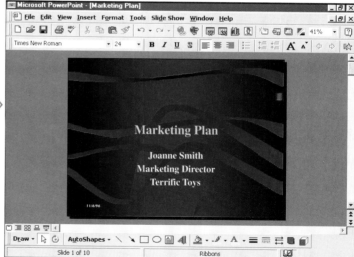

4 Repeat step 3 until the design you want to use appears.

5 To apply the design to all the slides in the presentation, move the mouse ▷ over **Apply** and then press the left mouse button.

■ The slides in the presentation display the new design.

■ The design you selected only changes the appearance of the slides. The content of the slides does not change.

You can select a different color scheme for your entire presentation.

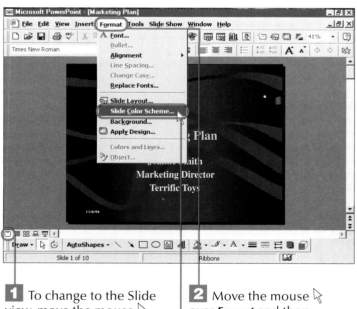

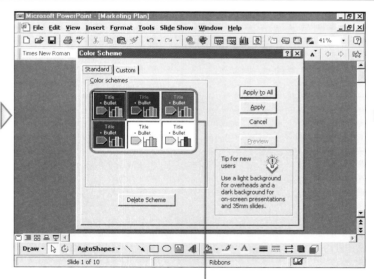

1 To change to the Slide view, move the mouse over ⬚ and then press the left mouse button.

2 Move the mouse over **Format** and then press the left mouse button.

3 Move the mouse over **Slide Color Scheme** and then press the left mouse button.

■ The **Color Scheme** dialog box appears.

■ This area displays samples of the color schemes that PowerPoint offers for a presentation.

Note: The color schemes offered depend on the slide design. To change the slide design, refer to page 254.

How can I emphasize one slide in my presentation?

You can make an important slide stand out from the rest of your presentation by changing the color scheme for only that slide.

To change the color scheme for only one slide, display the slide you want to change. Then perform steps 1 to 5 starting on page 256, selecting **Apply** in step 5.

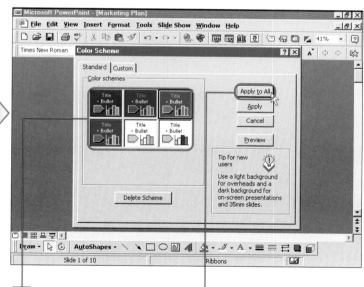

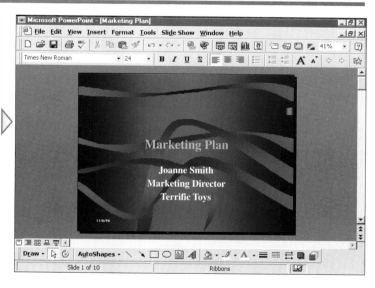

4 Move the mouse ▷ over the color scheme you want to use and then press the left mouse button.

5 To apply the color scheme to all the slides in the presentation, move the mouse ▷ over **Apply to All** and then press the left mouse button.

■ All the slides in the presentation display the new color scheme.

PowerPoint offers several styles that you can use to emphasize information on your slides.

Bold
Italic
<u>Underline</u>
Shadow

EMPHASIZE TEXT

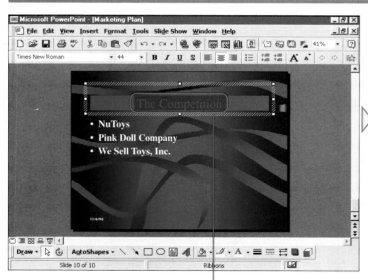

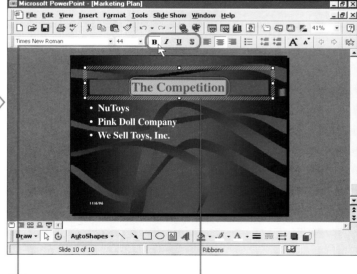

1 Display the slide containing the text you want to change.

2 Select the text you want to change. To select text, refer to page 228.

3 Move the mouse ⌖ over one of the following options and then press the left mouse button.

B Bold **U** Underline
I Italic **S** Shadow

■ The text you selected appears in the new style. To remove the style, repeat steps **2** and **3**.

> You can enhance the appearance of your slides by aligning text in different ways.

CHANGE ALIGNMENT OF TEXT

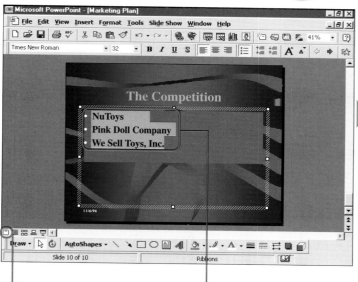

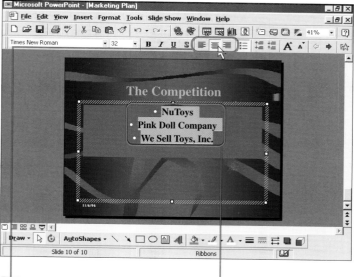

1 To change to the Slide view, move the mouse ⌖ over ▣ and then press the left mouse button.

2 Display the slide containing the text you want to align differently.

3 Select the text you want to align differently. To select text, refer to page 228.

4 Move the mouse ⌖ over one of the following options and then press the left mouse button.

▤ Left align

▥ Center

▦ Right align

■ The text you selected displays the new alignment.

> You can enhance the appearance of slides in your presentation by changing the design of the text.

CHANGE FONT OF TEXT

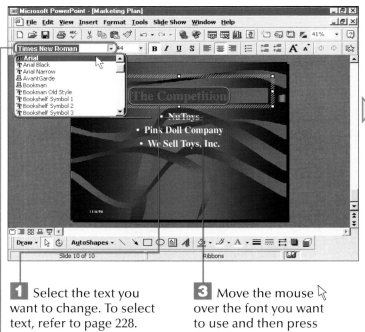

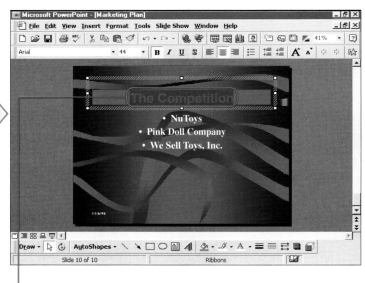

1 Select the text you want to change. To select text, refer to page 228.

2 To display a list of the available fonts, move the mouse ⌖ over ▾ in this area and then press the left mouse button.

3 Move the mouse ⌖ over the font you want to use and then press the left mouse button.

■ The text you selected changes to the new font.

You can increase or decrease the size of text in your presentation.

CHANGE SIZE OF TEXT

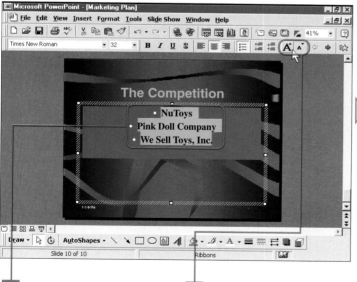

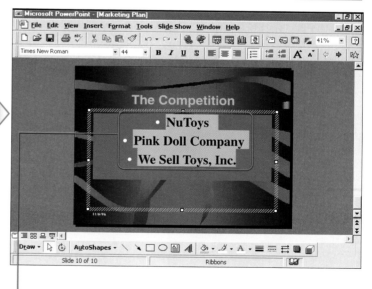

1 Select the text you want to change. To select text, refer to page 228.

2 Move the mouse ⌖ over one of the following options and then press the left mouse button until the text is the size you want.

$\boxed{A}$ Increase size of text

$\boxed{A}$ Decrease size of text

■ The text you selected changes to the new size.

CHANGE TEXT COLOR

You can change the color of text on a slide.

CHANGE TEXT COLOR

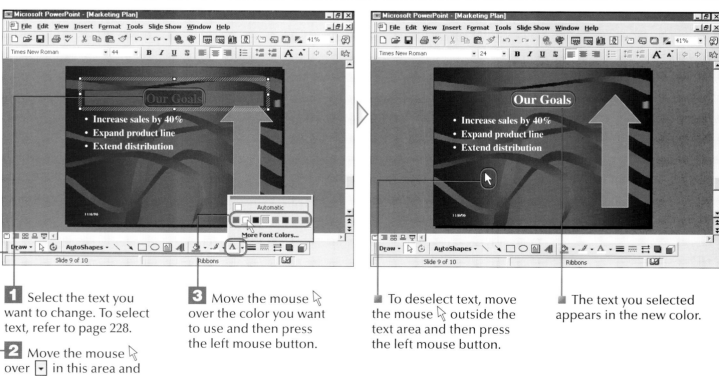

1 Select the text you want to change. To select text, refer to page 228.

2 Move the mouse ⌖ over ▾ in this area and then press the left mouse button.

3 Move the mouse ⌖ over the color you want to use and then press the left mouse button.

■ To deselect text, move the mouse ⌖ outside the text area and then press the left mouse button.

■ The text you selected appears in the new color.

CHANGE OBJECT COLOR

> You can change the color of an object on a slide.

CHANGE OBJECT COLOR

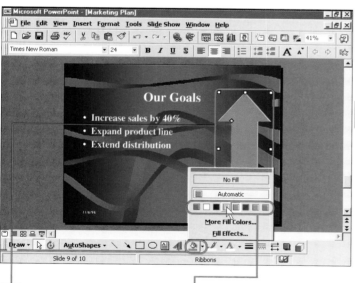

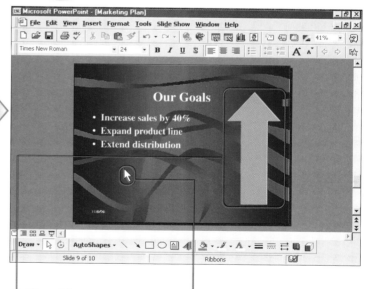

1 Move the mouse ⟨ over the object you want to change and then press the left mouse button.

2 Move the mouse ⟨ over ▾ in this area and then press the left mouse button.

3 Move the mouse ⟨ over the color you want to use and then press the left mouse button.

■ The object you selected appears in the new color.

■ To deselect the object, move the mouse ⟨ outside the object area and then press the left mouse button.

You can add information to every slide or page in your presentation.

ADD HEADER AND FOOTER

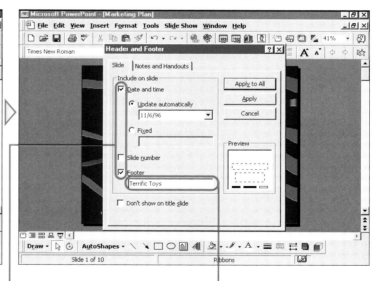

1 Move the mouse ⌖ over **View** and then press the left mouse button.

2 Move the mouse ⌖ over **Header and Footer** and then press the left mouse button.

■ The **Header and Footer** dialog box appears.

■ Each option that displays a check mark (✔) will appear on all the slides in the presentation.

3 To add or remove a check mark (✔) for an option, move the mouse ⌖ over the check box beside the option and then press the left mouse button.

4 To type the footer text you want to appear at the bottom of each slide, move the mouse Ⅰ over this area and then press the left mouse button. Then type the footer text.

What information can I add to my presentation?

Slides can include a date, footer and slide number.

Notes and handouts can include a header, date, footer and page number.

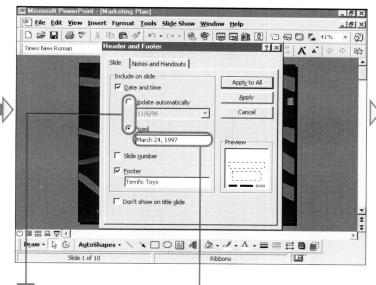

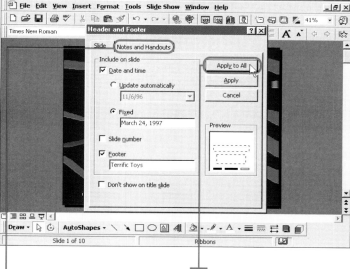

5 To select the date you want each slide to display, move the mouse ⬚ over one of these options and then press the left mouse button (○ changes to ◉).

Update automatically - Display the current date.

Fixed - Display the date you specify.

6 If you selected **Fixed** in step **5**, type the date.

■ To specify the information you want to appear on the notes and handout pages, move the mouse ⬚ over this tab and then press the left mouse button. Then repeat steps **3** to **6** to specify the information.

7 To apply the changes to all the slides and pages, move the mouse ⬚ over **Apply to All** and then press the left mouse button.

You can add movement and sound effects to the objects on your slides.

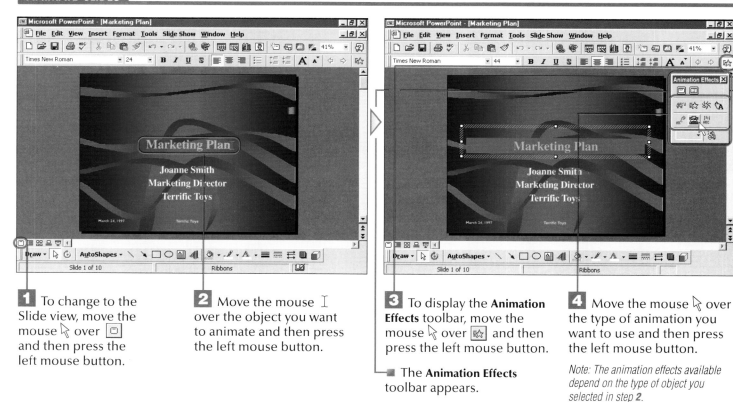

1 To change to the Slide view, move the mouse ⊳ over ▣ and then press the left mouse button.

2 Move the mouse I over the object you want to animate and then press the left mouse button.

3 To display the **Animation Effects** toolbar, move the mouse ⊳ over 🖾 and then press the left mouse button.

■ The **Animation Effects** toolbar appears.

4 Move the mouse ⊳ over the type of animation you want to use and then press the left mouse button.

Note: The animation effects available depend on the type of object you selected in step 2.

What animation effects can I add to my presentation?

 Drive-In

 Laser Text

 Flying

 Typewriter Text

 Camera

 Reverse Text Order

 Flash Once

 Drop In

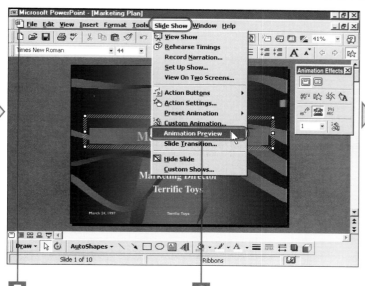

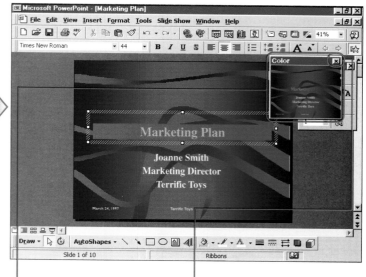

5 To view the animation, move the mouse over **Slide Show** and then press the left mouse button.

6 Move the mouse over **Animation Preview** and then press the left mouse button.

■ A preview window appears, displaying the animation.

Note: To view the animation again, move the mouse over the preview window and then press the left mouse button.

■ To close the preview window, move the mouse over ⊗ and then press the left mouse button.

■ To close the **Animation Effects** toolbar, repeat step 3.

REORDER SLIDES

You can easily change the order of the slides in your presentation.

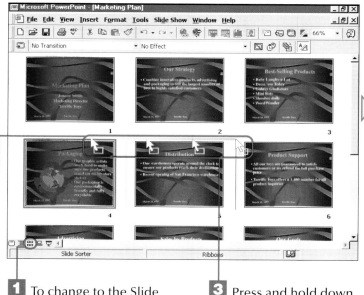

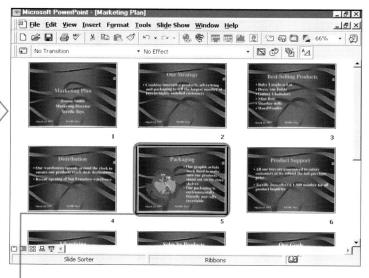

1 To change to the Slide Sorter view, move the mouse ↕ over 🔡 and then press the left mouse button.

2 Move the mouse ↕ over the slide you want to move.

3 Press and hold down the left mouse button as you move the slide to a new location.

■ A line shows the new location. The slide will appear to the left of the line.

4 Release the left mouse button and the slide appears in the new location.

268

You can remove a slide you no longer need.

DELETE A SLIDE

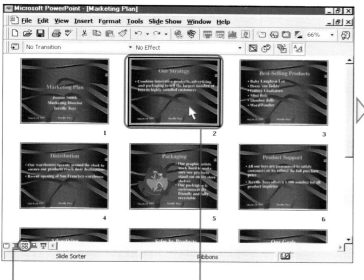

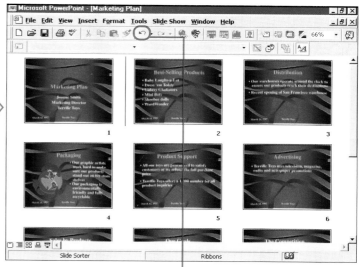

1 To change to the Slide Sorter view, move the mouse ⌖ over 🔲 and then press the left mouse button.

2 Move the mouse ⌖ over the slide you want to delete and then press the left mouse button.

3 Press **Delete** on your keyboard.

■ The slide disappears.

■ To immediately return the slide to the presentation, move the mouse ⌖ over 🔄 and then press the left mouse button.

CREATE SPEAKER NOTES

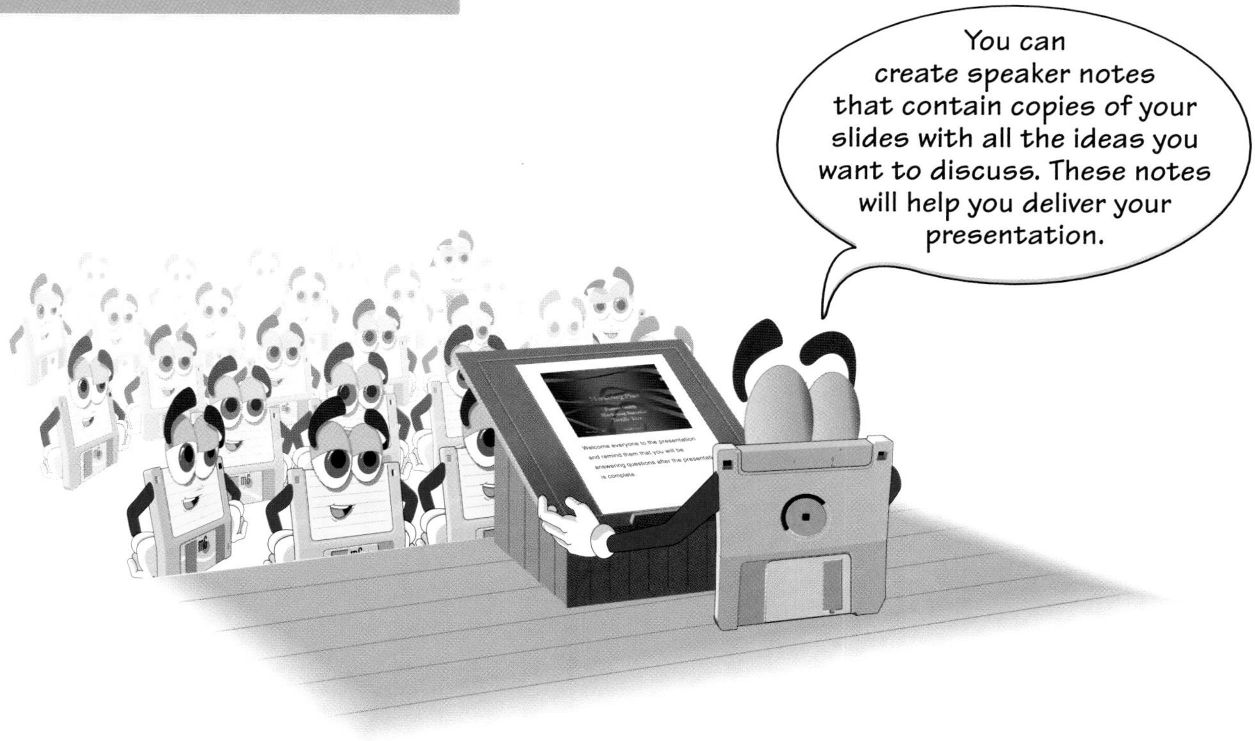
You can create speaker notes that contain copies of your slides with all the ideas you want to discuss. These notes will help you deliver your presentation.

CREATE SPEAKER NOTES

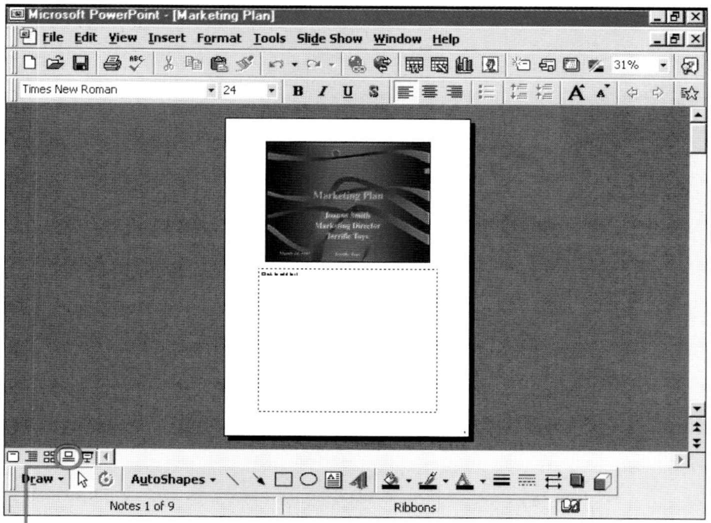
Microsoft PowerPoint - [Marketing Plan]
File Edit View Insert Format Tools Slide Show Window Help
Times New Roman
24
31%
Draw
AutoShapes
Notes 1 of 9
Ribbons

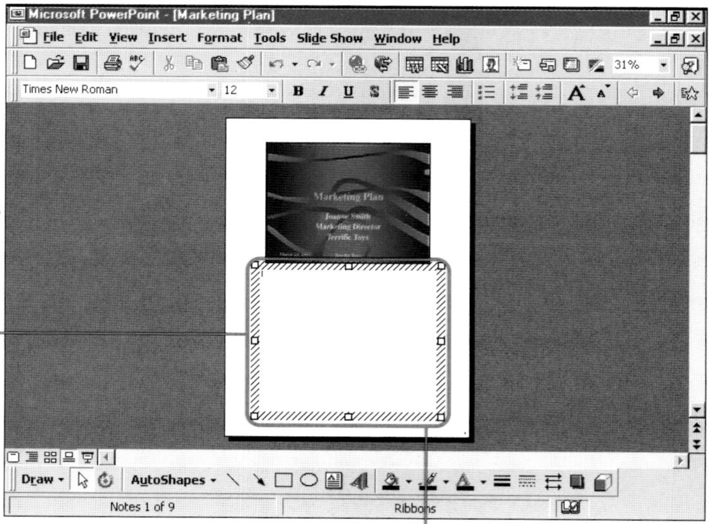
Microsoft PowerPoint - [Marketing Plan]
File Edit View Insert Format Tools Slide Show Window Help
Times New Roman
12
31%
Draw
AutoShapes
Notes 1 of 9
Ribbons

1 To change to the Notes Page view, move the mouse ↖ over ⊟ and then press the left mouse button.

2 Display the slide you want to create speaker notes for.

Note: You can add speaker notes to each slide in the presentation.

■ The notes page displays an area where you can add text.

3 Move the mouse I over the text area and then press the left mouse button.

■ A thick border appears around the text area.

What should I include in my speaker notes?

When creating speaker notes, include the key points you want to discuss during your presentation.

Speaker notes can also include statistics or additional information that will support your ideas and help you answer questions from the audience.

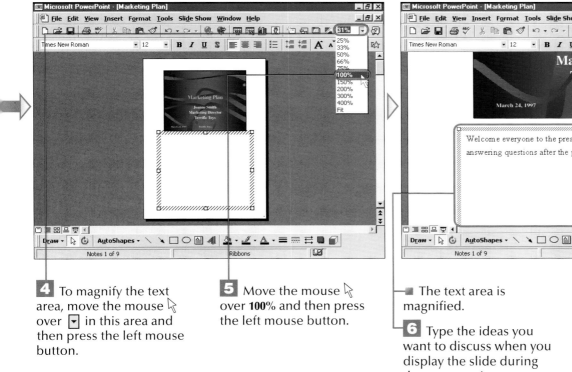

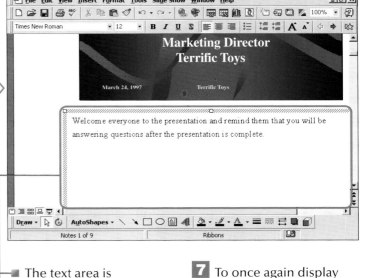

4 To magnify the text area, move the mouse ⬚ over ▼ in this area and then press the left mouse button.

5 Move the mouse ⬚ over **100%** and then press the left mouse button.

◼ The text area is magnified.

6 Type the ideas you want to discuss when you display the slide during the presentation.

7 To once again display the entire notes page on the screen, repeat steps **4** and **5**, selecting **Fit** in step **5**.

VIEW A SLIDE SHOW

You can view a slide show of your presentation on a computer screen.

VIEW A SLIDE SHOW

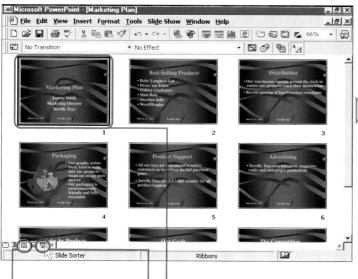

1 To change to the Slide Sorter view, move the mouse ⌖ over ▦ and then press the left mouse button.

2 Move the mouse ⌖ over the first slide in the presentation and then press the left mouse button.

3 To start the slide show, move the mouse ⌖ over 🖵 and then press the left mouse button.

■ The first slide fills the screen.

4 To display the next slide, press the **Spacebar** on your keyboard or press the left mouse button.

Is the speed at which I deliver a presentation important?

Make sure you rehearse the pace of your presentation before delivering it to an audience. A fast pace can overwhelm an audience whereas a slow pace may put the audience to sleep.

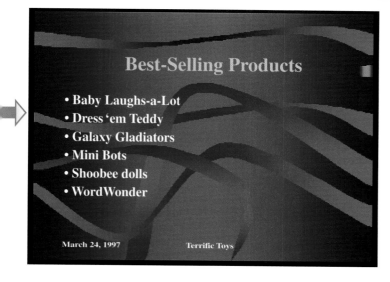

■ The next slide appears.

5 Repeat step 4 until you finish viewing all the slides in the presentation.

QUICK REFERENCE

You can use the keyboard to help you move through your presentation.

 Display the next slide — Press the **Spacebar**.

 Display the previous slide — Press ◆Backspace.

 Display any slide — Press the number of the slide on your keyboard and then press Enter.

 End the presentation — Press Esc.

Best-Selling Products

• Baby Laughs-a-Lot
• Dress 'em Teddy
• Galaxy Gladiators
• Mini Bots
• Shoobee dolls
• WordWonder

March 24, 1997   Terrific Toys

ADD SLIDE TRANSITIONS

> You can use special effects, called transitions, to help you move from one slide to the next. Transitions help to introduce each slide during an on-screen slide show.

ADD SLIDE TRANSITIONS

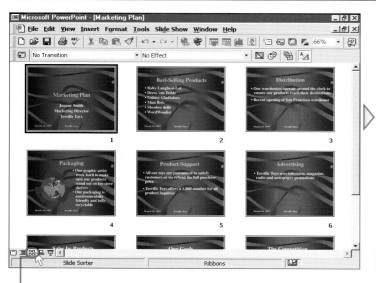

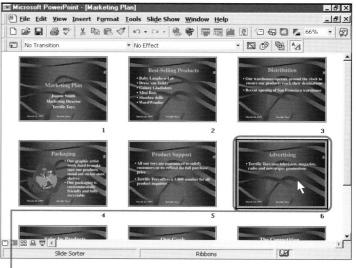

1 To change to the Slide Sorter view, move the mouse ⟷ over 🔳 and then press the left mouse button.

Note: PowerPoint automatically adds transitions to slides for some types of presentations. A symbol (🔁) appears below every slide with a transition.

2 To add or change a transition for a slide, move the mouse ⟷ over the slide and then press the left mouse button.

What slide transitions does PowerPoint offer?

These are a few of the slide transitions PowerPoint offers.

Blinds Vertical

Dissolve

Checkerboard Across

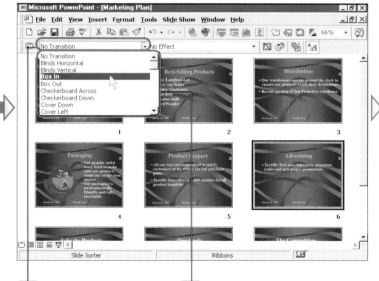

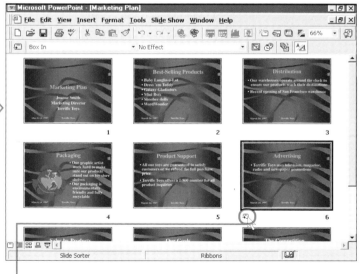

3 To display the available transitions, move the mouse ⬚ over this area and then press the left mouse button.

4 Move the mouse ⬚ over the transition you want to use and then press the left mouse button.

5 To view the transition for the slide, move the mouse ⬚ over the symbol (⬚) below the slide and then press the left mouse button.

PRINT A PRESENTATION

You can produce a paper copy of a presentation for your own use or to hand out to an audience.

PRINT A PRESENTATION

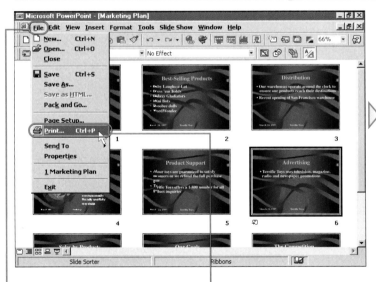

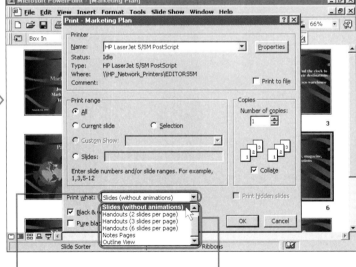

1 Move the mouse over **File** and then press the left mouse button.

2 Move the mouse over **Print** and then press the left mouse button.

■ The **Print** dialog box appears.

3 To select what you want to print, move the mouse over this area and then press the left mouse button.

4 Move the mouse over what you want to print and then press the left mouse button.

What can I print?

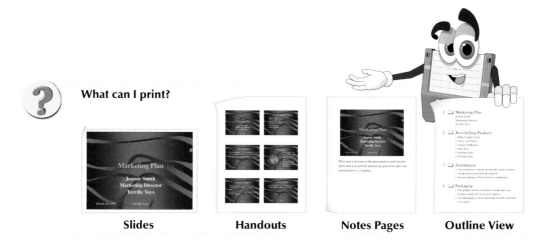

| Slides | Handouts | Notes Pages | Outline View |

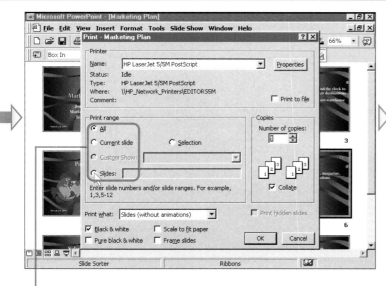

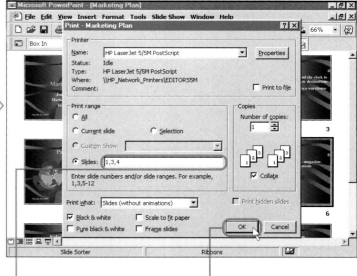

5 Move the mouse ⌖ over one of these options and then press the left mouse button (○ changes to ◉).

All - Prints every slide in the presentation.

Current slide - Prints the selected slide or the slide displayed on the screen.

Slides - Prints the slides you specify.

6 If you selected **Slides** in step **5**, type the slide numbers you want to print (examples: 1,3,4 or 2-4).

7 Move the mouse ⌖ over **OK** and then press the left mouse button.

Microsoft Outlook is a program that helps you keep track of your business and personal activities, including your appointments, contacts, tasks and e-mail messages.

Update a Contact
Page 308

Create a Note
Page 292

Open a Message
Page 284

Delete a Message
Page 285

Mark a Task as Complete
Page 298

OUTLOOK

View Calendar
Page 300

Start Outlook
Page 280

1 **Start Outlook**
   Pages 280-281

2 **Using Inbox**
   Pages 282-291

3 **Using Notes**
   Pages 292-295

4 **Using Tasks**
   Pages 296-299

5 **Using Calendar**
   Pages 300-305

6 **Using Contacts**
   Pages 306-311

7 **Using Journal**
   Pages 312-317

8 **Print**
   Pages 318-319

9 **Using Deleted Items**
   Pages 320-323

> Outlook can help you manage your messages, appointments, contacts, tasks and activities.

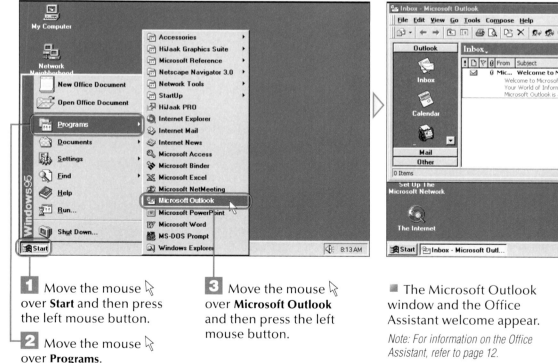

1 Move the mouse ⊳ over **Start** and then press the left mouse button.

2 Move the mouse ⊳ over **Programs**.

3 Move the mouse ⊳ over **Microsoft Outlook** and then press the left mouse button.

■ The Microsoft Outlook window and the Office Assistant welcome appear.

Note: For information on the Office Assistant, refer to page 12.

4 To start using Outlook, move the mouse ⊳ over **OK** and then press the left mouse button.

What can I do with Outlook?

Inbox
Send and receive messages.

Calendar
Schedule appointments.

Contacts
Maintain an address book.

Tasks
Create a list of things to do.

Journal
Keep track of activities.

Notes
Create brief reminder notes.

Deleted Items
Store items you delete.

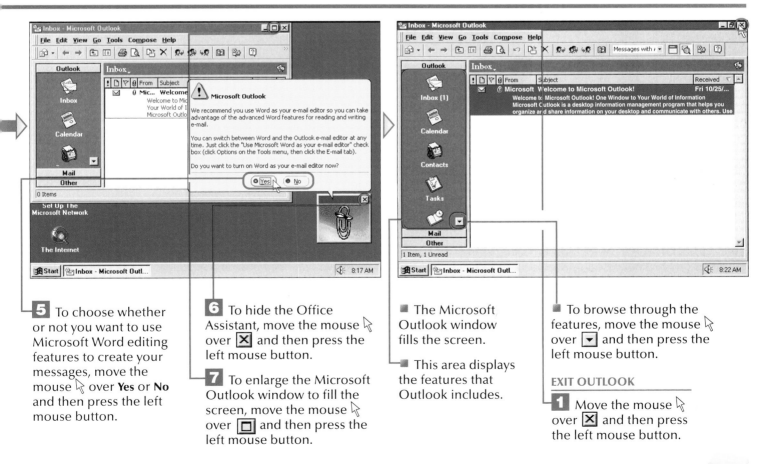

5 To choose whether or not you want to use Microsoft Word editing features to create your messages, move the mouse ⌖ over **Yes** or **No** and then press the left mouse button.

6 To hide the Office Assistant, move the mouse ⌖ over ☒ and then press the left mouse button.

7 To enlarge the Microsoft Outlook window to fill the screen, move the mouse ⌖ over ☐ and then press the left mouse button.

■ The Microsoft Outlook window fills the screen.

■ This area displays the features that Outlook includes.

■ To browse through the features, move the mouse ⌖ over ▼ and then press the left mouse button.

EXIT OUTLOOK

1 Move the mouse ⌖ over ☒ and then press the left mouse button.

VIEW INBOX

The Inbox lets you exchange electronic mail (e-mail) messages with friends, family members, colleagues and clients.

VIEW INBOX

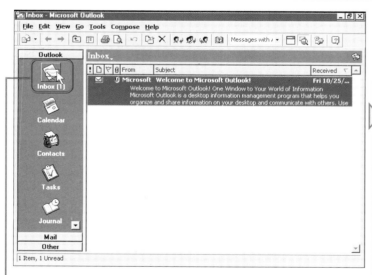

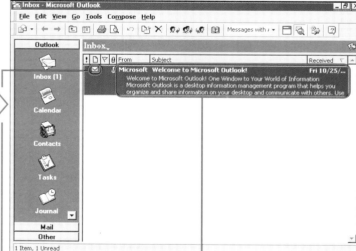

1 To view your messages, move the mouse ⬚ over **Inbox** and then press the left mouse button.

◼ If there are messages you have not read, the number of unread messages will appear in brackets beside **Inbox**.

◼ This area shows you whether or not you have read each message.

✉ Unread message

✉ Read message

◼ This area displays the author, subject and date of each message along with a few lines of text from each unread message.

Note: To view all the text in a message, refer to page 284 to open the message.

DISPLAY THE MAIL FOLDERS

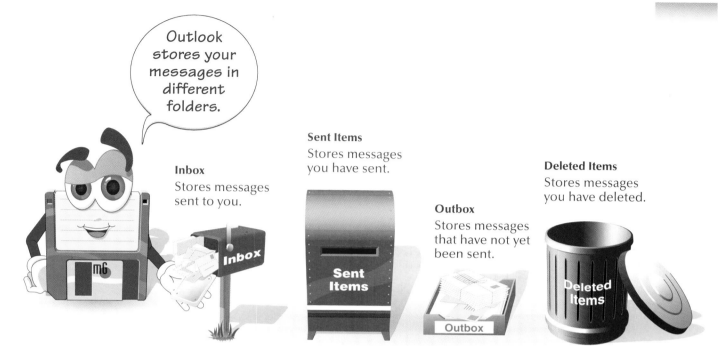

Outlook stores your messages in different folders.

Inbox
Stores messages sent to you.

Sent Items
Stores messages you have sent.

Outbox
Stores messages that have not yet been sent.

Deleted Items
Stores messages you have deleted.

DISPLAY THE MAIL FOLDERS

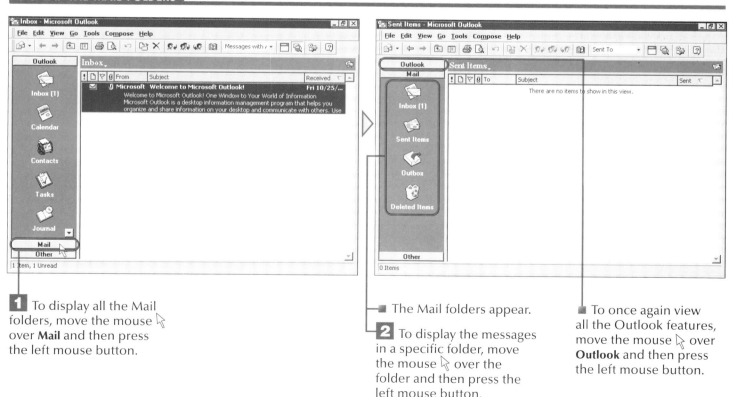

1 To display all the Mail folders, move the mouse over **Mail** and then press the left mouse button.

■ The Mail folders appear.

2 To display the messages in a specific folder, move the mouse over the folder and then press the left mouse button.

■ To once again view all the Outlook features, move the mouse over **Outlook** and then press the left mouse button.

You can easily open a message to view its contents.

OPEN A MESSAGE

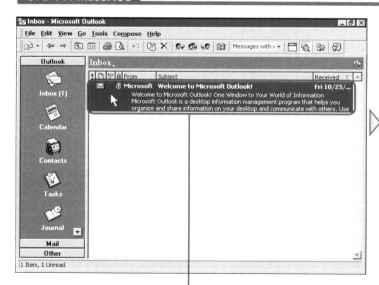

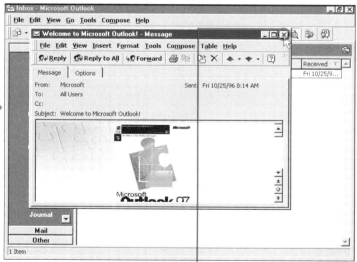

Note: To display the messages in a specific folder, refer to page 283.

1 Move the mouse over the message you want to open and then quickly press the left mouse button twice.

■ The contents of the message appear on the screen.

2 To close the message, move the mouse over **X** and then press the left mouse button.

DELETE A MESSAGE

You can delete a message you no longer need. This prevents your folders from becoming cluttered with messages.

DELETE A MESSAGE

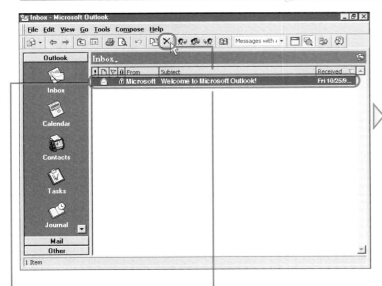

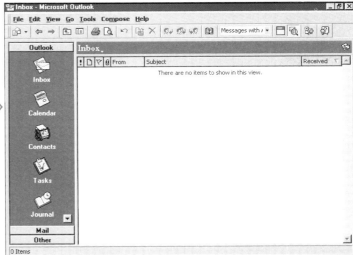

1 Move the mouse ⬚ over the message you want to delete and then press the left mouse button.

2 Move the mouse ⬚ over ☒ and then press the left mouse button.

■ The message disappears.

■ Outlook places the deleted message in the **Deleted Items** folder.

*Note: To display the messages in the **Deleted Items** folder, refer to page 283.*

285

You can send a message to exchange ideas or request information.

SEND A MESSAGE

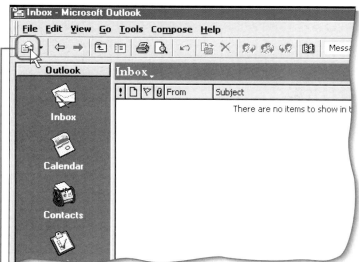

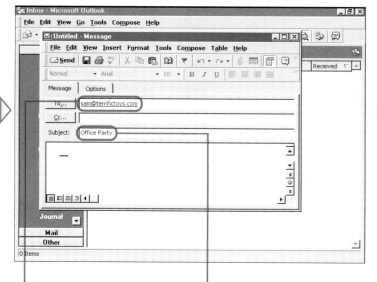

1 To create a message, move the mouse ⌖ over 🖆 and then press the left mouse button.

■ A window appears.

2 Type the e-mail address of the person you want to receive the message.

Note: You can practice sending a message by sending a message to yourself.

3 To enter a subject, press **Tab** twice on your keyboard. Then type the subject.

Why can't I send or receive messages?

Before you can send and receive messages, you must be connected to a service that allows you to exchange messages. These services include an office network, a commercial online service or an Internet service provider.

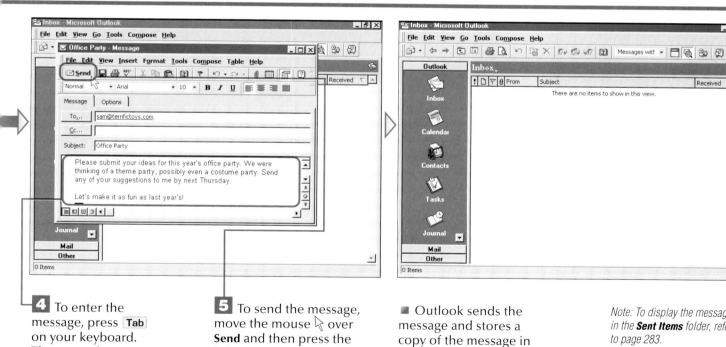

4 To enter the message, press `Tab` on your keyboard. Then type the message.

5 To send the message, move the mouse ⬚ over **Send** and then press the left mouse button.

▪ Outlook sends the message and stores a copy of the message in the **Sent Items** folder.

Note: To display the messages in the **Sent Items** folder, refer to page 283.

You can reply to a message to answer a question, express an opinion or supply additional information.

REPLY TO A MESSAGE

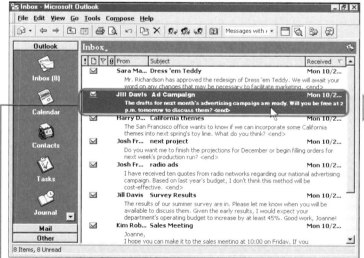

1 Move the mouse 🔈 over the message you want to reply to and then press the left mouse button.

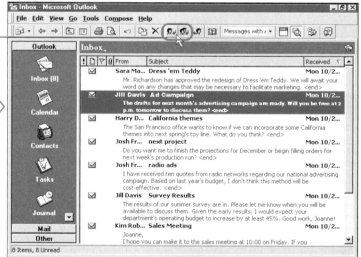

2 Move the mouse 🔈 over one of the following reply options and then press the left mouse button.

📧 Reply to sender

📧 Reply to sender and everyone who received the original message

Why haven't I received a response to my message?

When you send a message, do not assume the person receiving the message will read it right away. Some people may not regularly check their e-mail.

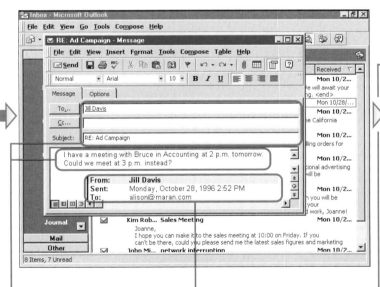

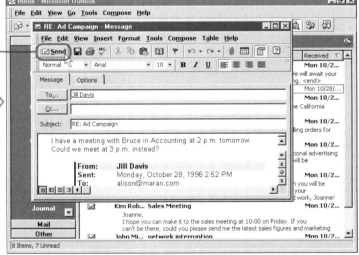

■ A window appears. Outlook fills in the e-mail address(es) and subject for you.

3 Type your reply to the message.

■ Outlook includes a copy of the original message. To save the reader time, you can delete all parts of the original message that do not directly relate to your reply.

4 To send the reply, move the mouse ⬚ over **Send** and then press the left mouse button.

■ Outlook sends the reply and stores a copy of the reply in the **Sent Items** folder.

*Note: To display the messages in the **Sent Items** folder, refer to page 283.*

FORWARD A MESSAGE

There is a 10th anniversary High School Reunion on August 8, 9 and 10 at Woodblock High School. We all hope to see you there. Contact Susan Hughes for more information.

Rick, I thought you might be interested in the reunion. Unfortunately, I will be out of town.

After reading a message, you can add comments and then send the message to a friend or colleague.

George Evans

Rick James
336 Stoney Lane
New York, NY
10010

FORWARD A MESSAGE

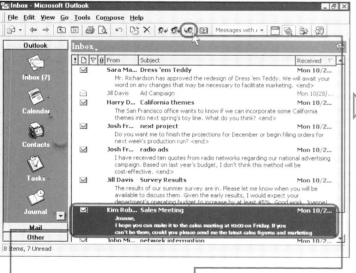

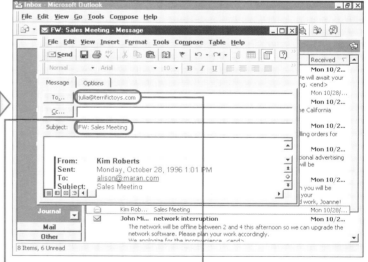

1 Move the mouse over the message you want to forward and then press the left mouse button.

2 Move the mouse over 🔲 and then press the left mouse button.

■ A window appears. Outlook fills in the subject for you.

3 Type the e-mail address of the person you want to forward the message to.

Can exchanging e-mail save me money?

Using e-mail can save you money on long distance calls to colleagues, friends and family. The next time you are about to use the telephone, consider sending an e-mail message instead.

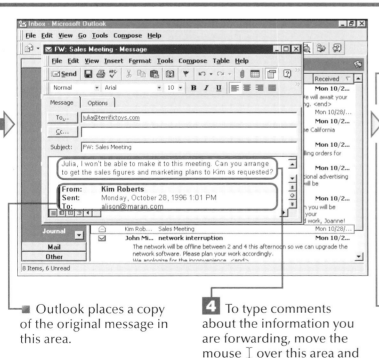

■ Outlook places a copy of the original message in this area.

4 To type comments about the information you are forwarding, move the mouse I over this area and then press the left mouse button. Then type your comments.

5 To forward the message, move the mouse ⬚ over **Send** and then press the left mouse button.

■ Outlook sends the message and stores a copy of the message in the **Sent Items** folder.

Note: To display the messages in the Sent Items folder, refer to page 283.

291

CREATE A NOTE

You can create electronic notes that are similar to paper sticky notes.

Doctor's Appointment Thursday 2 pm

Party at Steve's on Friday

Is the new sales report available yet?

Order latest catalog from ABC Computers Inc.

CREATE A NOTE

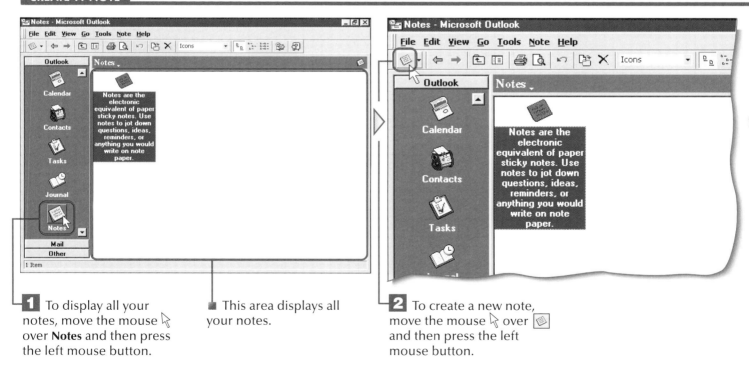

1 To display all your notes, move the mouse ⌖ over **Notes** and then press the left mouse button.

■ This area displays all your notes.

2 To create a new note, move the mouse ⌖ over 🗐 and then press the left mouse button.

What can I use notes for?

Notes are ideal for storing bits of information such as reminders, questions, ideas and anything else you would record on note paper.

Reminder
Pick up birthday cake after work.

Question ?
Is the meeting next Monday at 1:00 pm or 2:00 pm?

Idea
Hire an assistant to help out with extra work.

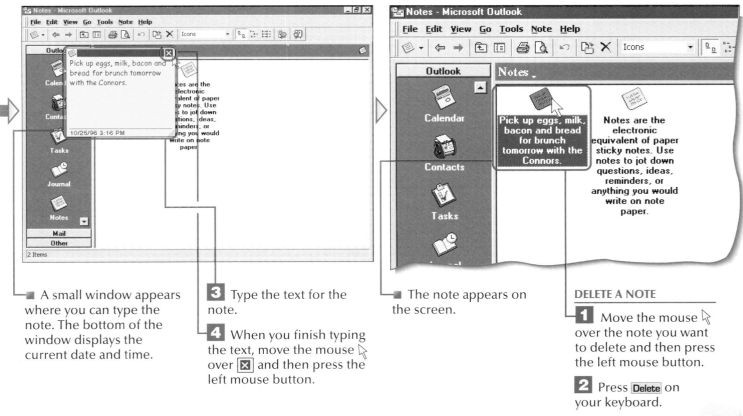

■ A small window appears where you can type the note. The bottom of the window displays the current date and time.

3 Type the text for the note.

4 When you finish typing the text, move the mouse over ☒ and then press the left mouse button.

■ The note appears on the screen.

DELETE A NOTE

1 Move the mouse over the note you want to delete and then press the left mouse button.

2 Press **Delete** on your keyboard.

OPEN A NOTE

You can easily open a note to view its contents.

OPEN A NOTE

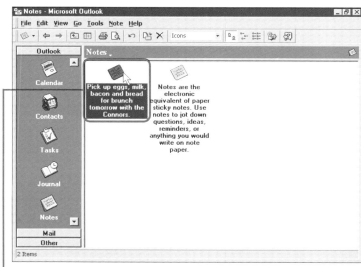

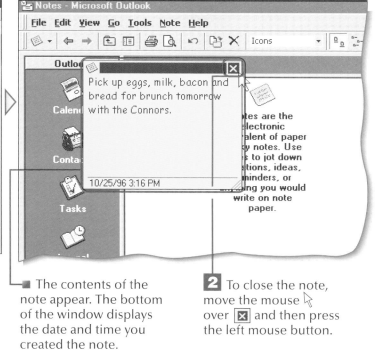

1 Move the mouse ⌖ over the note you want to open and then quickly press the left mouse button twice.

■ The contents of the note appear. The bottom of the window displays the date and time you created the note.

2 To close the note, move the mouse ⌖ over ⊠ and then press the left mouse button.

294

QUICK CHEESE MELT
For a quick and easy lunchtime
snack, try this delicious melt:
You will need white or whole wheat
bread, cheese, onions, bacon and
chives.
1. Microwave the bacon until crisp.
2. Lay thin slices of cheese, diced onion, bacon and chives
3. Cook this in the oven for 5-7 minutes, or until cheese is

You can change the size of a note. This is useful when the window is too small to display all the text.

RESIZE A NOTE

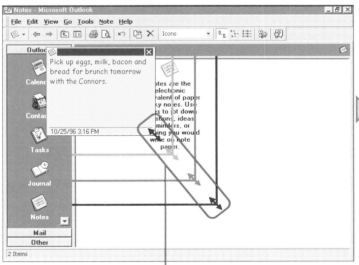

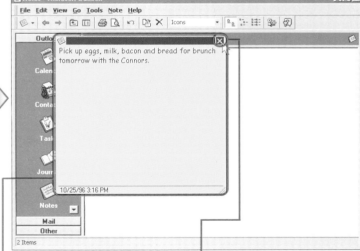

1 Open the note you want to resize. To open a note, perform step 1 on page 294.

2 Move the mouse ⬧ over the bottom right corner of the note (⬧ changes to ⬉).

3 Press and hold down the left mouse button as you move the mouse ⬉ until the outline of the note displays the size you want.

4 Release the mouse button and the note changes to the new size.

5 To close the note, move the mouse ⬧ over ☒ and then press the left mouse button.

CREATE A TASK

You can create a list of personal and work-related tasks that you want to accomplish.

CREATE A TASK

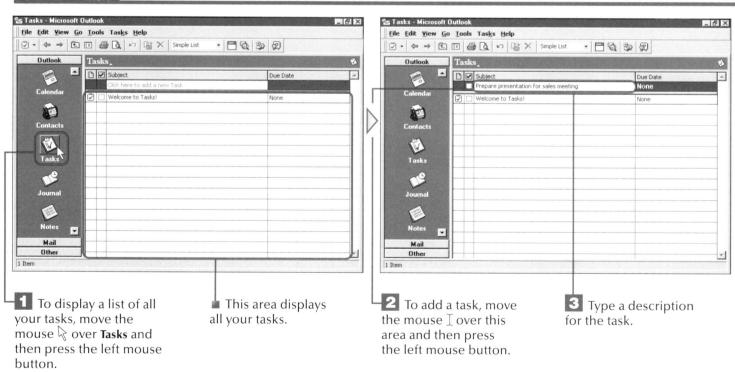

1 To display a list of all your tasks, move the mouse ⇧ over **Tasks** and then press the left mouse button.

■ This area displays all your tasks.

2 To add a task, move the mouse I over this area and then press the left mouse button.

3 Type a description for the task.

Where else can I see a list of my tasks?

There is a small area in the Calendar that displays a list of your tasks.

Note: For information on the Calendar, refer to page 300.

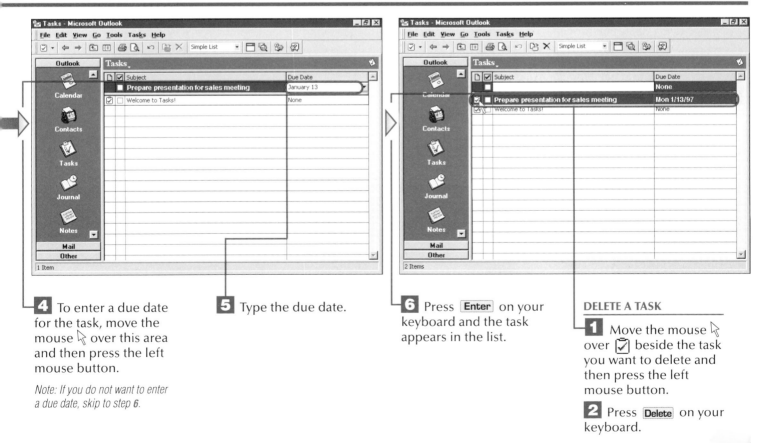

4 To enter a due date for the task, move the mouse ↳ over this area and then press the left mouse button.

Note: If you do not want to enter a due date, skip to step 6.

5 Type the due date.

6 Press **Enter** on your keyboard and the task appears in the list.

DELETE A TASK

1 Move the mouse ↳ over ☑ beside the task you want to delete and then press the left mouse button.

2 Press **Delete** on your keyboard.

297

When you complete a task, you can place a line through the task to remind you that it is complete.

MARK A TASK AS COMPLETE

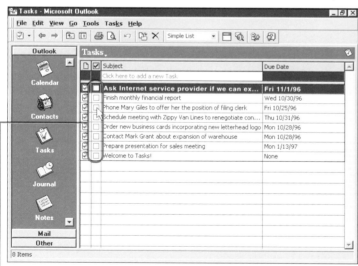

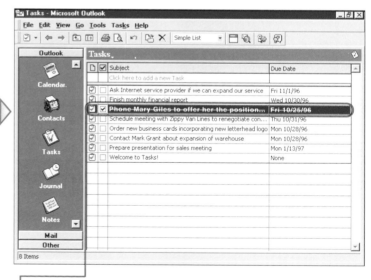

1 To mark a task as complete, move the mouse �️ over ☐ beside the task and then press the left mouse button (☐ changes to ☑).

■ A line appears through the task to show that the task is complete.

■ To remove the line through a task, repeat step **1**.

SORT TASKS

You can sort your tasks alphabetically by subject or by due date to help you quickly find tasks of interest.

SORT TASKS

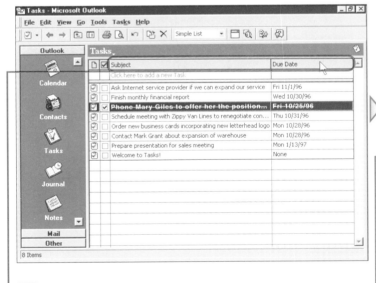

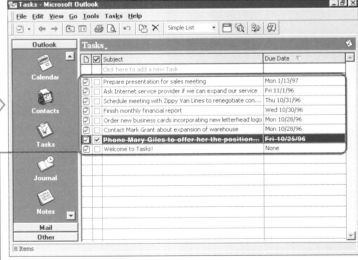

1 Move the mouse over the heading of the column you want to sort by and then press the left mouse button.

■ The tasks are sorted.

■ To sort the tasks in the opposite order, repeat step **1**.

The Calendar helps you keep track of your appointments.

VIEW CALENDAR

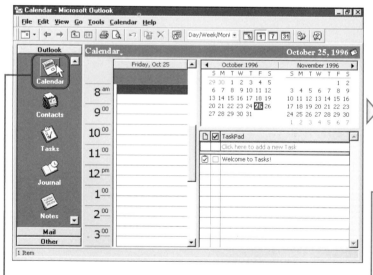

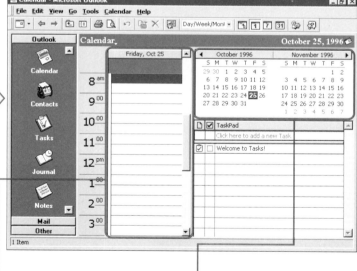

1 To display the Calendar, move the mouse ⍅ over **Calendar** and then press the left mouse button.

■ This area displays the appointments for the current day.

■ This area displays the days in the current month and the next month. Days with appointments are shown in **bold**.

Note: To add an appointment, refer to page 302.

How does Outlook know what day it is?

Outlook uses the date and time set in your computer to determine today's date. To change the date and time set in your computer, refer to your Windows manual.

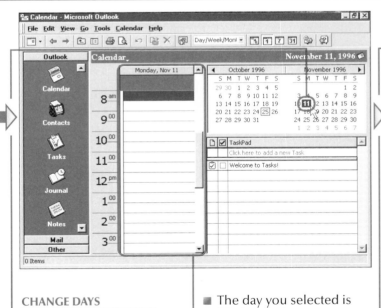

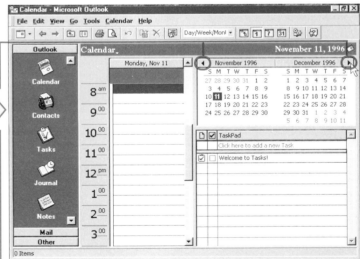

CHANGE DAYS

1 To display the appointments for another day, move the mouse ⍟ over the day and then press the left mouse button.

■ The day you selected is highlighted. The current day displays a red outline.

■ This area now displays the appointments for the day you selected.

CHANGE MONTHS

1 To display the days in another month, move the mouse ⍟ over one of the following options and then press the left mouse button.

◀ Display previous month

▶ Display next month

2 Repeat step 1 until the month you want to display appears.

ADD AN APPOINTMENT

You can add appointments to the Calendar to remind you of activities such as meetings, lunch dates and doctor's appointments.

ADD AN APPOINTMENT

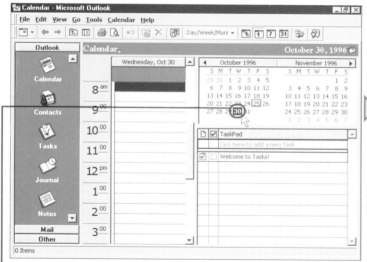

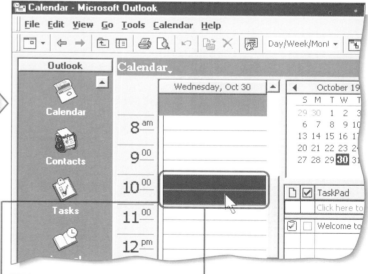

1 Move the mouse ⅄ over the day when you want to add an appointment and then press the left mouse button.

Note: To view the days in other months, refer to page 301.

2 Move the mouse ⅄ over the starting time for the appointment.

3 Press and hold down the left mouse button as you move the mouse ⅄ to select the time you want to set aside for the appointment. Then release the mouse button.

Outlook will play a brief sound and display a dialog box 15 minutes before a scheduled appointment.

RING
RING
RING

APPOINTMENT REMINDER

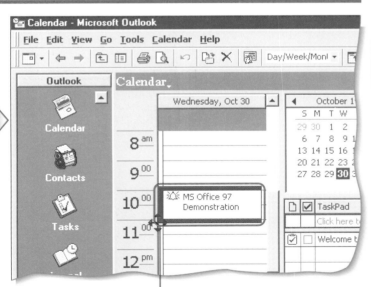

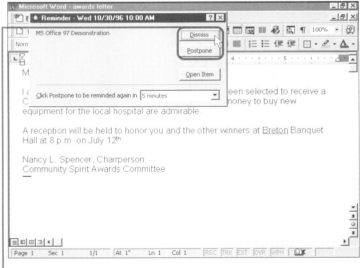

4 Type text to describe the appointment and then press **Enter** on your keyboard.

DELETE AN APPOINTMENT

1 To select the appointment you want to delete, move the mouse ↖ over the left edge of the appointment (↖ changes to ✛) and then press the left mouse button.

2 Press **Delete** on your keyboard.

1 To close the **Reminder** dialog box, move the mouse ↖ over one of the following options and then press the left mouse button.

Dismiss - Close the reminder

Postpone - Remind again in 5 minutes

DAY, WEEK AND MONTH VIEWS

You can view your appointments by day, week or month.

DAY, WEEK AND MONTH VIEWS

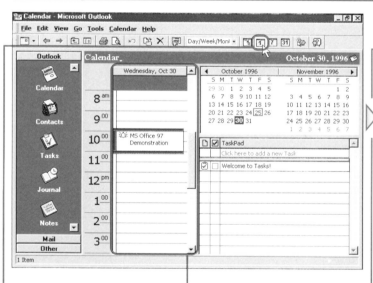

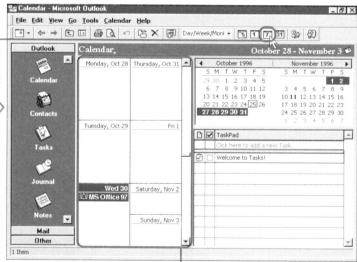

VIEW ONE DAY

1 To display the appointments for one day, move the mouse over ⬚ and then press the left mouse button.

■ This area displays the appointments for one day. You can use the scroll bar to browse through the day.

VIEW ONE WEEK

1 To display the appointments for one week, move the mouse ⬚ over ⬚ and then press the left mouse button.

■ This area displays the appointments for one week. You can use the scroll bar to browse through other weeks.

Can I schedule appointments months in advance?

You can schedule appointments months or even years in advance. Outlook will keep track of all your appointments no matter how far in advance you schedule them.

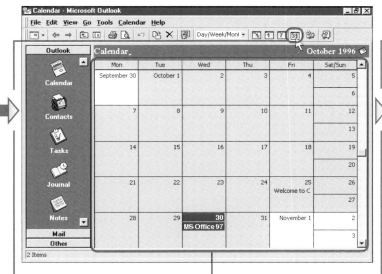

VIEW ONE MONTH

1 To display the appointments for one month, move the mouse ⌀ over 🗓 and then press the left mouse button.

■ This area displays the appointments for one month. You can use the scroll bar to browse through other months.

VIEW TODAY

1 To display the appointments for today in any view, move the mouse ⌀ over 🗓 and then press the left mouse button.

ADD A CONTACT

Outlook supplies an address book where you can keep detailed information about your friends, family members, colleagues and clients.

ADD A CONTACT

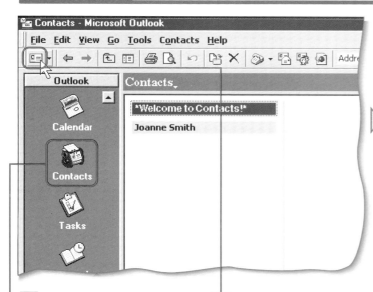

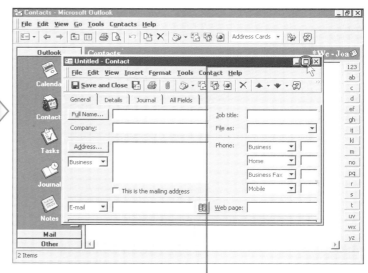

1 To display a list of all your contacts, move the mouse ⌖ over **Contacts** and then press the left mouse button.

2 To add a new contact, move the mouse ⌖ over 🔲 and then press the left mouse button.

■ A window appears with areas where you can enter information about the contact.

3 To enlarge the window to fill the screen, move the mouse ⌖ over 🔲 and then press the left mouse button.

Do I need to fill in all the information for a contact?

When entering information about a contact, you do not have to fill in all the areas. You can always add information later on. To update a contact, refer to page 308.

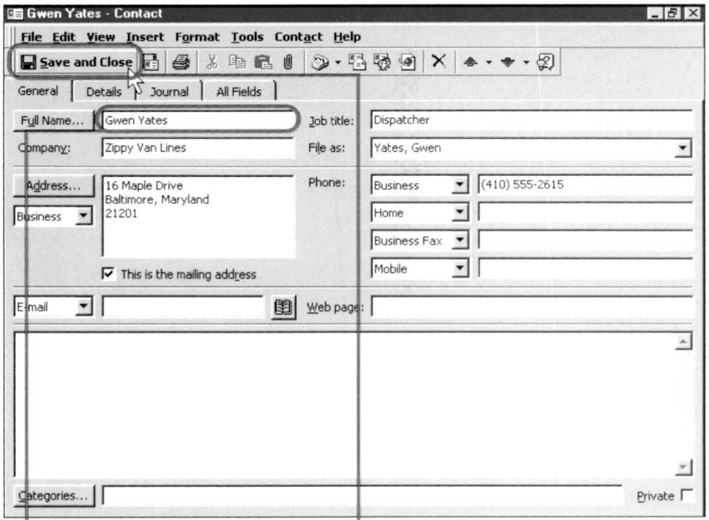

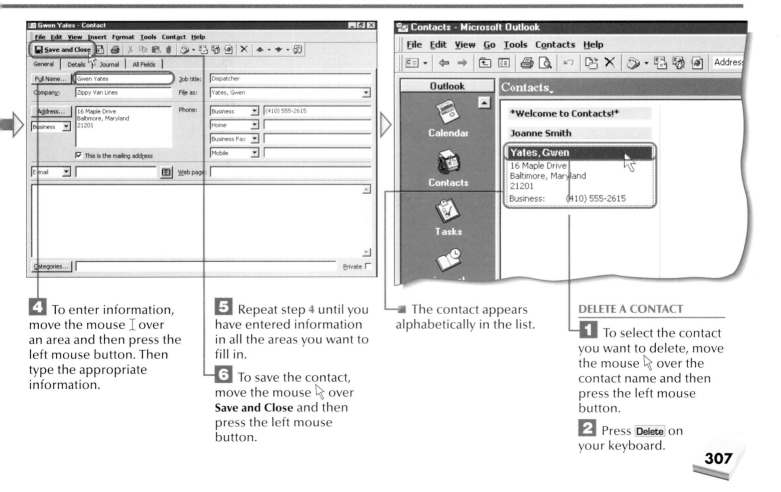

4 To enter information, move the mouse I over an area and then press the left mouse button. Then type the appropriate information.

5 Repeat step 4 until you have entered information in all the areas you want to fill in.

6 To save the contact, move the mouse over **Save and Close** and then press the left mouse button.

■ The contact appears alphabetically in the list.

DELETE A CONTACT

1 To select the contact you want to delete, move the mouse over the contact name and then press the left mouse button.

2 Press **Delete** on your keyboard.

You can easily update or add additional information to a contact in your list.

UPDATE A CONTACT

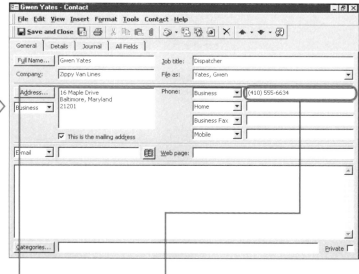

1 Move the mouse ⟨ over the name of the contact you want to update and then quickly press the left mouse button twice.

■ Information about the contact appears.

2 Move the mouse I over the information you want to change and then press the left mouse button.

3 Use ⟨Backspace⟩ and ⟨Delete⟩ on your keyboard to remove the existing text.

4 Type the new information.

When would I need to update my contacts?

Over time, friends and colleagues may move and you will need to record their new addresses.

Also, as you learn more about your contacts, you can add information such as directions to their house or the names of their children.

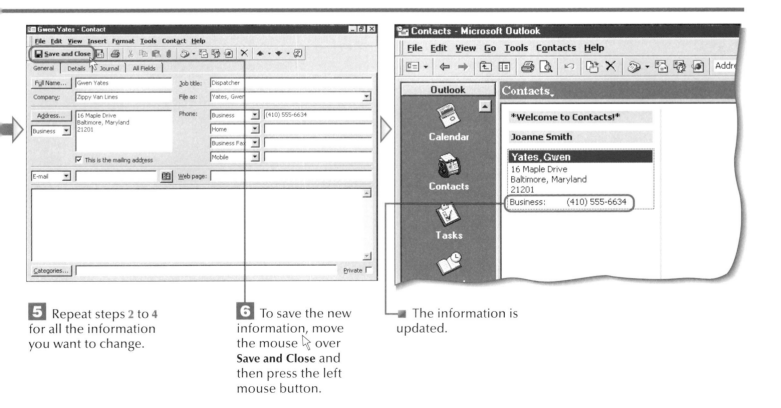

5 Repeat steps **2** to **4** for all the information you want to change.

6 To save the new information, move the mouse ⊹ over **Save and Close** and then press the left mouse button.

◼ The information is updated.

You can easily browse through your contacts to find information of interest.

BROWSE THROUGH CONTACTS

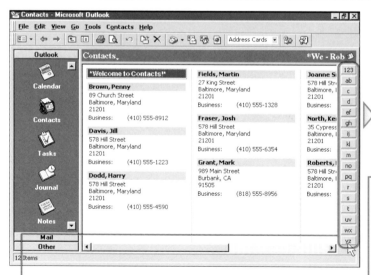

1 Move the mouse over the first letter of the contact you want to view and then press the left mouse button.

■ Contacts beginning with the letter you selected appear.

Address Cards   Detailed Address Cards   Phone List

CHANGE VIEWS

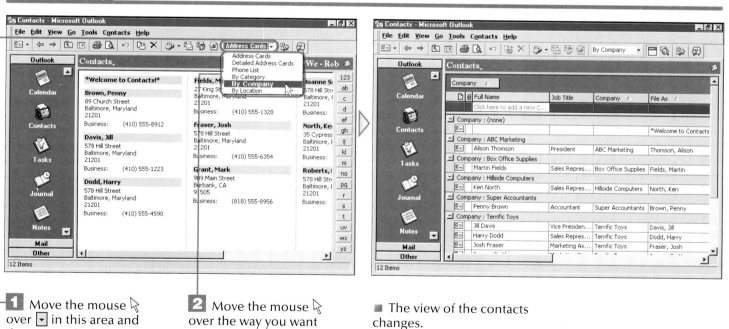

1 Move the mouse ▷ over ▾ in this area and then press the left mouse button.

2 Move the mouse ▷ over the way you want to view the contacts and then press the left mouse button.

■ The view of the contacts changes.

The Journal helps you keep track of all your activities. You can easily view the activities you accomplished on any day.

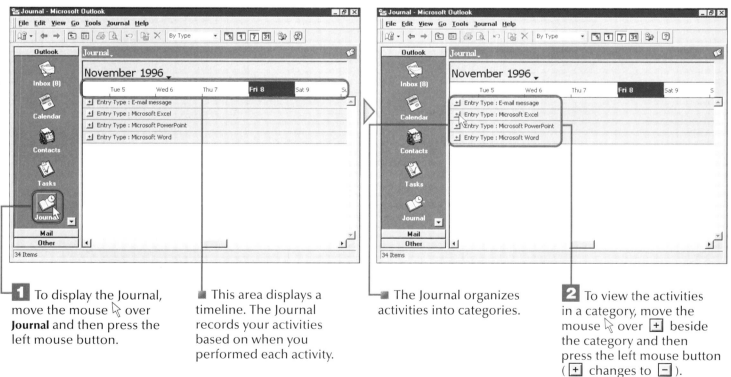

1 To display the Journal, move the mouse ⌖ over **Journal** and then press the left mouse button.

■ This area displays a timeline. The Journal records your activities based on when you performed each activity.

■ The Journal organizes activities into categories.

2 To view the activities in a category, move the mouse ⌖ over ⊞ beside the category and then press the left mouse button (⊞ changes to ⊟).

Can the Journal help me locate documents?

The Journal keeps track of the documents you work with each day. If you cannot remember where you stored a document, you can locate the document by looking in the Journal.

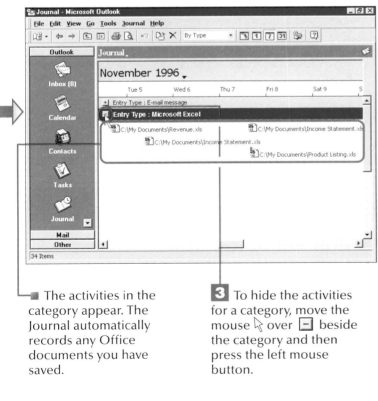

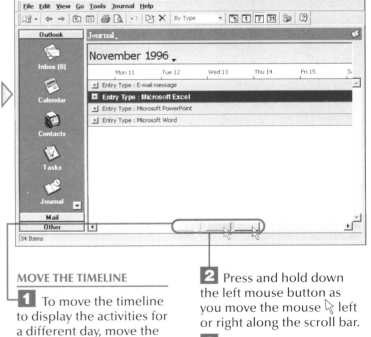

■ The activities in the category appear. The Journal automatically records any Office documents you have saved.

3 To hide the activities for a category, move the mouse ⇗ over ⊟ beside the category and then press the left mouse button.

MOVE THE TIMELINE

1 To move the timeline to display the activities for a different day, move the mouse ⇗ over the scroll box.

2 Press and hold down the left mouse button as you move the mouse ⇗ left or right along the scroll bar.

3 Release the mouse button when the day you want to view appears.

You can open a journal entry to view details about the activity or to open the document or item the entry refers to.

OPEN A JOURNAL ENTRY

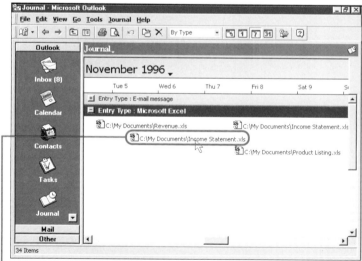

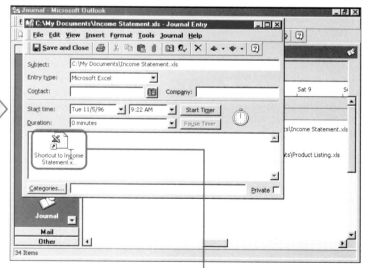

1 Move the mouse ⬚ over the journal entry you want to open and then quickly press the left mouse button twice.

■ A window appears, displaying information about the journal entry.

2 To open the document or item, move the mouse I over the shortcut and then quickly press the left mouse button twice.

What is removed from my computer when I delete a journal entry?

When you delete a journal entry, you do not delete the item or document the journal entry refers to. Only the entry itself is deleted.

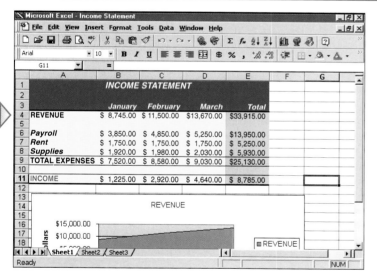

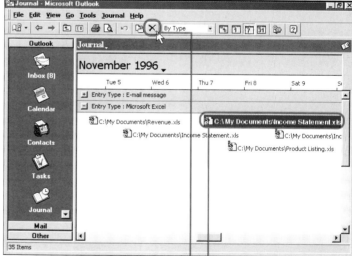

■ The document or item appears on the screen.

DELETE A JOURNAL ENTRY

You can delete a journal entry to make the Journal less cluttered.

1 Move the mouse ⌖ over the journal entry you want to delete and then press the left mouse button.

2 Move the mouse ⌖ over ⊠ and then press the left mouse button.

You can choose which activities you want the Journal to record.

SELECT ACTIVITIES TO RECORD

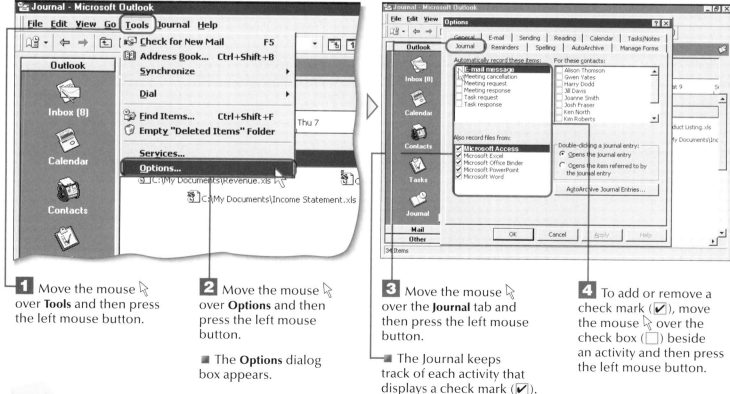

1 Move the mouse ⍩ over **Tools** and then press the left mouse button.

2 Move the mouse ⍩ over **Options** and then press the left mouse button.

■ The **Options** dialog box appears.

3 Move the mouse ⍩ over the **Journal** tab and then press the left mouse button.

■ The Journal keeps track of each activity that displays a check mark (✔).

4 To add or remove a check mark (✔), move the mouse ⍩ over the check box (☐) beside an activity and then press the left mouse button.

What activities can the Journal record?

The Journal can record communication with important contacts and work done in programs such as Word or Excel.

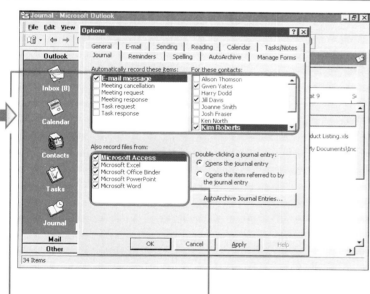

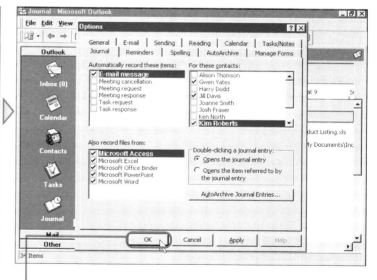

■ The Journal can keep track of items, such as e-mail messages, for the contacts you select.

Note: The list of contacts is the same list of contacts you entered into the Contacts feature. To add a contact, refer to page 306.

■ The Journal can also keep track of specific types of documents.

5 When all the activities you want the Journal to keep track of display a check mark (✔), move the mouse ⏳ over **OK** and then press the left mouse button.

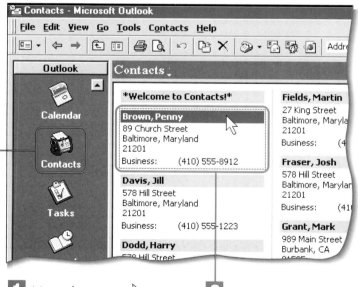

1 Move the mouse ⬚ over the feature that contains the information you want to print and then press the left mouse button.

2 To print the information for one item, move the mouse ⬚ over the item and then press the left mouse button.

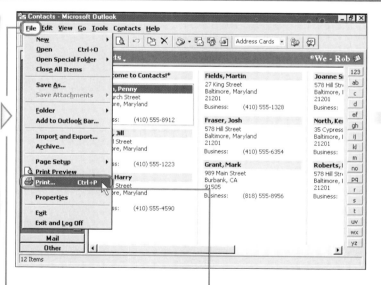

3 Move the mouse ⬚ over **File** and then press the left mouse button.

4 Move the mouse ⬚ over **Print** and then press the left mouse button.

■ The **Print** dialog box appears.

What are print styles?

Outlook lets you select the way you want to print information.

For example, you can print your calendar for one day, week or month.

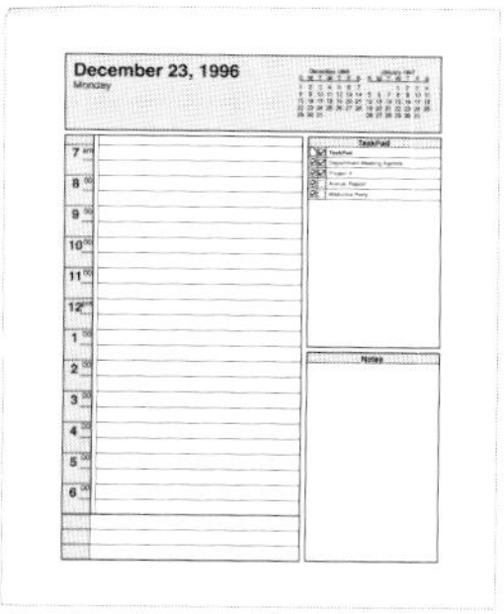

Daily Style

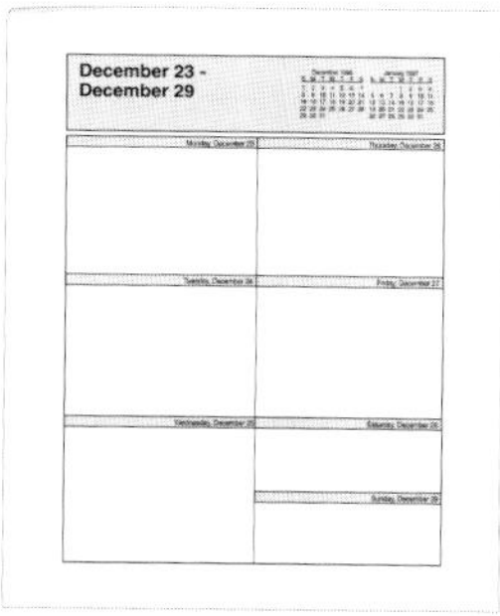

Weekly Style

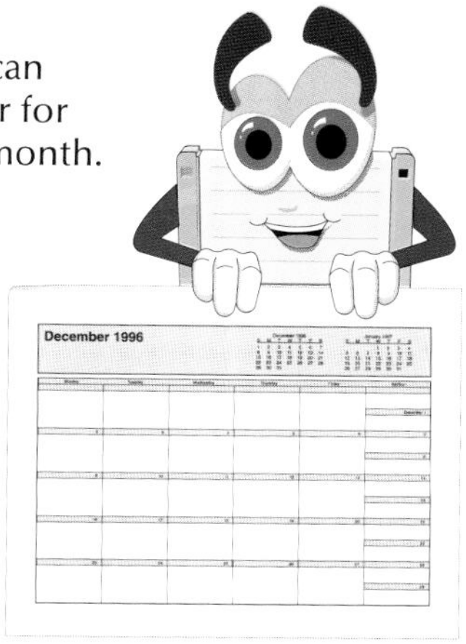

Monthly Style

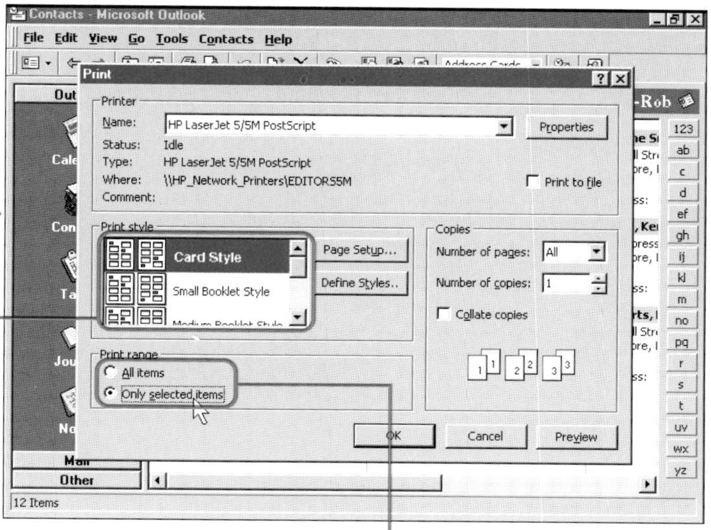

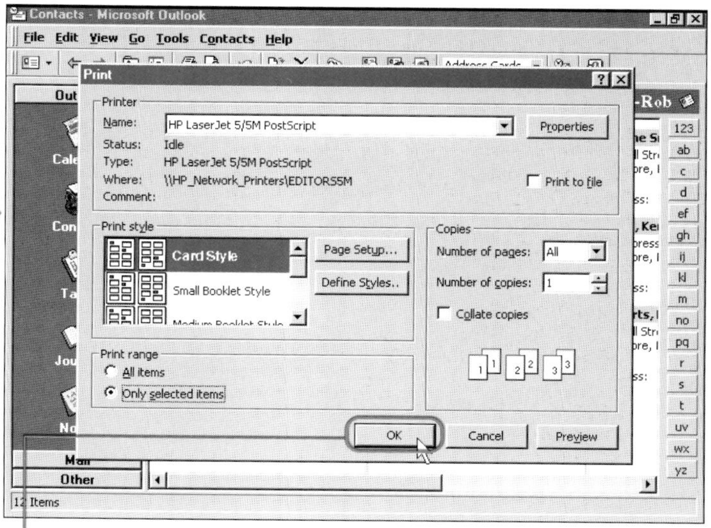

5 Move the mouse over the print style you want to use and then press the left mouse button.

Note: For information on print styles, refer to the top of this page.

6 Move the mouse over what you want to print and then press the left mouse button.

7 To print the information, move the mouse over **OK** and then press the left mouse button.

RECOVER A DELETED ITEM

The Deleted Items folder stores all the items you have deleted in Outlook. You can easily recover any of these items.

RECOVER A DELETED ITEM

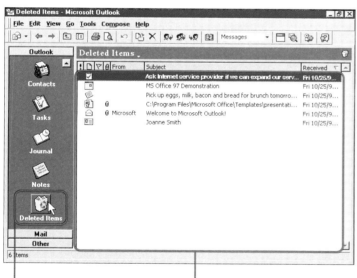

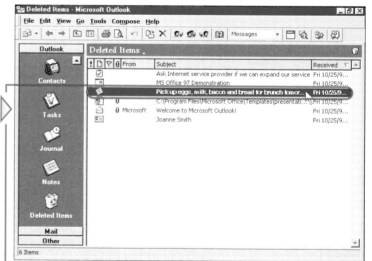

1 Move the mouse over **Deleted Items** and then press the left mouse button.

■ This area displays a list of all the items you have deleted.

2 To select the item you want to recover, move the mouse over the item and then press the left mouse button.

How can I identify the items in the Deleted Items folder?

Outlook places a symbol beside each deleted item.

 Calendar appointment

 Contact

 Journal activity

 Message

 Note

Task

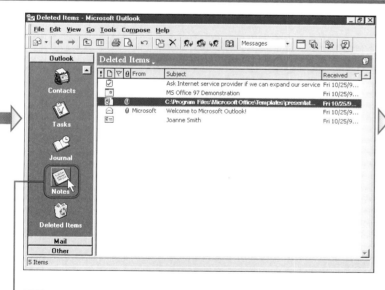

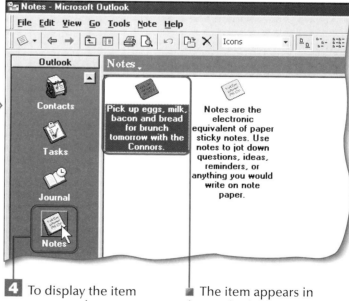

3 With the mouse still over the item, press and hold down the left mouse button as you move the item to the appropriate Outlook feature. Then release the mouse button.

■ The item disappears from the list. Outlook places the item in the feature you selected.

4 To display the item you recovered, move the mouse ⌖ over the feature you selected in step 3 and then press the left mouse button.

■ The item appears in the Outlook feature.

EMPTY DELETED ITEMS FOLDER

You should regularly empty the Deleted Items folder to save space on your computer.

EMPTY DELETED ITEMS FOLDER

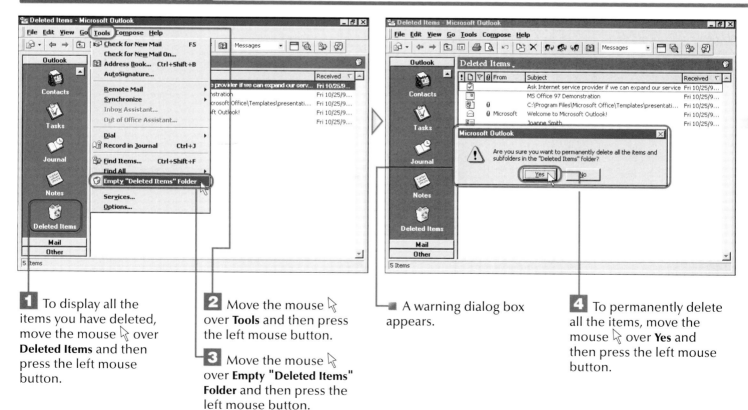

1 To display all the items you have deleted, move the mouse ⇨ over **Deleted Items** and then press the left mouse button.

2 Move the mouse ⇨ over **Tools** and then press the left mouse button.

3 Move the mouse ⇨ over **Empty "Deleted Items" Folder** and then press the left mouse button.

■ A warning dialog box appears.

4 To permanently delete all the items, move the mouse ⇨ over **Yes** and then press the left mouse button.

What if I may need an item in the future?

Deleting an item from the Deleted Items folder will permanently remove the item from your computer. Do not delete an item you may need in the future.

DELETE ONE ITEM

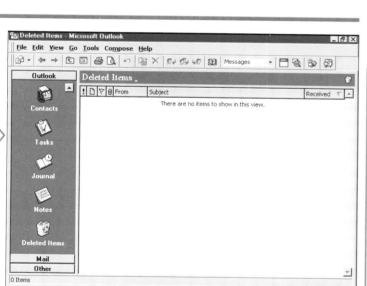

■ The items are permanently deleted.

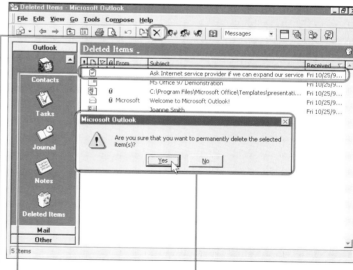

1 To permanently delete one item, move the mouse ⌖ over the item and then press the left mouse button.

2 Move the mouse ⌖ over ☒ and then press the left mouse button.

3 A warning dialog box appears. To permanently delete the item, move the mouse ⌖ over **Yes** and then press the left mouse button.

Microsoft Office has many features that make it easy for you to take advantage of the Internet.

Display the Search Page
Page 337

Display the Web Toolbar
Page 330

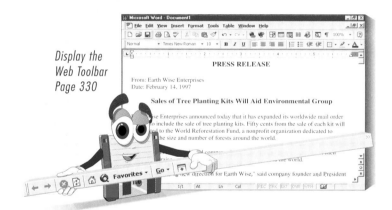

Open a Document
Page 332

Move Between Documents
Page 331

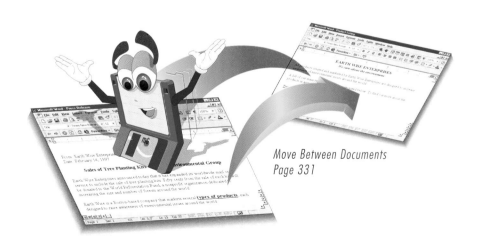

OFFICE AND THE INTERNET

Stop the Connection
Page 334

Create a Hyperlink
Page 326

Great Web Sites
You Can Visit!

1 BMW of Germany
2 Bank of America
3 IDG Books
4 maranGraphics
5 McDonald's
6 NFL Football
7 NBC News
8 WebWeather

You can create a hyperlink to connect a word or phrase in one document to another document or Web page. When you select the word or phrase, the other document appears.

Great Web Sites
You Can Visit!
1 BMW of Germany
2 Bank of America
3 IDG Books
4 maranGraphics
5 McDonald's
6 NFL Football
7 NBC News
8 WebWeather

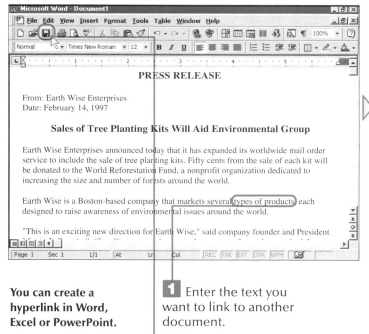

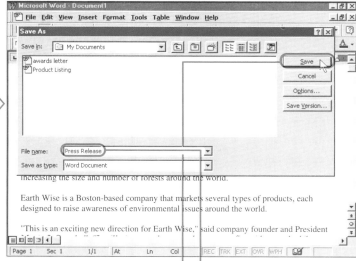

You can create a hyperlink in Word, Excel or PowerPoint.

1 Enter the text you want to link to another document.

2 To save the document, move the mouse ⬚ over 🖫 and then press the left mouse button.

■ The **Save As** dialog box appears.

*Note: If you previously saved the document, the **Save As** dialog box will not appear since you have already named the document.*

3 Type a name for the document.

4 Move the mouse ⬚ over **Save** and then press the left mouse button.

Where can a hyperlink take me?

You can create a hyperlink that takes you to another document on your computer, network, corporate intranet or the Internet.

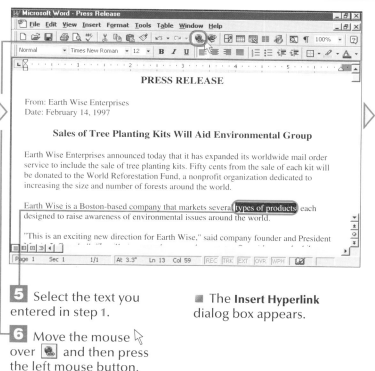

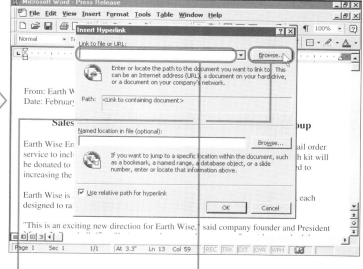

5 Select the text you entered in step **1**.

6 Move the mouse ⅃ over 🔲 and then press the left mouse button.

■ The **Insert Hyperlink** dialog box appears.

7 To link the text to a document on your computer or network, move the mouse ⅃ over **Browse** and then press the left mouse button.

■ To link the text to a Web page, type the address of the Web page (example: http://www.maran.com). Then skip to step **10** on page 328.

CONT🌐NUED➡

EARTH WISE ENTERPRISES

We care about the environment.

All products created and marketed by Earth Wise Enterprises are designed to increase awareness of environmental issues around the world.

A list of our main types of products is presented below. To find out more about the products in any category, select the category name.

Tree planting kits

Recycle bins

Compost kits

> You can easily see hyperlinks in a document. Hyperlinks appear underlined and in color.

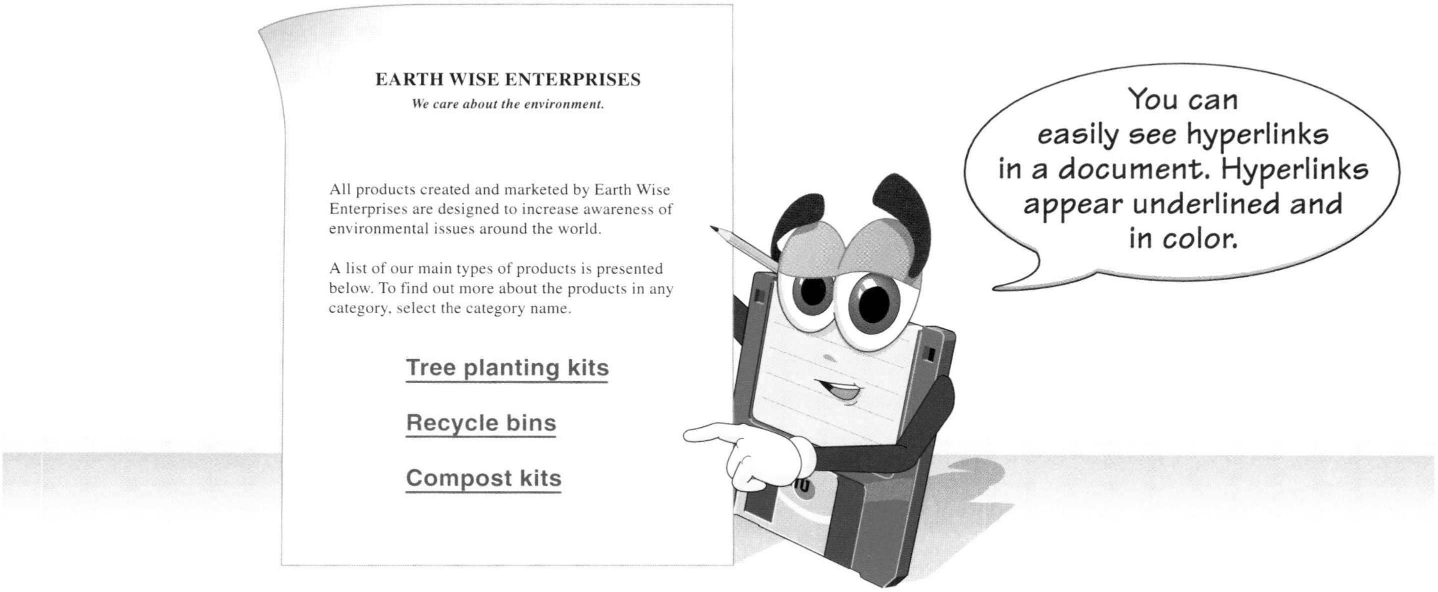

CREATE A HYPERLINK (CONTINUED)

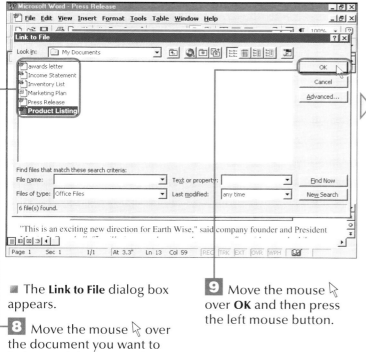

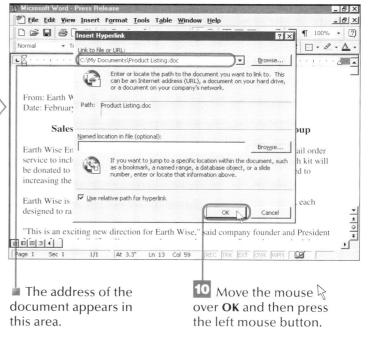

■ The **Link to File** dialog box appears.

8 Move the mouse � over the document you want to link to and then press the left mouse button.

9 Move the mouse � over **OK** and then press the left mouse button.

■ The address of the document appears in this area.

10 Move the mouse � over **OK** and then press the left mouse button.

Can Word automatically create hyperlinks for me?

When you type the address of a document located on a network or on the Internet, Word automatically changes the address to a hyperlink.

http://www.maran.com

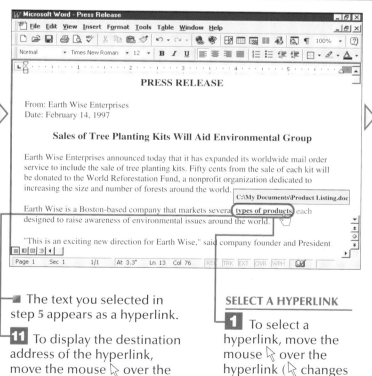

🔳 The text you selected in step 5 appears as a hyperlink.

11 To display the destination address of the hyperlink, move the mouse ▷ over the hyperlink (▷ changes to 👆). After a few seconds, the address appears.

SELECT A HYPERLINK

1 To select a hyperlink, move the mouse ▷ over the hyperlink (▷ changes to 👆) and then press the left mouse button.

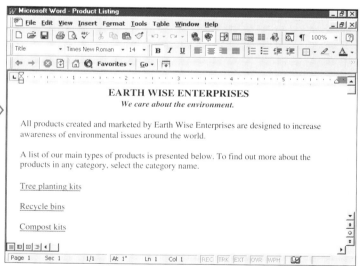

🔳 The document connected to the hyperlink appears.

🔳 If the hyperlink is connected to a Web page, your Web browser opens and displays the Web page.

DISPLAY THE WEB TOOLBAR

You can display the Web toolbar to help you browse through documents containing hyperlinks.

DISPLAY THE WEB TOOLBAR

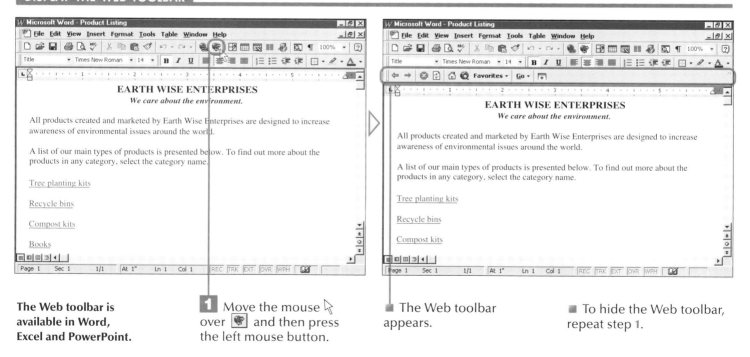

The Web toolbar is available in Word, Excel and PowerPoint.

1 Move the mouse 🖰 over 🌐 and then press the left mouse button.

■ The Web toolbar appears.

■ To hide the Web toolbar, repeat step **1**.

MOVE BETWEEN DOCUMENTS

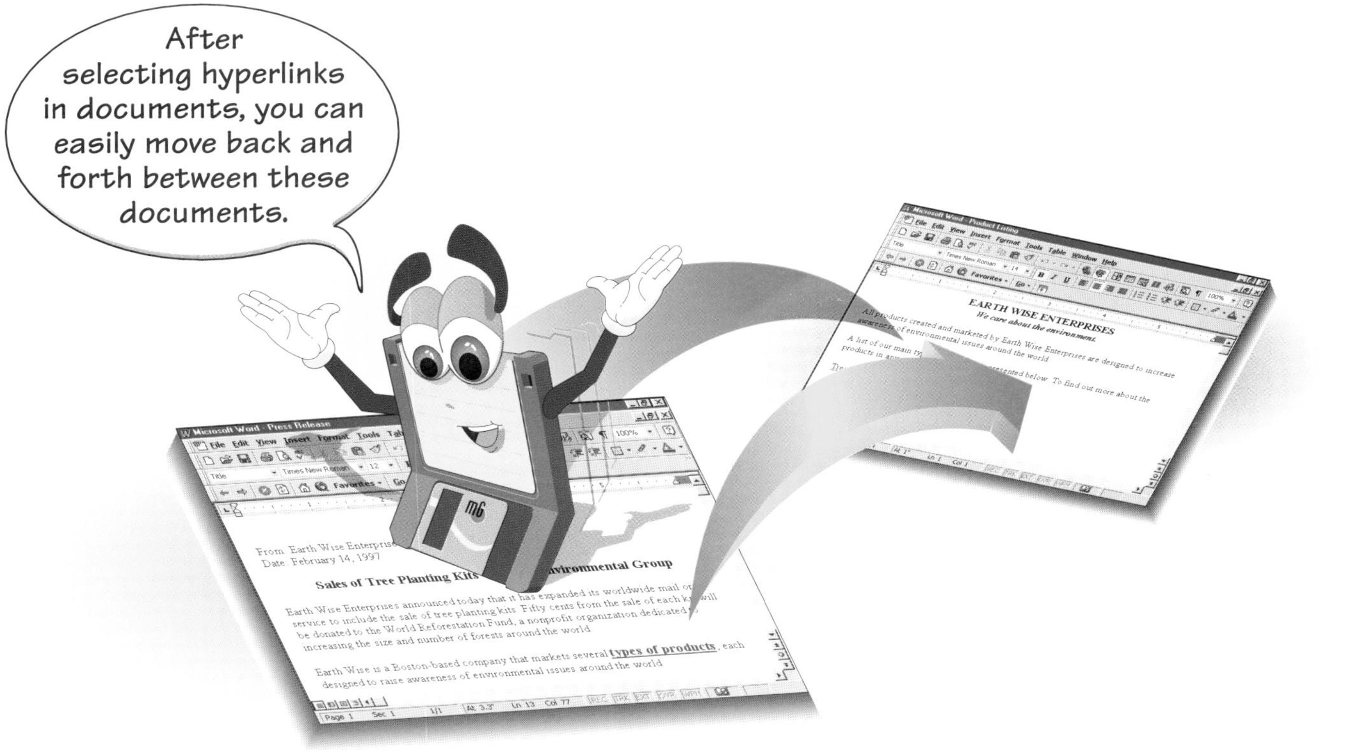
After selecting hyperlinks in documents, you can easily move back and forth between these documents.

MOVE BETWEEN DOCUMENTS

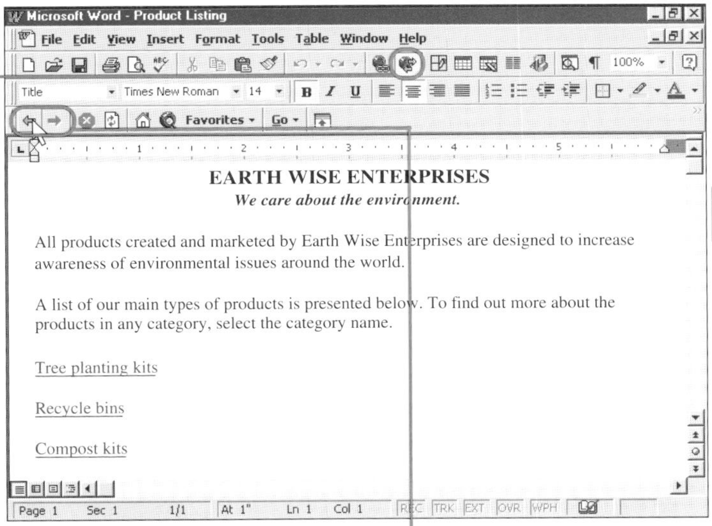
Microsoft Word - Product Listing
EARTH WISE ENTERPRISES
We care about the environment.
All products created and marketed by Earth Wise Enterprises are designed to increase awareness of environmental issues around the world.
A list of our main types of products is presented below. To find out more about the products in any category, select the category name.
Tree planting kits
Recycle bins
Compost kits

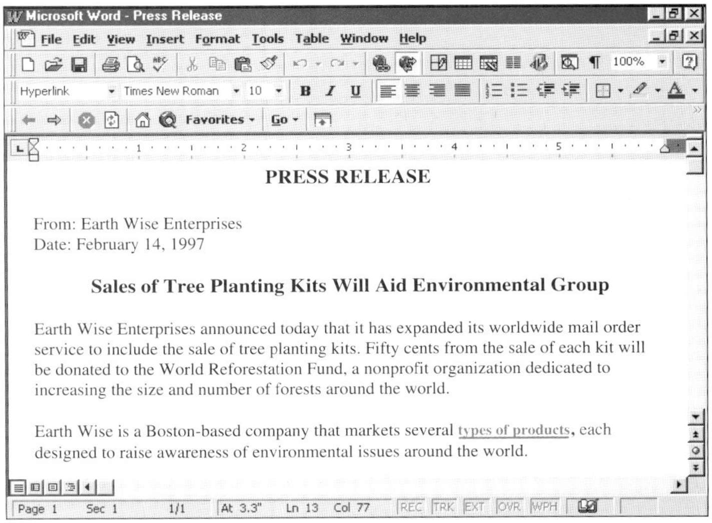
Microsoft Word - Press Release
PRESS RELEASE
From: Earth Wise Enterprises
Date: February 14, 1997
Sales of Tree Planting Kits Will Aid Environmental Group
Earth Wise Enterprises announced today that it has expanded its worldwide mail order service to include the sale of tree planting kits. Fifty cents from the sale of each kit will be donated to the World Reforestation Fund, a nonprofit organization dedicated to increasing the size and number of forests around the world.
Earth Wise is a Boston-based company that markets several types of products, each designed to raise awareness of environmental issues around the world.

■ To display the Web toolbar, move the mouse over and then press the left mouse button.

1 Move the mouse over one of the following options and then press the left mouse button.

- Move back
- Move forward

■ The document you selected appears.

You can quickly open a document that is on your computer, network, corporate intranet or the Internet.

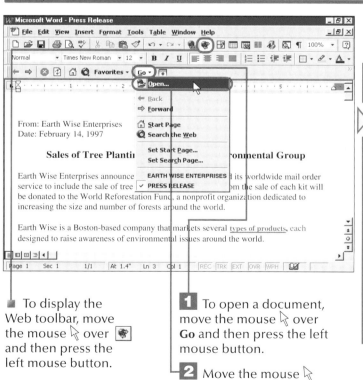

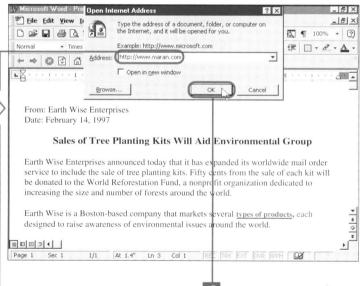

■ To display the Web toolbar, move the mouse ⟋ over 🌐 and then press the left mouse button.

1 To open a document, move the mouse ⟋ over **Go** and then press the left mouse button.

2 Move the mouse ⟋ over **Open** and then press the left mouse button.

■ The **Open Internet Address** dialog box appears.

3 Type the address of the document you want to open.

4 Move the mouse ⟋ over **OK** and then press the left mouse button.

Microsoft Office remembers the last documents you visited. You can instantly return to any of these documents.

RETURN TO A DOCUMENT

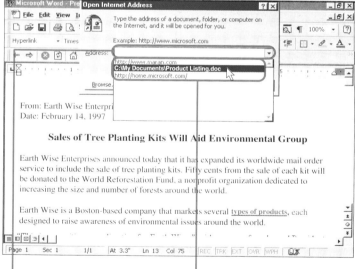

■ The document appears.

■ If the document you opened was a Web page, your Web browser opens and displays the Web page.

1 In the **Open Internet Address** dialog box, move the mouse ⤧ over ▾ in this area and then press the left mouse button.

2 Move the mouse ⤧ over the document you want to open and then press the left mouse button.

3 Press **Enter** on your keyboard to open the document.

STOP THE CONNECTION

If a Web page is taking a long time to appear, you can stop the transfer of information.

STOP THE CONNECTION

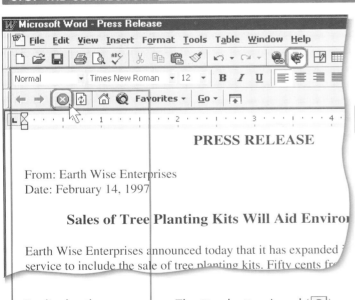

■ To display the Web toolbar, move the mouse ⬚ over 🌐 and then press the left mouse button.

■ The **Stop** button is red (🔴) when information is transferring to your computer.

1 To stop the transfer of information, move the mouse ⬚ over 🔴 and then press the left mouse button.

■ The **Stop** button turns gray (⬜). Information is no longer transferring to your computer.

REFRESH A DOCUMENT

While you are viewing a document, the author may make changes to the document. You can easily transfer a fresh copy of the document to your computer.

REFRESH A DOCUMENT

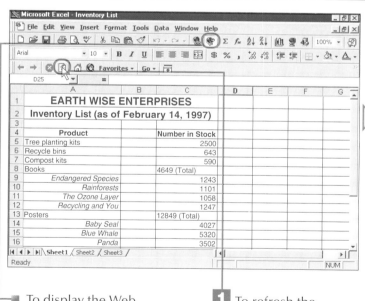

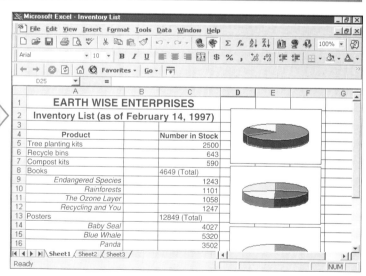

■ To display the Web toolbar, move the mouse over 🌐 and then press the left mouse button.

1 To refresh the document, move the mouse over 🔄 and then press the left mouse button.

■ An up-to-date copy of the document appears.

DISPLAY THE START PAGE

The start page is the first page that appears when you start a Web browser.

The start page includes instructions and hyperlinks that let you quickly connect to interesting documents.

DISPLAY THE START PAGE

■ To display the Web toolbar, move the mouse ⇖ over 🌐 and then press the left mouse button.

1 To display the start page, move the mouse ⇖ over 🏠 and then press the left mouse button.

■ The Web browser opens and displays the start page.

The search page helps you find information of interest.

DISPLAY THE SEARCH PAGE

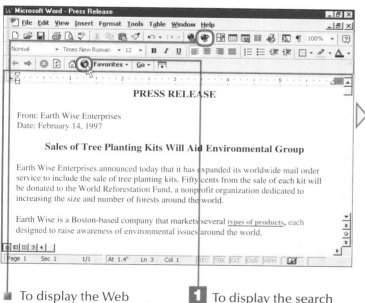

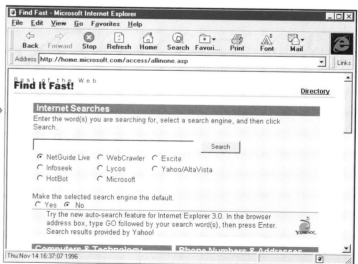

■ To display the Web toolbar, move the mouse over 🌐 and then press the left mouse button.

1 To display the search page, move the mouse over 🔍 and then press the left mouse button.

■ The Web browser opens and displays the search page.

You can add documents you frequently use to the Favorites folder. This lets you quickly open these documents at any time.

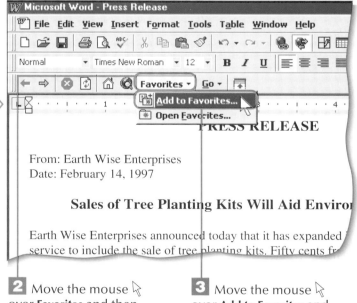

1 Open the document you want to add to the Favorites folder.

■ To display the Web toolbar, move the mouse ▷ over 🌐 and then press the left mouse button.

2 Move the mouse ▷ over **Favorites** and then press the left mouse button.

3 Move the mouse ▷ over **Add to Favorites** and then press the left mouse button.

When I add a document to the Favorites folder, does the document change locations?

When you add a document to the Favorites folder, you create a shortcut to the original document. The original document does not change its location on your computer.

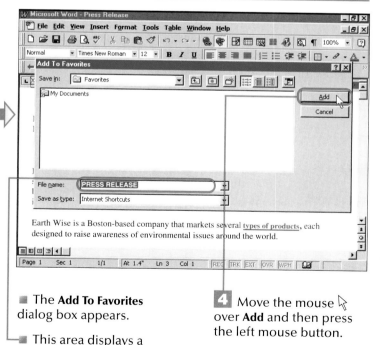

■ The **Add To Favorites** dialog box appears.

■ This area displays a name for the document. To change the name, type a new name.

4 Move the mouse ⬚ over **Add** and then press the left mouse button.

OPEN DOCUMENT IN FAVORITES

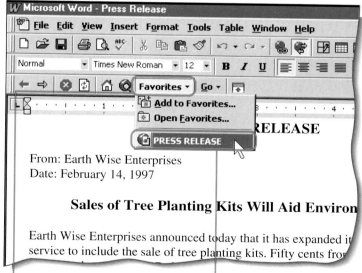

1 To open a document in the Favorites folder, move the mouse ⬚ over **Favorites** and then press the left mouse button.

2 Move the mouse ⬚ over the document you want to open and then press the left mouse button.

SAVE DOCUMENT AS A WEB PAGE

You can save a document as a Web page. This lets you place the document on your company's intranet or on the Web.

SAVE DOCUMENT AS A WEB PAGE

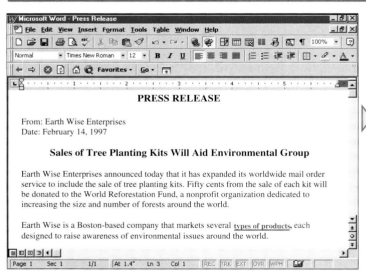

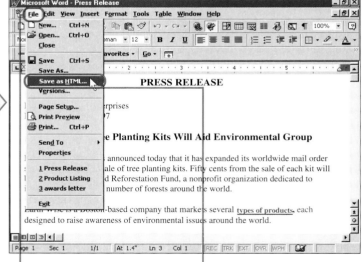

You can save a Word, Excel or PowerPoint document as a Web page.

1 Open the document you want to save as a Web page.

2 Move the mouse ⬚ over **File** and then press the left mouse button.

3 Move the mouse ⬚ over **Save as HTML** and then press the left mouse button.

*Note: If the **Save as HTML** command is not available, you need to add the Web Page Authoring (HTML) component of Microsoft Office to your computer.*

Why do Excel and PowerPoint ask me a series of questions?

When you save an Excel or PowerPoint document as a Web page, you will be asked a series of questions. Your answers help customize the resulting Web page to suit your needs.

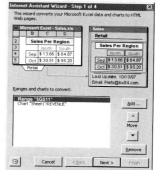

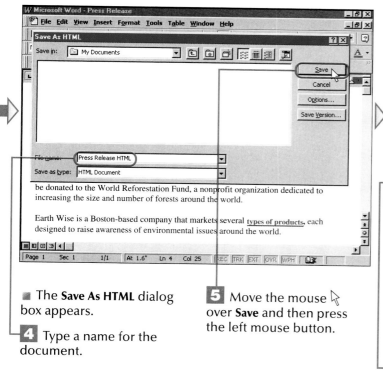

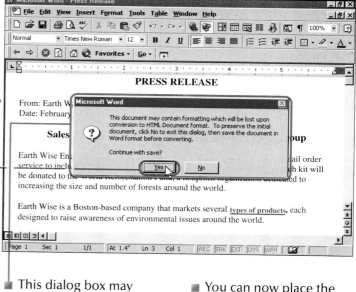

■ The **Save As HTML** dialog box appears.

4 Type a name for the document.

5 Move the mouse ⬉ over **Save** and then press the left mouse button.

■ This dialog box may appear to warn that the document contains formatting that will be lost.

6 To save the document as a Web page, move the mouse ⬉ over **Yes** and then press the left mouse button.

■ You can now place the document on a corporate intranet or the Web for others to view.

INDEX

A

absolute cell references, 164-165
active cells, 114
add list of numbers, 158-159
addition. *See* formulas; functions
align
    data, 172
    text, 61, 259. *See also* indent; tabs
animate slides, 266-267
animation effects, 267
appointments
    add, 302-303
    delete, 303
    reminders, 303
    view in calendar, 300-301
art in slides, 244-245
asterisk (*) in formulas, 146
AutoCalculate feature, 156-157
autocomplete data, 117
AutoFormat
    feature, 180-181
    tables, 108-109
automatic correction, spelling, 57, 135, 239
AutoShapes, 250-251
Average
    automatic calculation, 156-157
    function, 151

B

black and white, print in, 190-191
blank lines
    delete, 45
    insert, 43
bold
    data, 169
    text, 60, 64, 258
borders, 69, 174-175
breaks
    pages, 88-89, 192-193
    sections, 90-91
browse
    through contacts, 310
    through presentations, 222-223
    through worksheets, using tabs, 195
bulleted lists, 72-73

C

calculations. *See* formulas; functions
calendar
    appointments, 302-303
    days, change, 301
    display, 300-301
    months, change, 301
    print, 318-319
    views, change, 304-305

caret (^) in formulas, 146
cell references
    absolute, 164-165
    defined, 114
    in formulas, 146
    relative, 162-163
cells
    active, 114
    borders, 174-175
    color, 176
    data. *See* data
    defined, 101, 114
    designs, apply, 180-181
    formats, copy, 178
    print, 186-187
    replace data in, 135
    select, 120-121
center
    data
        across columns, 179
        in cell, 172
        on page, 188
    text, 61, 259
        vertically, 92-93
changes, undo, 47, 137, 231
characters. *See also* data; presentations, text; text
    delete, 44, 234
    insert, 42, 232
    special. *See* symbols
charts
    add, 246-249
    create, 200-203
    delete, 203, 249
    edit, 249
    as Excel feature, 112
    move, 206
    print, 208-209
    resize, 207
    titles, 202
    types, 204-205, 249
circular reference (error message), 161
click, using mouse, 7
clip art, 244-245
close
    documents, 32
    Excel, 131
    messages, 284
    notes, 294, 295
    Outlook, 281
    PowerPoint, 225
    programs, 11
    Word, 33
    workbooks, 130
colons (:) in functions, 150
color
    cells, 176
    data, 177
    highlighted text, 67

object, 263
slides, 256-257
text, 66, 262

columns
  center data across, 179
  defined, 114
  delete, 145
  in documents, 96-97
  headings, print, 190-191
  insert, 143
  select, 121
  in tables
    add, 105
    defined, 101
    delete, 106
    width, 101
  width, 166

commas (,) in functions, 150

connections, stop, 334

contacts
  add, 306-307
  browse through, 310
  change views, 311
  delete, 307
  display, 306
  print, 318-319
  update, 308-309

copy
  data, 140-141
  formats, 68, 178
  formulas, 162-165
  text, 50-51

Count
  automatic calculation, 156-157
  function, 151

Count Nums, automatic calculation, 156-157

D

#DIV/0! (error message), 160

data. *See also* charts; formulas; functions; numbers; text
  align, 172
  autocomplete, 117
  bold, 169
  center
    in cell, 172
    across columns, 179
    on page, 188
  color, 177
  copy, 140-141
  delete, 136
  edit, 134-135
    as Excel feature, 112
  enter, 116-117
  fonts, 170
  format, as Excel feature, 112
  indent, 173
  italicize, 169

move, 138-139
replace in cell, 135
series, complete, 118-119
size, 171
underline, 169
undo changes, 137

delete
  appointments, 303
  autoformats
    from cells, 181
    from tables, 109
  blank lines, 45
  borders, 69, 175
  bullets, 73
  characters, 44, 234
  charts, 203
  color, 66, 176, 177
  columns
    in documents, 97
    in tables, 106
    in worksheets, 145
  contacts, 307
  data, 136
  footnotes, 85
  highlights from text, 67
  images from slides, 245
  items in Outlook, 322-323
  journal entries, 315
  lines in tables, 102
  messages, 285
  notes, 293
  numbers from lists, 73
  page breaks, 89
  rows
    in tables, 106
    in worksheets, 144
  section breaks, 91
  slides, 269
  tables, 107
  tabs, 81
  tasks, 297
  text, 44-46, 234-235
  worksheets, 197

deleted items, recover, 320-321

Deleted Items folder, empty, 322-323

designs
  cells, 180-181
  slides, 254-255
  tables, 109
  types, 255

display
  calendar, 300-301
  contacts, 306
  documents, 36-37
  journal entries, 312-313
  mail folders, 283
  messages in Inbox, 282
  ruler, 39

343

search page, 337
start page, 336
toolbars, 40-41, 330
division. See formulas; functions
documents. See also pages; paragraphs; text; worksheets
add to Favorites, 338-339
blank lines, 43, 45
change views, 36-37
close, 32
columns of text, 96-97
connect to other documents, 326-329
create, 30
display, 36-37
edit
in Print Preview, 27
as Word feature, 16
footers, 86-87
footnotes, 84-85
format, as Word feature, 16
grammar, check, 56-57
headers, 86-87
line spacing, 74-75
magnify, 38
margins, 94-95
move through, 22-23
newspaper columns, 96-97
open, 34-35, 332-333
in Favorites, 339
page breaks, 88-89
page numbers, 82-83
preview, 26-27
print, 28-29
as Word feature, 16
refresh, 335
rename, 25
save, 24-25
as Web pages, 340-341
section breaks, 90-91
select all text, 21
spelling
check, 56-57
errors, automatic correction, 57
switch between, 31, 331
tables. See tables
tabs, 78-81
undo changes, 47
views, 36-37
dollar signs ($) in absolute cell references, 165
double-click, using mouse, 7
draft quality, print in, 190-191
drag and drop, using mouse, 7

E
electronic mail. See messages
electronic notes. See notes
e-mail. See messages
equal signs (=)
in formulas, 146
in functions, 150
errors
in formulas, 160-161
spelling, automatic correction, 57, 135, 239
Excel. See also specific subject or feature
documents. See workbooks; worksheets
exit, 131
overview, 5, 112
screen, overview, 115
start, 113
exit
Excel, 131
Outlook, 281
PowerPoint, 225
programs, 11
Word, 33
exponents. See formulas; functions

F
Favorites
add documents, 338-339
open documents, 339
files
Excel. See charts; workbooks; worksheets
PowerPoint. See presentations; slides
Word. See documents; pages
find, text, 52-53
fonts
data, 170
size, 63, 171, 261
text, 62, 64-65, 260
footers, 86-87, 264-265
footnotes, 84-85
format
data, as Excel feature, 112
documents, as Word feature, 16
tables, 108-109
formats. See also designs; text
copy, 68
to other cells, 178
formatting toolbar, 19, 40, 125
formula bar, 115
formulas. See also functions
and AutoCalculate feature, 156-157
cell references, 146
copy, 162-165
edit, 149
enter, 148
errors, 160-161
as Excel feature, 112
overview, 146-147

forward messages, 290-291
functions. *See also* formulas
    enter, 152-155
    as Excel feature, 112
    overview, 150-151
    types available, 153
    typing, 155

G

grammar, check, 56-57
graphics
    AutoShapes, 250-251
    clip art, 244-245
gridlines, print in worksheets, 190-191

H

handouts
    as PowerPoint feature, 212
    for presentations, 217
    print, 276-277
hanging indents, 77
headers, 86-87, 264-265
headings, row and columns, print, 190-191
height
    charts, 207
    objects, 253
    rows, 100, 167
help, 12-13
hide
    ruler, 39
    toolbars, 40-41, 125, 330
highlight text, 67
hyperlinks
    create, 326-329
    select, 329

I

images
    AutoShapes, 250-251
    clip art, 244-245
Inbox, view, 282
indent
    data, 173
    text, 76-77
insertion point, 18
    move, 22
IntelliMouse, Microsoft, 23, 123
    described, 7
Internet, 326-341
italicize
    data, 169
    text, 60, 64, 258

J

join paragraphs, 45
journal
    entries
        delete, 315
        open, 314-315
        view, 312-313
    print, 318-319
    record activities, 316-317
justify text, 61

L

landscape orientation, 189
layout, slides, 240-241
left align
    data, 172
    text, 61, 259
lines
    blank. *See* blank lines
    spacing between, 74-75
    in tables, delete, 102
lists, bulleted and numbered, 72-73

M

magnify, 7, 38, 124
mail folders, display, 283
margins, 94-95, 184-185
Max
    automatic calculation of, 156-157
    function, 151
menu bar
    Excel, 115
    vs. toolbar, 9
messages
    close, 284
    delete, 285
    forward, 290-291
    in Inbox, display, 282
    open, 284
    print, 318-319
    reply to, 288-289
    send, 286-287
Microsoft
    Excel. *See* Excel
    IntelliMouse, 23, 123
        described, 7
    Office, overview, 4-5
    Outlook. *See* Outlook
    PowerPoint. *See* PowerPoint
    Word. *See* Word
Min
    automatic calculation, 156-157
    function, 151
minus sign (-) in formulas, 146
mouse, using, 6-7

INDEX

move
    charts, 206
    data, 138-139
    mouse, 6
    objects in slides, 252
    tabs, 80
    text, 48-49, 236
    through documents, 22-23
    timeline, 313
    toolbars, 99
    worksheets, 199
multiplication. See formulas; functions

N

#NAME? (error message), 161
Normal view, 37
notes
    close, 294
    create, 292-293
    delete, 293
    open, 294
    print, 318-319
    resize, 295
Notes Page view, 220, 221
notes pages
    display, 222
    print, 276-277
number keys, 117
number series, complete, 118-119
number signs (#) as error messages, 117, 159, 160
numbers. See also charts; data; formulas; functions; text
    add list of, 158-159
    appearance, 168
    in lists, 72-73
    pages, 82-83, 265
    scientific form, 117
    slides, 264-265

O

object, color, 263
Office. See Microsoft Office
Office Assistant, 9, 12-13, 17, 113, 213, 280-281
Online Layout view, 37
on-screen presentations, as PowerPoint feature, 212
open
    documents, 34-35, 332-333
    Excel, 113
    Favorites documents, 339
    journal entries, 314-315
    messages, 284
    notes, 294
    Outlook, 280-281
    PowerPoint, 213
    presentations, 226-227
    programs, 8-9
    Word, 17
    workbooks, 132-133

operators in calculations, 146
orientation, pages, 189
outline, print, 276-277
Outline view, 37, 220, 221, 223
Outlook. See also specific subject or feature
    exit, 281
    features, 281
    overview, 5
    start, 280-281
overheads, as PowerPoint feature, 212

P

Page Layout view, 37
pages. See also documents; paragraphs; text; worksheets
    breaks, 88-89, 192-193
    center data, 188
    center text vertically, 92-93
    columns, 96-97
    display
      search, 337
      start, 336
    footers, 86-87, 264-265
    footnotes, 84-85
    headers, 86-87, 264-265
    magnify, 38
    margins, 94-95, 184-185
    numbers, 82-83, 265
    orientation, 189
    Print Preview feature, 26-27, 182-183
    sections, 90-91
    Web, save documents, 340-341
paragraphs. See also pages; text
    indent, 76-77
    join, 45
    select, 21
    split, 43
    tabs, 78-81
parentheses ( )
    in formulas, 146
    in functions, 150
pictures in slides, 244-245
plus sign (+) in formulas, 146
point sizes, 63. See also fonts
pointers, mouse, 6
points
    insert, 233
    select, 228
portrait orientation, 189
PowerPoint. See also specific subject or feature
    exit, 225
    overview, 5, 212
    start, 213
presentations
    browse through, 222-223
    categories, 215
    create, 214-219
    footers, 264-265

346

headers, 264-265
open, 226-227
output types, 217
print, 276-277
save, 224-225
scroll through, 222-223
slide show, 272-273
slides, insert, 242-243
speaker notes, create, 270-271
spelling, check, 238-239
text
    first slide, 218
    select all, 229
types, 215
views, 220-221
preview
    documents, 26-27
    worksheets, 182-183
print
    in black and white, 190-191
    calendar, 318-319
    charts, 208-209
    contacts, 318-319
    documents, 28-29
    in draft quality, 190-191
    gridlines, 190-191
    journal, 318-319
    messages, 318-319
    notes, 318-319
    presentations, 276-277
    preview, 26-27, 182-183
    row and column headings, 190-191
    styles in Outlook, 319
    tasks, 318-319
    as Word feature, 16
    worksheets, 186-187
Print Preview feature, 26-27, 182-183
programs
    exit, 11
    start, 8-9
    switch between, 10

R

#REF! (error message), 145, 161
record activities in journal, 316-317
recover deleted items, 320-321
refresh documents, 335
relative cell references, 162-163
rename
    documents, 25
    worksheets, 198
replace text, 54-55, 230
reply to messages, 288-289
resize
    charts, 207
    notes, 295
    objects in slides, 253

right align
    data, 172
    text, 61, 259
Round function, 151
rows
    defined, 114
    delete, 144
    headings, print, 190-191
    height, 167
    insert, 142
    select, 121
    in tables
        add, 104
        defined, 101
        delete, 106
        height, 100
ruler, 19
    display or hide, 39

S

save
    documents, 24-25
    documents as Web pages, 340-341
    presentations, 224-225
    workbooks, 126-127
scientific form, numbers in, 117
screen
    Excel, overview, 115
    Word, overview, 19
scroll, 7
    through documents, 23
    through presentations, 222-223
    through worksheets, 122-123
search page, display, 337
sections, 90-91
select
    cells, 120-121
    hyperlinks, 329
    text, 20-21, 228-229
selected text, delete, 46, 235
send messages, 286-287
sentences, select, 20
series of text or numbers, complete, 118-119
shadow, text, 258
size. See also resize
    data, 171
    text, 63, 64-65, 261
slash (/) in formulas, 146
slide show, view, 272-273
Slide Sorter view, 220, 221
Slide view, 220, 221
slides
    animate, 266-267
    AutoShapes, insert, 250-251
    charts, insert, 246-249
    clip art, insert, 244-245
    colors, 256-257

INDEX

delete, 269
design, 254-255
display, 222
footers, 264-265
headers, 264-265
insert, 242-243
layout, 240-241
move through, 273
objects
    move, 252
    resize, 253
pictures, insert, 244-245
as PowerPoint feature, 212
print, 276-277
reorder, 268
select, 229
text. *See* text
transitions, 274-275
sort tasks, 299
spacing, lines, 74-75
speaker notes
    create, 270-271
    as PowerPoint feature, 212
special characters. *See* symbols
special effects, text, 65
spelling
    check, 56-57, 238-239
    errors, automatic correction, 57, 135, 239
spreadsheets. *See* worksheets
standard toolbar, 19, 40, 125
start
    Excel, 113
    Outlook, 280-281
    PowerPoint, 213
    programs, 8-9
    Word, 17
start page, display, 336
status bar, 19, 115
stop connections, 334
subtraction. *See* formulas; functions
Sum
    automatic calculation, 156-157
    function, 151
switch
    between documents, 31, 331
    between programs, 10
    between workbooks, 129
    between worksheets, 194-195
symbols, insert, 43, 70-71

T

tables
    cells, defined, 101
    columns
        add, 105
        defined, 101
        delete, 106
        width, 101

create, 98-99
delete, 107
format, 108-109
lines, erase, 102
rows
    add, 104, 105
    defined, 101
    delete, 106
    height, 100
text, enter, 103
tabs
    add, 78-79
    delete, 81
    move, 80
    using, 79
    worksheet, browse through, 195
tasks
    create, 296-297
    delete, 297
    help performing, 12-13
    mark as complete, 298
    print, 318-319
    sort, 299
text. *See also* charts; data; documents; numbers; pages; paragraphs
    align, 61, 259
    autocorrect spelling, 57, 135, 239
    bold, 60, 64, 258
    borders, 69
    bullets, 72-73
    center, 61, 259
        vertically, 92-93
    color, 66, 262
    columns, 96-97
    copy, 50-51
    delete, 44-46, 234-235
    edit, as Word feature, 16
    effects, 65
    emphasize, 258
    enter, 18
    find, 52-53
    font, 62, 64-65, 260
    footers, 86-87
    footnotes, 84-85
    formats, copy, 68
    grammar, check, 56-57
    headers, 86-87
    highlight, 67
    importance, 237
    indent, 76-77
    insert, 42, 232-233
    italicize, 60, 64, 258
    line spacing, 74-75
    move, 48-49, 236
    numbers, 72-73
    print, 28-29
    replace, 54-55, 230
    select, 20-21, 228-229
    series, complete, 118-119

shadow, 258
size, 63, 64-65, 261
special characters. *See* symbols
special effects, 65
spelling
    check, 56-57, 238-239
    errors, automatic correction, 57, 135, 239
in tables, enter, 103
tabs, 78-81
underline, 60, 65, 258
    styles, 65
undo changes, 47, 231
Thesaurus feature, 58-59
timeline, move, 313
toolbars
    button names, 13
    display, 40-41, 125, 330
    Excel, 115
    hide, 40-41, 125
    move, 99
    vs. menu bar, 9
transitions, slides, 274-275

U

underline
    data, 169
    text, 60, 65, 258
underline styles, 65
Undo feature, 47, 137, 231

V

#VALUE! (error message), 161
view
    calendar, 300-301
    day in calendar, 304
    Inbox, 282
    journal entries, 312-313
    month in calendar, 305
    slide show, 272-273
    today in calendar, 305
    week in calendar, 304
views
    calendar, 304-305
    contacts, 311
    documents, 36-37
    presentations, 220-221

W

Web pages
    create hyperlinks, 326-329
    save documents, 340-341
Web toolbar, 330
width
    chart, 207
    columns, 101, 166
    object, 253

Word. *See also* specific subject or feature
    exit, 33
    overview, 4, 16
    screen, overview, 19
    start, 17
words
    connect to other documents, 326-329
    select, 20, 228
workbooks. *See also* worksheets
    close, 130
    create, 128
    defined, 115
    open, 132-133
    print, 186-187
    save, 126-127
    switch between, 129
    vs. worksheets, 127
worksheet tabs, 115
worksheets. *See also* cells; columns; data; pages; rows; workbooks
    browse through tabs, 195
    charts in. *See* charts
    delete, 197
    insert, 196
    magnify, 124
    margins, 184-185
    move, 199
    overview, 114
    preview, 182-183
    print, 186-187
    rename, 198
    scroll through, 122-123
    select all cells, 121
    switch between, 194-195
    undo changes, 137
    vs. workbooks, 127

Z

zoom, 7, 38, 124